ariel, stop. Nothing's as bad as you think."

"Yes it *is* and even worse." She stared up at him for a moment, searching for something, and then she pushed away, turning her face from him. "You just don't know what I've tried to do."

He put his hands on her shoulders, holding her so firmly that she couldn't escape, and his voice was stern and unwavering. "I'm sorry, Mariel, but God is bigger than your efforts. Even those men can't thwart him. He doesn't give up. He won't change his mind."

"Oh, stop," she cried.

His hand on her face was gentle again, his breath on her forehead as tender as a blessing. "With them, it's his wrath, Mariel, the smell of death, but not with you. Can't you accept life? Love?"

Palisades.
Pure Romance.

FICTION THAT FEATURES CREDIBLE CHARACTERS AND
ENTERTAINING PLOT LINES, WHILE CONTINUING TO UPHOLD
STRONG CHRISTIAN VALUES. FROM HIGH ADVENTURE
TO TENDER STORIES OF THE HEART, EACH PALISADES
ROMANCE IS AN UNDILUTED STORY OF LOVE,
FROM BEGINNING TO END!

A PALISADES CONTEMPORARY ROMANCE

GLORY

MARILYN KOK

PALISADES

GLORY
published by Palisades
a part of the Questar publishing family

© 1995 by Marilyn Kok
International Standard Book Number: 0-88070-754-2

Cover illustration by George Angelini
Cover designed by David Carlson
Edited by Deena Davis

Printed in the United States of America

For information:
QUESTAR PUBLISHERS, INC.
POST OFFICE BOX 1720
SISTERS, OREGON 97759

95 96 97 98 99 00 01 02 — 10 9 8 7 6 5 4 3 2 1

Dedication

As always, for Randy, my husband and friend.
And for the teacher and friends we met at Morrison Academy:
Beth, Peter, Gordon, Karen, Julie, Vincent, Janet, Vinnie,
Kathy, and...Donnie Joe.
May His face shine upon you. Soli deo gloria.

And we, who with unveiled faces all reflect the Lord's glory, are being transformed into his likeness with ever-increasing glory, which comes from the Lord, who is the Spirit.
2 CORINTHIANS 3:18

One

Mariel Forrest looked up warily at the imposing gateway of the Hudson Christian Academy in Taichung, Taiwan. Not yet noon, the August morning had warmed up quickly and the sultry summer humidity had already left a sticky sheen of moisture over her. Mariel pulled her dress away from her back and lifted her hair off her neck, letting the air touch her skin with brief comfort.

As a new teacher, Mariel's interview with the school superintendent was a predictable necessity, but for her most unwelcome. She was, after all, living a lie.

Her secrets felt like clothes that were too tight. Mariel's fingers fluttered over the buttons of her dress, irrationally checking that they were still fastened. She made herself stop, take a deep breath, and calm down. This superintendent, Adam Lyons, was entrusted with the spiritual well-being of the missionary children at Hudson. How would he react if he discovered that this good Christian teacher hadn't been to church in three years? Would he welcome her then?

Last night at the Carltons' mission guest house, her eyes bright with a gossip's delight, Gladys Carlton had eagerly told Mariel about Mr. Lyons's past, his wife's death in childbirth, the daughter he had raised alone.

"After eleven years we've decided he's become a confirmed bachelor," Mrs. Carlton said. "Who could believe it, a nice man like Adam?"

"Nice" Adam Lyons. Was it too much to hope that he might also be a little blind and not too bright and much too casual in what he expected from his teachers?

Reluctantly, Mariel made her way across the gravel driveway, through the red-brick arch that announced the name of the school, and toward the glass doorway labeled "Office."

The middle-aged Chinese woman behind the desk in the lobby smiled sympathetically when she saw Mariel fanning herself. "Are you Miss Forrest?" she asked. "Please go on in. Mr. Lyons is expecting you."

At the open inner door Mariel paused a moment. The room gave an immediate impression of shabbiness—worn blue carpet, two hard-backed chairs in front of a large desk, drapes in a fabric that would have been contemporary in Eisenhower's day.

And at the desk, Adam Lyons.

Mariel almost smiled. So this was the mission field's most eligible bachelor. Her first impression was of graying hair and glasses, a relaxed demeanor at his desk, and strong shoulders and arms. He stood. In his late thirties, she guessed, and not much taller than she, perhaps 5'10". She thought at first that his looks were almost bland.

Then Mariel met his eyes, and all thought of a mild-mannered missionary receded into oblivion. The strength of his person-

12

ality came through his eyes. His gaze was compelling, sharply intelligent, and deeply unsettling to Mariel, who gave an involuntary shiver. Her senses, already heightened, quickened to an acute perception. Here was a man who would not easily be fooled. "Nice," Mrs. Carlton might call him. Yet this man had the power to look within her and lay bare not only her secrets but her most closely held hopes and desires.

Mariel wondered helplessly how much of her reaction he could now sense. *Anything, anything, please, but not this. Not now.*

By sheer force of willpower, Mariel gathered the shreds of her dignity around her, made herself breathe deeply and evenly, and then advanced to take his outstretched hand.

As she feared, the contact was electric.

She had hesitated so long at the door that Adam thought at first she must be very shy, and then he wasn't sure. Did those eyes hold fear or judgment? Was her chin, turned a little to one side, defensive or superior?

Adam had welcomed many new teachers to Hudson Christian Academy in his five years as superintendent, and on paper Mariel Forrest certainly fit a common pattern: late twenties/early thirties and still unmarried, with excellent credentials but perhaps a little bored by her position in the States. On paper a close fit, but in person she was far from typical. In the world of missionaries, where inhabitants almost prided themselves on ignoring their appearance, she had an obvious flair about her, a sense of style that came from an inborn confidence in the way she looked—and she looked great. Tall, slender, blond hair, subtle makeup, and an almost regal bearing.

He shook her hand, and his interest sparked. *Why, of all places, had this woman come to Hudson?*

"Please sit down," Adam said, pointing toward one of the two chairs. He came around from behind his desk to take the other chair, a move deliberately designed to set people at ease. His first question was chosen for the same reason. "Well, Miss Forrest, what do you think of Taiwan?"

She raised her eyebrows.

"Oh, I know," Adam grinned. "Not exactly an original opening, but useful. What has impressed you? The heat? The smells? The crowds?"

She took her time choosing an answer. "Yes," she agreed finally. "All those, but the traffic has been the biggest surprise."

Adam nodded. "Back in the States, you probably saw motorcycles only occasionally. Here, during rush hour, you might see 500 around a single intersection."

She barely smiled, and Adam's eyes narrowed. Something in the tilt of her head gave him the distinct impression that she was looking down on him. He wondered again whether her poise was inbred or whether she had learned to use it as a defense. He began to suspect the latter. When his expression softened, Mariel's chin rose even higher.

"What brought you overseas, Mariel—may I call you Mariel?"

"Of course. Please do," she said, but refused to return the compliment. "I came overseas for all the standard reasons: a change, a challenge, a desire to see a new place and meet new people."

Adam flicked through her papers again and nodded. "You certainly have an active appetite for change. Since college you've lived in Ohio, Washington, D.C., Illinois, and now you've moved here. Why so many moves?"

"As you said—a taste for change."

This time Adam studied her openly for a moment, noting the signs of tension in her face and hands, and he tried unsuccessfully to lighten things up with a smile. "Well, Hudson will offer you plenty of that," he finally said.

He then turned the interview to her course load, which she knew from their correspondence in the spring. Mariel would have three classes in the mornings: grammar, a writing course for sophomores, and senior thesis. In the afternoon she would have a two-hour journalism lab.

"Senior thesis?"

"Our seniors write on a topic related to theology. We hope they will graduate with a firmer grasp on their beliefs." Adam caught a small frown moving across her face. "Is that a problem?"

"I know next to nothing about theology!"

"Oh, don't misunderstand. Thomas Cartwright, the school pastor, teaches the content side; you handle the writing—a team-teaching approach that has worked well for us. After sitting through Thomas's lectures this fall, you'll feel more ready to help in the spring when they write their papers, and Thomas will be on hand as well."

Adam paused for a moment, waiting for a further question or comment, but Mariel Forrest was clearly a woman who preferred silence.

He proceeded with another of his standard questions. "Speaking of theology, how did you become a Christian?"

Blankness fell over her expression the way window shades fall at the approach of a bill collector. Adam hadn't realized the question would so demoralize her—it never had this effect on other teachers. His curiosity heightened.

"Do you want my testimony? I thought I covered that in my application."

"I'd still like to hear it again."

She took a small breath and began. "I accepted Christ when I was a child through my parents' witness. I attended church through my childhood and maintained Christian contacts through college. As to how I came to Hudson, in college Amanda Harrison—you might remember her, she graduated from Hudson about ten years ago—she suggested that I look into teaching at a missionary kids' school, and here I am."

Adam had the sensation of a neatly wrapped package thrown to him. "And God, Mariel? Do you believe God wants you here?"

"Of course."

He said nothing, waiting her out.

"Mr. Lyons, I have never been as capable as others seem to be at divining God's will. Amanda suggested; I followed up on it. As far as I'm concerned, that's how God's will works itself out for me."

"If a student asked you, what would you say God means to you?"

She took another breath, longer this time and slower. "I believe God made the world—he's my creator. I believe he sent Jesus to redeem me, so I belong to him. He rules me. He's the ultimate authority in all life whether a person acknowledges him or not." From his expression she knew she still hadn't found the right words. Impatiently, she added, "What else should I say?"

"Nothing, nothing, not if you have nothing to add," Adam said, shifting in his chair. "That's fine. Then let's talk about your living arrangements. As you know, we provide housing free of charge as part of your salary. You'll have an apartment next to another young teacher, Katy Martin. Our houses and apartments are built up alongside the school, so you'll find yourself among other teachers. They'll be good neighbors. As I understand it, Chet Carlton has already lined up some used furniture for you, so you can move in anytime." He suddenly grinned. "You'll like Katy Martin, although watch out! For your sake and hers I hope she's settled down since the days she spent here in high school. If not, perhaps you can be a calming influence!"

Before concluding the interview, Adam escorted her around campus. The school sat within a large fenced-in compound surrounded by rice fields on three sides and bordered on the fourth by a narrow road that ran toward the city of Taichung. The playing fields, a large, modern gymnasium, and a swimming pool filled the back of the compound. Dormitories skirted one wall and faculty housing the other.

Even to Adam, the buildings in the main part of campus looked depressingly plain: the ever-present gray concrete walls, the simplest possible rectangular shapes, a walkway along the bottom floor, and a wide balcony along the second. There didn't seem to be any pattern to the position of the buildings, and indeed they had been planted as second and third thoughts in response to a growing need for space. The one saving feature of the area was a shady plaza sandwiched between the classroom buildings and the library. Ten or twelve eating areas, each with its own tree, hugged the perimeter, leaving the center area free. And for now, very quiet.

Without the students, the school sat waiting and watchful.

Adam wondered if Mariel realized how very different this teaching experience would be from her past ones. She must know, for like the school she was waiting and watchful, clearly on her guard.

Back in his office now, Adam closed the interview with a firm handshake. "Well, Mariel, if you have no further questions, let me formally welcome you to our staff."

Drawn irresistibly to the window, Adam watched Mariel walk across campus to the entrance. He had thought at first she was too thin; her hands especially seemed fragile. Watching her move now, he realized that hers was the build of a dancer, each ounce tuned to move with elegance and grace. Through the interview she had seemed poised, though whether for flight or battle, he didn't know. She had stood her ground like a fighter, yet he thought her oddly reluctant to confront spiritual matters. *Had she some hidden failing, perhaps, some old sin that haunted her?* Only once had he seen her falter and that had been over God's role in her life. In response to his simple request for her testimony, he had seen in her eyes what could only be called fear. *Odd.*

On the main road, as Mariel waited in the heat for a taxi to take her back to the Carltons' guest house, she lifted her hands to warm cheeks, smiling ruefully. How predictably she had responded to Adam Lyons! No wonder Mrs. Carlton had felt compelled to warn her.

Yet, if the mission field truly was full of single women, Mariel's was not the first heart to beat more rapidly in Adam Lyons's presence. She dropped her hands, willing herself to leave thoughts of him behind. She did, at least, have enough presence of mind to avoid that complication, didn't she?

As for the other problem…the old familiar languor settled over her as she glanced back up at the gateway of the school. Hudson Christian Academy. The name was emblazoned in both English and Chinese across the arch leading into the school compound. Emphasis on the *Christian*.

Mariel had first heard of Hudson from Amanda, a friend at college. Amanda had spoken fondly of the missionary kids' school she had attended through high school, and as the two women had neared graduation, Amanda had tried to interest Mariel in applying for a teaching position at the school straight out of college. No chance, not with David waiting for her. She and David had moved to Ohio and lived there for four years.

Lived? More like suffered. But that wasn't entirely true. The years after Annie was born had been wonderful. It was what followed that had been so awful.

During those horrible days after Annie's death, lying in the dark beside David, trying desperately to deal with her pain, she had pictured God as a willful child playing with tiny Lego blocks, Annie a small figure he could crush at will, and Mariel standing nearby in plastic immobility, unable to stop him. He must have noticed them one day and, on a whim, plucked up all Mariel loved and threw it across His cosmic room, momentarily amusing Himself but leaving her eternally bereft.

Capricious, spoiled, unkind. That was her God and David's death did nothing to change her mind.

Amanda came to visit Mariel after David died and again suggested Hudson as a partial solution to Mariel's loneliness and grief. Amanda sounded like an armed forces commercial: Apply to Hudson and see the world. At least it would mean a new start.

Mariel had scoffed at the idea. *She, become a missionary, with her twisted view of God?*

But Mariel *was* restless, so she took Amanda's suggestion for a change and moved from Ohio to a teaching job in Washington, D.C. The change didn't help and after a year she moved back to Illinois where she had grown up. Maybe a return to her roots was what she needed.

It only hurt more. The reasons for so many of her attitudes and habits became clear to her, and Mariel felt even more bound by behaviors she couldn't change, trapped and imprisoned.

The image of that capricious and willful God hardened and choked her, and her malice distilled into a toxic bitterness that made her literally sick.

An ulcer, the doctor had said a year ago, and asked about her diet. Something in Mariel's laughter must have alarmed him for he recommended a psychiatrist, and Mariel was desperate enough to try, but the psychiatrist's endless reflecting and steadfast unwillingness to advise her had not helped at all.

In despair, last summer, three years after David's death, Mariel went reluctantly to visit Amanda at her midwestern seminary. Amanda, the missionaries' daughter, the Bible student, blunt, uncompromising, the friend she had been most avoiding. After Amanda's initial surprise at seeing Mariel, she welcomed Mariel and returned to her studies, uncharacteristically silent over the reasons for Mariel's visit. Amanda gave Mariel free use of a cot in her spare bedroom and an unspoken willingness to listen whenever Mariel wanted to talk.

Mariel had stayed in Amanda's tiny apartment all summer, compulsively putting puzzles together, sometimes wandering through a nearby nature reserve, and so often sleeping and then waking to sleep again. Days and weeks with everything on hold, until finally she had spoken, disgorging her doubts like a vile discharge.

Amanda calmly heard her out, sorting dispassionately through everything and leading Mariel to acknowledge what she had most feared: Somehow in spite of her worst accusations, Mariel was unable to deny her desperate need for God.

"We humans are capable of incredible feats of self-delusion," Amanda said gently. "Some people live their entire lives in obvious paradox and contradiction. They survive, who knows how? But *you* can't, Mariel. Temperamentally, you can't delude yourself that way—not about God. You want to change him, but you know you can't, and it's screwing you up. Mentally, you seem to be coping. Physically, not so good. Spiritually, you're in big trouble."

Disgusted, Mariel turned her spite inward, mocking herself for clinging to a child's fantasy of God.

Amanda merely shook her head: Was it foolish to have faith or foolish to deny the need for it?

"Find out which it is for you," Amanda had said. "Are you a Christian or aren't you? I think you should do what I suggested that first summer after David died. Go out to Hudson and live among men and women who have committed their lives to Christ and left family and home to serve him. Find out there what you really believe. God will find you anywhere, but I think he'll heal you more quickly among Christians."

Mariel had put it off for six months, then finally applied to Hudson during a bleak day after Christmas. Thirty-two years old, and she was purposely challenging God to prove himself to her. Even the angels didn't test God. Talk about a fool.

Having decided to come to Hudson, however, Mariel lied about her past, listing herself as single and childless. She wanted to hide her lingering grief and avoid everyone's pity. Why clue these people in and let them tailor themselves to whatever they imagined she needed from them?

The taxi pulled up outside the school gate and Mariel climbed in wearily, settling herself back uncomfortably against the patchy plastic seat. As the taxi bounced and jolted through the crowded streets, she let the unfamiliar scenes of Taichung slip past in an unfocused blur until she finally slumped against the side window and closed her eyes. This was the arena in which Amanda had been so certain God would confront her. So be it.

He could take his best shot, but he'd better not expect any help from her.

Two

A week after that first interview with Adam Lyons, just as dusk was falling, Mariel paid off another taxi at the school gate and carried her small bag of groceries down the row of buildings toward her own apartment. From Gladys Carlton, she had received guided tours of both the earlier warren of stalls in the block-size traditional market and the more modern Western-style stores. After a week in Taichung, she could quickly maneuver the taxi ride downtown for her shopping.

The humid August weather oppressed her, and Mariel walked slowly. The early evening offered no relief from the heat of the sun. Only the dust seemed to have energy, dancing brief dirges around her to the wind's tune.

She had been given a small, second-story, one-bedroom apartment identical to the one next door and the two apartments downstairs. They all had three-and-a-half rooms: a rather spacious living/dining room that took fully the front half of the floor space, a minuscule kitchenette through the door on the right, a smallish bedroom on the left, and a cramped bathroom tucked behind the kitchenette.

A long, screened-in balcony porch ran the length of the two second-story apartments, with stone steps giving access from one end. Having settled in first, Mariel had chosen the apartment farthest from the steps.

Now as she climbed the stairs, she heard voices overhead. Mariel paused for a moment and leaned against the wall, wishing she could avoid meeting whoever was up there. Then she shrugged fatalistically and went on.

Two people sat on the porch. The young woman stood up and exclaimed, "You must be Mariel! How nice to meet you! I'm Katy Martin. Come sit down and talk with us!"

Katy Martin's uninhibited black curls and diminutive stature couldn't contain the energy of her smile.

The young man, like Katy in his early twenties, leaned indolently against a balcony pillar. His easy stance failed to prepare Mariel for the alert gaze he turned upon her.

"I...I don't think..." Mariel stammered, trying to find a way to refuse and escape.

Katy laughed. "Of course. I forgot to introduce you. This is Luke Shepard. We're talking about school starting next week. Go dump your groceries and I'll get you some iced tea. Isn't this heat *awful?*"

As Mariel settled into the patio chair a few minutes later, she studied Katy's friend. Dressed in shorts and a rough-cut muscle shirt, Luke Shepard looked deceptively average, height under 6', his build so lean he bordered on skinny, his dusty blond hair cut a little too short for Mariel's liking.

Luke smiled, and a glint in his eyes betrayed his amusement at Mariel's perusal. She dropped her eyes, feeling her cheeks flush. *Far from average,* she admitted to herself. Almost ten years younger than she was and still able to make her feel very much a woman. How close *were* he and Katy?

Katy came out with iced tea and handed the glass to Mariel. "Luke and I went to college together," she said, finishing her introduction. "He's teaching chemistry and physics and senior math, I think?" After a nod from Luke, she went on. "We met in college, hung around together, had the same friends. If you ever find yourself playing volleyball, be sure Luke's on your side. He's got a wicked serve."

His smile was merely friendly now. "All wickedness reserved for volleyball, I assure you," he said. A comfortable strength coursed through Luke's hand as he gripped Mariel's. "So where are you from?"

Mariel told them and asked her own polite questions in turn. The conversation eventually turned to teaching, specifically Luke's inexperience.

"Even if Luke hasn't ever taught before," Katy said, "he'll be great. I should know. In college I had some foolish notion of becoming a physical therapist, so the very first year I signed up for chemistry. I would have dropped out before the first big test if Luke hadn't rescued me. He was my lab partner."

Luke's lips twitched.

"Oh, don't look like that," Katy said, and then laughed. "He's thinking of our first lab together, Mariel. I connected the Bunsen burner to the water spout instead of the gas outlet. When I turned the burner on, water sprayed all over us and most of the lab!"

Under cover of their laughter, Mariel studied them. Friends, obviously, of long standing if they had met as freshmen, but judging from Katy's casual attitude, not much more than friends.

"Actually, I'm surprised you got a job here without at least some student teaching like I had," Katy said. "Hudson's one of the best missionary schools in the world."

"Not biased are you?" Luke teased.

"What if I am? It's still true. At the beginning, the school board recruited teachers from people already out here, mostly wives, of course. Now, with almost six hundred students, Hudson hires its own teachers—although we all have to form some kind of affiliation with a mission board so that we have a support structure here. You did, didn't you, Mariel?"

"Yes, with the Evangelical Christian Mission."

"Luke and I are with my parents' mission board. Anyway, based on being a student myself here, I think the administration's pretty selective."

"How *did* you qualify, Luke?" Mariel asked.

Luke gave a lopsided grin. "Good grades, I suppose. And science teachers are hard to find anywhere these days."

"Will you stay a while?" Mariel asked.

"Only one year, and then I'm going to graduate school."

"Why Hudson?" Mariel persisted.

Luke smiled again at Katy. "No mystery there. Through my lab partner here, I met a lot of missionary kids, ended up rooming with one from Kenya and hung around with some others. When I decided to take a year off, going overseas naturally appealed. Hudson was the only one of the three schools with vacancies that needed someone for one year only."

"Mr. Avery, our usual science teacher, is on furlough," Katy explained.

"And, of course, Katy would be here," Mariel said mildly, still trying to discover their relationship.

"Oh, I had nothing to do with it!" Katy exclaimed. "I decided before Christmas, got Adam Lyons to hire me, and Luke did the same later in January without either of us knowing the other was coming. I think all our friends breathed a collective sigh of relief. They're glad Luke's here to keep me in protective custody."

Luke grunted in denial, and Katy jumped up to throw an arm around his shoulders. "Really, Mariel! Since the days of freshman chemistry Luke's been my knight in shining armor, beating off all my dragons!"

"Dragons," Mariel said. "What dragons?"

Katy settled back down into her chair, tucking one foot comfortably under her. "Here's the worst," she began. "We went to a college named Crocker—Crocker College, in Crocker, California. Small, Christian, liberal arts, conservative right down to its rule on alcohol—which was don't drink *any!* Anyway, my roommate's name was Christie and I was Katy, of course, and we decided one night—and we hadn't broken the rule on alcohol, I promise you; we hadn't drunk anything stronger than Seven-Up laced with orange juice—anyway late one night when we were kind of silly from writing a paper on Kafka, which could make a saint insane, we decided that what our room really needed," and here Katy grinned ruefully at Luke, who rolled his eyes in mock disgust, "we decided what we really needed were the 'C' and 'K' from the CROCKER COLLEGE sign out in front of the campus."

"Katy!"

"Sure. We had a place picked out on our wall, the one touch of class in a room of cast-offs and garage-sale buys. Heavy brass letters about eight to ten inches high—absolute glitz."

"So somewhere between 2:00 and 3:00 A.M.," Luke continued, "Christie and Katy put on black pants and dark sweatshirts, crept over to the CROCKER sign, and filched the letters."

Katy smiled warmly. "A deed that brought on the first dragon Luke fought off for me."

The glance Luke and Katy exchanged was so familiar that Mariel wondered again about their relationship. Could they really be just friends?

"You can smile now," Luke said, "but I remember a time when you could hardly speak for crying."

Katy shuddered. "In chapel the next morning, the dean gave a long sermon on honesty, responsibility, and morality, and all manner of other admirable characteristics in which the perpetrators of this criminal act—in a word, thieves—were obviously deficient. To help supply those traits, let it be known that upon discovery this person or persons would be summarily reprimanded, chastised, punished, and suspended. If it sounds as if I'm making light of it, I am, on purpose, because even now thinking about that awful day makes me feel as if someone is cutting a chunk out of my stomach. The dean ended by saying that not only was our spiritual character of concern, but the silly letters cost $350 each."

"Chemistry lab came right after chapel," Luke said. "By the time Katy finally showed up forty-five minutes later, she was ready to tell me everything. She was really rattled. She couldn't think of anything to do except trying to put the letters back that night. I suggested a much wiser action."

"Confessing?" Mariel supplied helpfully.

Katy and Luke laughed. "Hardly!" Katy said with a further giggle. "Luke was as devious as I was dumb. Right after lab we took the wretched things down to a self-service post office—so we couldn't be recognized, you understand—and sent them to the dean, post-paid, with the president's return address!"

Try as she might, Mariel couldn't keep from laughing. "All this time, no one knows you took them?"

Sobering, Katy shook her head. "I finally told the dean at the end of my junior year. Christie had transferred to a state university by that time—" here Luke interjected a grunt that sounded like "Good riddance," which brought a squelching look from Katy, "so she didn't mind my telling. I felt like I had to confess when the Board of Trustees recommended me for the CRS Award."

"It's an annual award for service and scholarship," Luke explained, "which Katy deserved to win. She worked all four years with CRS—Christian Relief Services—a group of ministries that students at Crocker can work in. Like a prison ministry or nursing homes or inner city kids' clubs. Katy went once a week to Haven House, a home for battered women."

"I cooked meals and played with the kids. It was no big deal."

"You also helped them during your vacations, didn't you?"

"Mom and Dad were over here, so why not?"

"And there was the playground—"

Katy nodded. "Right. My first year there I decided the place needed a playset. The mothers wouldn't go to the park, of course, and the backyard was pretty dull stuff. We raised some money and went around and lined up volunteer labor, and I think that's what got me the service award, all that fund-raising."

"Not only that," Luke objected. "Grades and commitment and a lot more, too, though the playground alone should have been enough. No little swing set, you understand. Katy talked local merchants into donating supplies and raised money to hire a nearby playground designer, then lined up the students who could do the actual work. In the end the kids had what looked like a cross between a castle and a three-dimensional labyrinth with places to climb and hide and crawl across and swing from and slide down. It was incredible."

"The kids loved it. I think it really helped the women to see their children having such fun."

"But what does all this have to do with stealing the letters?"

"Oh, I refused the award," Katy said. "How could I take an award like that—it was a full year's tuition—when I'd done something so crazy? When the dean told me I had won, I confessed the whole sorry story, told him I couldn't possibly accept, and had to watch it go to someone else."

"You could have taken it." Luke sounded as if he'd said the same thing before, many times. "The dean accepted your apology and said the award was still yours. Everyone knew you should have gotten it."

"Maybe. But I felt better refusing it. Besides if I hadn't told the dean, I might be sitting here tonight wondering if my degree itself were in jeopardy!"

Luke shook his head in hopeless denial.

"Anyway," Katy said, "I'm glad Luke's here and that I'm going to be living next to you, Mariel. I'm so excited about being back at Hudson, and I just know this is going to be a *great* year!"

Luke smiled at Mariel over Katy's head, and Mariel smiled back, sensing an unexpected and, for once, not unwelcome bond between them.

The sunshine had turned golden as it neared the horizon, and its oppressive heat had abated. Its warmth on Mariel's face felt like a caress now. She leaned back into her chair and took a deep breath, for the first time in so long, without tension.

In the following days, Katy introduced Mariel and Luke to a side of Taichung Mrs. Carlton had neglected in her routine introductory tour: the theaters where American movies were incredibly cheap, the bookstores selling pirated best-sellers and cassettes, beauty parlors where a shampoo and set cost hardly more than a dollar. Best of all, Katy led them into the flower stalls where Mariel purchased a massive bouquet of fresh-cut roses for next to nothing.

"An apple costs a fortune, but you can buy a rose for what a stick of gum would cost in the States," Katy said, shrugging. "I'd call it even, wouldn't you?"

Mariel and Katy agreed to share a cleaning lady, someone to tidy the apartment, do their shopping, and keep a supply of fresh flowers. Reluctant at first to hire anyone as a servant or to give up her privacy, Mariel finally saw the sense of such an arrangement. They would pay the woman well, and she would do the jobs they preferred to avoid. It was a fair bargain, Katy said, and Mariel finally agreed.

Mariel was surprised to find herself so at ease in Katy's company and in Luke's, who came often in the evenings to sit with them on their porch. They never pried into Mariel's past and seemed willing to tolerate Mariel's moods and occasional demands for privacy. They did most of the talking, with Mariel sitting and listening, enjoying their optimism and youth. *They brought as much sunshine to the porch,* she thought, *as the sun itself did.*

With their friendship Mariel took a first step, a big one.

The next had to be going to church.

Until Katy moved in, Mariel had avoided going at all, but she knew now that Katy would expect Mariel to go with her. And really, Mariel had known she would have to attend. The Hudson community was so small that her absence would be obvious. No one had said church attendance was actually required, but what missionary would not want to attend church?

Well...Mariel, for one.

After Annie died, she and David had attended church only once, months after her funeral, during the time they were seeing a counselor. Sitting there in a pew, an image of that small malicious child she thought of as God had risen up before her and repelled her, so that she couldn't join in with the songs and prayers that had once been so routine for her. She felt pity and contempt for the faith of those around her, but hated herself even more for the deep regret she felt over her own loss of that faith. Finally, unable to bear the confusion, Mariel had risen and walked out, and David had followed.

If she had stayed...? If David hadn't followed her...?

The answers to those questions threatened unavoidable guilt, and she had not allowed herself to follow through on them.

So, even more than she had dreaded meeting Adam Lyons, Mariel dreaded meeting the school pastor. He seemed the obvious choice to be God's champion, if God needed someone like that. She had heard a lot about Thomas Cartwright from Adam when he told her about the theology classes and from Katy, who spoke of him with great fondness and respect. In her mind, Mariel made him out to be God's great warrior, probably a foolish notion but one that lingered and unnerved her.

She first met Pastor Cartwright a few days after she met Katy. He called and asked her to come to the school and discuss the theology class.

The afternoon was another distressingly warm one, and as with Adam she felt drained before she even entered the classroom. She didn't see him at first. He was at the back, looking out the window toward the faculty housing. He must have been watching her approach. *Wonderful. An advance reconnaissance.*

Then he turned to greet her, and the image of a mighty warrior vanished. He was a short, small-boned man, around sixty, with bushy white hair, a friendly face, and a quiet, gentle voice. *An absentminded scholar,* she thought, then heard the hope in the thought. She could handle a scholar, couldn't she? After he introduced himself, he smiled and looked at her with interest, but after only a few questions, sensing her reticence, he turned quickly to business.

He began by running through the theology course outline with her: how God reveals himself, the attributes of God, Christ, the Holy Spirit, the doctrine of man and the fall, salvation, and several other topics.

"I do hope you'll feel free to join in the discussion," he said. "We spend a good part of the class exploring issues related to these doctrines. In the past, my team teachers have been among the most vocal participants, but..." he smiled and shrugged, "it's good for kids to know that many issues aren't settled, that we're all growing—even me."

He paused, waiting for some comment from Mariel, but her silence held.

"Now you, Mariel, will really start working the second semester when students begin writing. They prepare a personal creed first and then a fifteen- to twenty-page paper on an issue related to theology. They present this report orally in class. I'll help anytime you want with the content, but I'll leave the presentation for you to work on with the students. Sound okay?"

Mariel nodded slowly. Moments later, assured that she had no questions, he rose and walked her back across campus to her apartment, speaking of his own children and their experiences in college and his desire to help the students make the transition easily.

Not a word about church.

He must have known that she'd been in Taiwan a few weeks and hadn't yet come to church, but…nothing.

Apprehension crept over Mariel after he left her at her apartment, again the dread of a warrior in a mismatched battle. Curiosity, pity, unwanted advice, or blame—she had become adept at dealing with those. She had met her share of pompous, self-focused ministers without the intelligence or mental courage to see two sides of an issue. But Pastor Cartwright, who must have sensed her unfriendliness, had been resolutely kind.

Disliking him would have been so much easier to sustain, she thought regretfully. Instead his gentleness had drawn her to him.

In her inexorable march toward a confrontation with God, she had now met his champion, and she was far from confident.

In church the next Sunday, she tried hard to relax, forcing herself to replace the capricious child with her former image of God, a stern, elderly judge, and wished she could believe instead that God was like Thomas Cartwright.

"He looks a little like an elf, doesn't he?" Katy whispered, and Mariel managed a stiff smile in response.

He preached like a scholar, logically, calmly, steadily, answering questions even as she silently raised them, and she realized there was nothing childish about his faith. He was speaking from Colossians, and he brought into his sermon a wealth of information from church history and theology, scholarly interpretation, and practical application.

Some preachers had the effect of a stick of dynamite, loud, forceful, and dramatic; Thomas Cartwright had the power of a slow and steady stream of wisdom—and his quiet reasoning probably altered his listeners more effectively than louder, more explosive speakers would. The thought was little comfort to Mariel.

In the first weeks of his theology class she discovered how right her apprehension was but not for the reason she thought. He was an excellent teacher. When class began she immediately sensed the students' affection and respect for him. Easygoing, friendly bantering between the students and Pastor Cartwright quickly quieted to attentive silence when he began his lecture. His relaxed delivery encouraged student response, and he soon began asking them questions: how each had become a Christian, what they considered most important to their Christian growth, why they were Christians.

She must have shown her panic that day and in the ones following, for within a week he asked her quietly after class to wait. He wanted to speak with her. His was the last class before lunch, so he knew she would have time.

The students filed out, and then he turned to her, studying her thoughtfully. "Mariel, tell me what you think—why should we study theology?"

She sighed and turned away from him and concentrated on what she thought he wanted to hear. "To know more about God, to grow in our faith." He didn't seem satisfied. "All that you've said, Pastor Cartwright. It sounds good."

"No, Mariel. Tell me yourself."

A difficult swallow. "He's...God. A major player—whether we want him to be or not. I mean, whether a person believes in him or not. It's...it's good to know what we're up against."

35

Something in his eyes—pity? compassion?—made her realize what she had said, and she shook her head helplessly. "That came out wrong. I'm sorry. I don't mean to make him our opponent."

He nodded, as if she had confirmed something for him, and she wanted to cry in frustration. Half-turning toward the door, she mumbled something about lunch.

He touched her arm to stop her, and she looked up miserably.

"Mariel," he said, so gently, "you seem very troubled, but whatever it is, please don't be afraid of me. I will not ask you questions about your faith, ever, in this class or out of it. When you can talk, when you are ready to work through whatever's troubling you…" he paused, his eyes filling with compassion, "when it becomes impossible, then come to me, and by God's grace I'll try to help you. Until then, please believe me, you have nothing to fear from me."

Tears sprang to her eyes, drawn by his gentleness. For one brief moment she faltered and then with a muttered apology she fled to her lunch. No wonder she was afraid.

Three

Mariel loved sports. As an only child in a neighborhood with mostly older children and with a father who spent hours of every weekend watching the sport of the season, Mariel had become hooked very early. She eventually realized that athletics was a sop to her thirst for justice: clearly defined rules, handy judges, quickly enforced verdicts.

"Wouldn't it be nice if life had rules like sports does?" she had asked her father once.

"Of course we have rules," he had said, everything so simple for him. "In the Bible. God Himself will judge whether you keep them!"

It must have seemed to her father that God had judged *him* worthy. He had a beautiful wife, a well-behaved daughter, a prosperous business, and an expensive suburban home—health, wealth, and ease.

"Anyone can have a good life," he told her. "Work hard and live a clean life. God will reward you."

What had sounded so simple to him, however, caused

increasing anxiety in Mariel, for she had little confidence in the outcome of God's judgment on her own life. Consequently, as she grew, she purposely limited her expectations. She took risks like a three-toed sloth did—not at all—so that even though she loved sports, she never actually tried out for a sports team.

She never stopped loving sports, though, and had long been a fan and involved on the periphery. So when Katy asked Mariel soon after school started if she would like to help coach volleyball—keep stats and supplies and generally cheer Katy as she took on the team—Mariel agreed. Her after-school hours became busy.

In the evenings Mariel managed to keep up on her classes. She had been quickly drawn into the familiar patterns of teaching, reading papers, working through revisions with students, drilling on editing skills, and then making new assignments.

To encourage the students to express themselves, she proposed a regular column called "The Debater's Choice" to Steven Williams, the student editor of the school newspaper. He readily accepted the idea and included a notice asking other teachers to recommend papers.

During the third week of school, Ned Waters, the history teacher, brought an offering.

"I got this from Steven himself," Ned said, reflexively smoothing his hair back. Ned was young, newly graduated from college, with strong ideals and still-fresh ambitions for his students. "We've been studying the place of war in history, and the juniors read *Walden* in English, so I suppose it was natural that Steven would write on civil disobedience. It's worth publishing, I think."

It was indeed. Mariel read the piece to her journalism class and filed it in the "Print" folder for the coming issue.

The next morning, Mariel found a note from Adam Lyons in her mailbox, asking her to come to his office at the beginning of the lunch hour. A flicker of alarm swept through Mariel at the thought of meeting with Adam. Each time she was in the same room with him she had to force herself to function as if all was normal, and yet with him nearby, his presence compelled her attention, whatever she did.

Fortunately, she had seen Adam rarely since school began, usually in meetings or the faculty lounge. Once, during someone's report, she had glanced up at a faculty meeting and found him watching her. It must have been a coincidence, for he had merely smiled and turned his attention back to the speaker. Even so, his brief study stole her composure.

Another day he dropped by her journalism class, but she was hard at work and didn't notice him immediately. When she looked up and saw him by the door, he continued watching her for a moment more, his thoughts a mystery to her. Then he smiled, said, "Carry on," and was gone. *This was not odd,* she told herself repeatedly. *He probably walked through the school routinely, checking on things.* But the memory of that moment before he smiled, when their eyes met and held, continued to haunt her.

Adam's daughter, Holly, was in two of Mariel's classes, journalism and freshman grammar, and from her Mariel learned a little more about Adam. Holly was an adequate writer and had a natural flair for layout, so she promised to be an important asset to both the newspaper and yearbook staffs. Cheerful and adventurous, she was immensely popular with her classmates. She was also precocious and playful, and just a little wild, with a flair all her own. Mariel imagined Adam must be very proud of Holly, if also a little concerned by how far she pushed the limits of good behavior. More than once, Mariel caught herself thinking about Adam as she watched Holly work. *Had Holly's rebellious streak come from Adam himself, a reflection of his own adolescence?*

So far, Mariel had avoided investigating that and other questions about Adam firsthand. Now she had another command visit.

Mariel stood looking down at the note so intently that Luke, passing her in the mailroom, had to speak twice before she heard him. Mariel sighed. Once again that man had dominated her thoughts.

"Bad news?" Luke asked.

Mariel shook her head slowly. "No. I don't think so. I hope not."

When she entered his office, Adam rose to greet her. "Thank you for coming so quickly," he said.

Mariel forced herself to offer a cool smile in response to his greeting, her sophistication a handy mask for the troubled emotions inside.

He gestured to a chair. "Please sit down, Mariel. I don't want to take any more of your lunch hour than necessary, so let me get to the point immediately: your 'Debater's Choice' column."

"I don't understand."

"The column's an excellent idea, don't get me wrong, but I don't want you to publish Steven's civil disobedience piece." He came around the desk, leaned against its front edge, and looked down at her.

Overdoing the authority bit, aren't you, she thought grimly.

As if aware of her thoughts, he shifted to the chair beside her. "You and Ned Waters weren't to know, as it's so foreign to those of us raised in a country that values free press so much, but putting something into print that justifies disobeying the government—well, it's not a diplomatic thing to do in another country, especially one without our freedoms. Thoreau's book is here, and we study it in our school, but I think in deference to the standards of this country, we'll pass on publishing Steven's paper."

Adam was looking across at her now, but with no less authority than before. Still a command from on high.

"As you wish," she said, starting to rise. "Thanks for explaining in person."

Adam put out a hand to stop her. "There's something else. A request this time. We have our new teachers speak in chapel soon after school starts so the entire school can meet them. Usually they give their testimony and tell a little about their professional background. We schedule two to a chapel, so you'll have about fifteen minutes."

"My testimony?"

"And perhaps something from the Bible."

Mariel took a deep breath and concentrated on lowering the pitch of her voice. "I don't think so, Mr. Lyons."

"Stage fright? Most teachers are a little nervous, Mariel."

"No. That's never been a problem for me."

His eyes narrowed. Too late, she realized she should have taken the excuse he offered. Now he was obviously trying to decide what was the problem. She hurried to interrupt his thoughts.

"Look, I'll speak if you want...on...on something. I could talk about persuasion, if you want. That could have some religious applications, I would think. Or about why writing is such an important life skill. But not my testimony."

He studied her, considering her words. He was obviously not used to being denied. "You won't give your testimony?" He sounded like her unwillingness was a capital offense. He lifted his eyebrows in a clear indication of criticism. "Very well; we'll postpone it." He rose and stood looking down at her. "Mariel—" he began, stopped himself, shook his head, and moved to open the door for her. "Fine. That's all for now. You may go."

She felt an overpowering urge to slam the door behind her.

After she left, Adam stood at the window as he had in August, watching her walk across the plaza. Something was very wrong for her, and it was not surprising it had reached into her spiritual life. Trouble finds its way there for all Christians, he knew, either to be resolved or to fester and do damage. *Probably a man,* he decided, *one who had hurt her. A woman so attractive did not reach her age without some involvement with a man. She had suffered a loss,* he thought, *and for some reason had turned against God. Perhaps she had lived with the man, become pregnant, perhaps even had an abortion...*

He felt the need somehow to face the worst of possibilities with her, but as his suspicions spiraled further down into the darkest of sins, he felt even more the grip of compassion and a desire to shield her from pain.

Mariel Forrest. He said her name again, slowly, letting the sound echo softly through the room. He had met many women since Jenny died, some very attractive, a few even intriguing. What was it about this woman that put such an overwhelming desire in his heart to protect her, and why did it mean so much to see her smile? Most incredibly, how had he known within thirty seconds of meeting her that she would plant herself so deeply into his thoughts, inhabit his dreams, even shape his ambitions?

Courage, he told himself, and knew he would need it.

With Jenny, he was so young. At that age, he easily fit into a pattern of mutual pleasure, mutual gratification. Only with time did he come to understand how much of love requires sacrifice. With Mariel, if God really did want this, he would have to begin with that knowledge. It was a daunting thought, to be drawn to someone so troubled, and yet he also had fallen short of the glory of God. His own sins, if less grievous than whatever he was imagining with Mariel, had ruled his soul no less completely. Who was he to judge?

Across campus Mariel was asking herself the same question, but with a far different feeling behind her words: Just who was Adam Lyons to judge her? She sat down on a bench in the plaza to eat her lunch, but was too angry to unwrap it.

"Share this bench with you, Mariel?"

She looked up to find Luke standing before her. "Sure. Have a seat." She took out her sandwich but still couldn't eat.

Luke stretched his legs, massaged his neck, and then leaned back in a lanky expanse of relaxed muscles.

"This teaching is hard work!" he said. "They look skeptical in senior math and dazed in chemistry and downright frightened in physics. What am I trying to do here?"

"Disabuse them of the notion they can understand this world. They have to grow up sometime."

Too late, she realized how bitter she sounded. Luke turned thoughtful eyes on her.

"Perhaps," he said, a little gently, "they'll appreciate God's genius, as a result?"

Mariel grunted. "As in 'Who has known the mind of the Lord? Or who has been his counselor?'"

"Is it so bad for us to answer, 'no one'?"

When she didn't answer, he touched her shoulder and asked instead, "Mariel, what's wrong?"

She found it suddenly hard to breathe, as if walls were closing in on her, the walls of a maze without an exit, and in desperation she spilled out words: "Nothing's wrong. I'm okay, really. Don't worry about me."

But he waited, and into the silence came words she couldn't control: "It's just so hard to figure God out sometimes, to know what he requires."

"Requires?"

She knew she should stop, give an excuse and walk away, but somehow she couldn't hold the words back. "I've always been a Christian and always tried to do what's right. I liked church and my Christian friends and was too sensible to try drugs or sex or alcohol or anything like that. I knew God made us, and it made sense that he knew what was best. So I've never ever really stepped out of line very much." Her sandwich was disintegrating in her hands, torn strip by strip into shreds. "But none of it matters in the end, does it? None of the obeying or discipline or praying or anything. None of it counts with him; I know. We can try and try and try, but—oh, God!"

And surely angels in Heaven must have shivered, for her cry was the first prayer she had uttered in years.

She stopped speaking abruptly. *Fool! Why had she gone on so? Give her one kind, caring, attentive male, and she couldn't control herself.*

"What was it, Mariel?" Luke finally asked. "What hurt so badly?"

She would give him nothing else, not even tears.

"Mariel, when did you discover that none of it mattered to God?"

She finally shrugged, a stiff, defiant little movement, like a traitor might make after being sentenced. "It really doesn't matter anymore. I've got to go now, Luke."

She felt his eyes on her all across the plaza. She entered her classroom, closed the door behind her, and leaned back against it, weak with rage. She was stupid to speak so carelessly. It was Adam's fault, needling her into admitting her problems, and Luke's, for not leaving her alone.

But mostly her own. Why couldn't she keep her distance as she had planned?

Because you can't, she taunted herself. *You're a weak, undisciplined piece of putty, and you know you're dying to unload this on someone.*

Of all the things she had to admit to herself since coming to Taiwan, this was the hardest to accept. For three years, she had kept so much inside, and she thought it had been safely covered. Then the ulcer had boiled up, and now she was losing control. Her words to Luke had risen like gurgling bubbles from a foul-smelling pot. She *had* to unburden herself to someone, and quickly, or as Amanda had warned, her body would rebel again.

She sat on the porch that night in the gathering dusk, listening to the crickets and the bugs and the muffled street sounds, and she forced herself to acknowledge it. It frightened her to need someone so badly, but she could no longer ignore it.

Perhaps she should have stayed longer with that psychiatrist, but he had always seemed to be so much in the dark. The blind leading the blindfolded.

Who then? Katy was too young, in so many ways. Luke she

liked too much. Adam Lyons was out of the question. Pastor Cartwright? She wasn't ready yet to walk over the spiritual coals he would undoubtedly put before her.

It was Katy who provided the solution and that very evening, so soon after Mariel admitted the need that even Mariel suspected cosmic maneuvering. Katy climbed the stairs around 9:30 P.M., collapsed into the chair beside Mariel, and said, "I thought college was exhausting, but it was nothing compared to teaching!"

"What did you have tonight?"

"A Girls' Athletic Association meeting. Afterwards, some of them stayed behind to talk and then suddenly it was curfew, and I still have reams of papers to grade. I'll be up all night."

"It's tough."

"Anyway, I'm ready for a break. How about coming home with me this weekend?"

"Home?"

"To my parents' house in Tainan."

Mariel instinctively drew back. "I don't know, Katy. I've got a lot of work."

"You always do this!" Katy exclaimed. "How many invitations have you turned down since you came here? You're a recluse, did you know that? Oh, don't tighten up on me like that, Mariel. It's me—Katy. Are you really this shy?"

"I wish it were shyness," Mariel said. She felt spent, her earlier rage leaving her defenseless. "The truth is, I don't like people that much."

"But these are nice people around here!"

"Like Mrs. Carlton? She's an old gossip who picks away at everyone she knows until she finds something awful about them.

Adam Lyons is so smug—I can't stand it. Pastor Cartwright's all right, I suppose, but I feel like I'm under a microscope when I'm with him. It makes me nervous. As for the teachers—most of them simply don't interest me. It's always been like this with me. I'd rather be alone."

Katy was quiet, and Mariel's heart contracted in a sudden fear that she would lose her. "I suppose you think that's awful," she said, daring Katy to turn her away.

"Well," Katy said slowly, "I've never heard anyone admit it. Luke and I should be honored that you've spent so much time with us."

When Mariel flinched, Katy leaned over to grab her hand. "No, I really mean it. I'm glad you like us. You know—" she hesitated, obviously weighing the wisdom of her next words. "You could pray about this. Ask God to let you see the good in people."

Mariel made a scornful sound. *Like worrying about a dent on the fender,* she thought, *when the engine had burned out.*

"So you don't want to come for the weekend? We're really a non-threatening bunch."

Mariel wondered briefly if Luke had suggested the invitation after lunch, but she didn't care. She suddenly found Hudson oppressive, her apartment imprisoning, and Katy's parents' house was as good a change as any. She would go.

They went by train on Saturday morning and sat down almost immediately to a family lunch. Spencer Martin sat at the head: tall, deceptively serious, with a ready humor that frequently cracked his thick beard into a grin. At the other end of the table sat Rebecca Martin, small like Katy, warm-hearted, with a smile that lingered even when her face was in repose. Arrayed around

47

the table were Billy, eleven; Peter, fourteen; Troy, fifteen; Katy, and Mariel.

Anyone besides Mariel would have been gratified by their interest in her. They asked her questions, but with so many children eager to speak, they managed not to put her too much on the spot.

Mostly they laughed. For Mariel's benefit, they threw stories around the table like hot potatoes, with Rebecca occasionally starting a new one and Spence adding a droll comment. All seemed blessed with an ability to take the joke, laughing with the rest when the mud was on their face.

At one point, Mariel asked why missionaries seemed to have such big families. Many had four or five or even more children.

"Insanity," muttered Peter.

Troy had a different idea: "Overactive hormones."

"Troy!"

"Well, then, cold January nights."

"Troy Spencer Martin!"

"I think it's ready help around the house," said Katy.

"Having a maid is nice," Rebecca admitted, "but remember, I didn't have any disposable diapers for you."

"Lousy TV," whispered Troy.

Another scowl from Rebecca.

"Maybe they like kids," suggested Billy tentatively.

"I *know* that was our reason, Billy," confirmed Rebecca, clasping his hand. "If Christians all paid less attention to what they could give children and let themselves enjoy their children more, we'd all have more children. I'm sure of it."

Troy wasn't done. "Faulty pharmaceuticals?"

Spence laughed and then looked around the table. "I remember what it was for me. It was when you learned to walk. You'd be across the room, catch sight of me; your eyes would light up and out would come those little arms. You'd stumble across the room to me with such single-minded purpose, and I could read it in your eyes: profound joy at seeing me, supreme confidence in my ability to make you happy. Nothing can compare. That's when I'd know that we'd be wanting another one. We were never sorry."

"And we make life so interesting, don't we, Dad?" Peter said, grinning.

"Seven children would tend to do that, yes," he agreed.

Seven? Counting Katy's sister Bridget, who had stayed at Hudson for the weekend, Mariel counted only five Martin children.

After lunch, when Katy wandered into her father's study to talk to him, Mariel offered to help Rebecca with the dishes.

"Thank you. We do have a maid, but she doesn't come in on the weekends. Actually, when the children are at school, she only comes on weekday mornings."

Over the sudsy sink, Mariel asked about the other children. "I only count five," she said, with no premonition. "Are the others at college?"

For a moment, Rebecca stopped rinsing, then spoke slowly. "We had two other sons, Mariel, older than Katy. Nick was a year older and Christopher two years. We had those three right after we got married, when Spence was teaching. Then we waited for him to finish seminary before having any more. With that five-year gap between Katy and Bridget, the three older ones were closer than kin, I always thought, real kindred spirits to the end."

She put a glass into the drainer, moving deliberately, then continued. "One terrible day when Katy was fifteen, on a weekend like this when the children were home, we went on a picnic to one of the rivers up in the mountains. The older three wandered off after lunch to swim. According to Katy, Nick got caught in an eddy, Christopher shouted for her to get help, and then plunged in after him. We found them both later, much later, downriver, drowned."

Water from the dish drainer dripped ever so slowly into the sink. Mariel stared at Rebecca, her thoughts a whirl of shock and grief and sudden searing memory. Then Rebecca sighed, patted Mariel's arm to reassure her, and began to rinse again. "These things happen," she said absently.

"Yes, I know," Mariel said carefully. "I have a friend—her little girl died in a car accident. Maybe it wouldn't have been so bad, but her husband couldn't handle it and started drinking and—"

Mariel bit her lip. *A friend? If she couldn't control her voice, she wouldn't fool anyone, least of all Rebecca.*

"And?"

"Went out one night and crashed his car into a tree."

"And died?"

"Instantly."

"Oh, Mariel." Rebecca's voice shook with feeling.

Struggling to breathe evenly, Mariel continued. "Well, it was three years ago. I...I suppose my friend is getting over it. Their marriage wasn't all that good anyway, and the accident put an end to it."

"Mmmm." Rebecca had been rinsing the same glass since Mariel had begun her story, compulsively rubbing it under the water until it squeaked, but she didn't hear it. "How awful."

"I have to tell you," Mariel went on and spoke truly—she did have to tell Rebecca, "my friend's never been able to forgive God. Does that sound awful? She doesn't trust him anymore."

Rebecca hesitated a moment, then finally put the glass in the drainer. She dried her hands and reached out to put her palm on Mariel's bent head, almost in benediction.

Mariel knew she hadn't fooled Rebecca. An eddy of grief had begun spinning within her, and she was fighting to hold back tears. Without looking up to confirm the compassion she knew she would find in the other woman's eyes, Mariel asked, "How did you cope?"

"Dreadfully at first," Rebecca responded, turning to lean back against the sink and gazing down at the floor. "I kept setting nine places, just like always, which the children kindly removed without comment. I felt so relieved when they all went back to school because then I could fool myself, thinking Nick and Chris would be coming home again at the next break. I even spoke once of Christopher's plans for college. When I finally acknowledged their death, I was bitterly angry, just...just at everyone. Nick and Christopher for being such wonderful sons, Spence for giving them to me, and especially God. How could he do this? We had served him so faithfully and loved him and put him first through so many years. But I had loved God longer than I had loved my sons, and one day I couldn't bear the bitterness any longer, so I stopped screaming my prayers at him and sank back into his love."

"His love?"

"Yes, his love. I was like a child who has to seek comfort from the very mother who removed a treat. Children do that constantly, haven't you noticed? They turn for reassurance to the very person they're angry at. It's so poignant. They know better than we do that love's the only thing that can heal the pain.

"It's odd. During all that time of anger, I felt as if God were holding back from me, angry and vindictive. Then I remembered that he'd lost a Son himself, that he must know my anguish. Why had I expected to escape? If the Father himself bore such pain, why should I think myself above it?

"Mariel, he was waiting for me to reach out, patiently waiting, coveting my faith in him, longing to comfort, agonizing at my sorrow, but waiting for me. C.S. Lewis said it: God will not ravish, only woo. When I turned to him and poured out my anguish, I felt his own sorrow and compassion for my grief and only then did I get some sense of his eternity, some sense of his perspective. I had mourned so for what the boys lost here—their youth and manhood. I grieved for that horribly. After coming to God, I sensed their wholeness over there on the other side. They are, right now, all that God intended them to be. Isn't that wonderful? Completely free of sin and disappointment and pain. They have the glorious freedom we all want."

Rebecca turned back to the sink and began rinsing again. "I sympathize with your friend, Mariel. I held back from God, and it was awful while it lasted. That way is terribly dangerous, because that little corner of our soul we think we can withhold from him finally festers and rots and spreads throughout our lives until its stench putrefies our entire relationship with God, until every shred of devotion spoils away. Then we're no more than straw Christians, incapable of service or worship or love. All that we do, however good in the world's eyes, he'll burn away, for none is to his glory, and we're left with nothing to leave before his throne."

Mariel crouched against the sink, unwilling to face Rebecca, unwilling to soften or repent. All good and fine to describe her condition so eloquently, stench and uselessness and straw efforts and all. Mariel couldn't deny any of it, not with the ulcer such tangible physical evidence. But whose fault was it? The prodigal son returned home from his rebellion, all sorry and repentant, to a wonderful feast. But what if the father had stolen the birthright to begin with, banished the son, dealt out the hardship and inflicted the pain? How likely would the son be then to return?

"What about Katy?" Her words sounded forced and tight.

"Katy?" Rebecca asked.

"How did she react to losing her brothers, her kindred spirits, you called them?"

"Well, better and worse than I did, I think. Better because she never held out against God. Worse, too, because she has held her sorrow too long. When all of her friends in high school were 'going steady,' Katy refused anything but the most casual relationships, which means she didn't date much since steady dating is the norm at Hudson. It's not the norm at college, of course, and she dated there quite often, but never seriously. Somehow she was always the friend boys talked to about their girlfriends. In fact, she's always said she would never marry."

"Oh, I can't believe that!"

"I don't either. But I think she's still afraid of loving again the way she loved Christopher and Nick. Christopher especially was a brother to her soul and when he died that day something died in her that only love can revive. Perhaps now...I'm praying..."

Seeing Mariel's puzzled look, Rebecca laughed. "We'll see."

Then seriously, with her hand warm on Mariel's arm: "If your friend ever…well, tell your friend to remember that God has loved her much longer than she could know, longer than she's drawn breath or known thought, and that he'll hold out for her return to the end. The waiting for her return—I think that waiting is an agony for him, the way it would be if our children ran away. He longs to share her grief; he wants to comfort her. He wants her to be all she was made for, and she can't become that until she's returned to him. Don't forget, Mariel."

Finally turning, Mariel saw more than compassion. In Rebecca's eyes shone the love of a fellow sufferer.

Double Ten, the tenth day of October, the tenth month, marked Taiwan's Independence Day, and Hudson Academy recognized the event by giving the students Thursday and Friday off. Katy and Luke, with two young married couples, were spending the four-day weekend cycling.

"Two days down-island to Tainan, a day at my parents' house, and then the train home," Katy explained, as she sat with Luke and Mariel over iced tea at her dining table on Tuesday night. "Think of the muscles we'll develop."

"Think of the pains we'll develop," Luke said, a hand on his backside.

"Oh, don't," Katy said. "On Monday I'll be doing my teaching standing up, and my students will know why. Horrible thought."

Luke turned to Mariel. "You're heading south, too, aren't you?"

"Yes. The Evangelical Christian Mission spends every Double Ten at Chengching Lake for meetings and relaxation and fellowship, and I have a command appearance." She shrugged.

"Well," Katy said, "Adam is ECM, so you'll know one person there anyway."

"I suppose."

But Mariel couldn't see any reason to rejoice at Adam's presence. Of all she had expected from this year in Taiwan, her reaction to Adam was the most surprising. It made her angry, this ripple of emotion she felt near him. Surely that small pool could have been left in peace? And that it should be Adam: so sure of himself, so unquestioning in his authority! What was she thinking?

Thinking? a little voice inside murmured. *As if this had anything to do with thinking!*

Mariel drove down to the lake Thursday morning with three other women, Vivian Sewell, Wendy Engstrom, and Felicity Dwyer. Vivian, the oldest of the group, taught at the ECM seminary located in a small town south of Taichung. Wendy, a few years past thirty and a career missionary, taught third grade at Hudson, and Felicity, a short-term missionary like Mariel, taught music.

Soon after they started, Felicity turned around in the front seat. She was not a pretty woman. Her makeup was a little too heavy, and she had almost beady eyes. Her brassy auburn hair, piled high, looked as if it would fall with one good shake.

Her manner was no more attractive. "Well, the other three of us all know each other, so you tell us about yourself, Mariel. What are you doing at Hudson—I mean you don't fit anyone's idea of a missionary, you're much too sophisticated." She made the word sound dirty. "So what's up? Why are you here?"

Mariel stared silently back at Felicity, stunned. If Felicity thought she was making a friendly overture with her question, Mariel could set her straight!

Something of Mariel's feelings must have shown through, for Felicity flushed and added petulantly, "Well, I was curious."

Wendy reached over to touch Mariel's arm. "Never mind, Mariel. I'm sure you'd rather wait your turn. Felicity, why don't you tell Mariel about your Hollywood exploits instead."

Felicity happily launched into a description of her short-lived career in show business—apparently she had sung the ditty for a gourmet popsicle commercial. Mariel turned a grateful smile on Wendy. She had often noticed Wendy on campus and rather unkindly thought of her as a typical "unclaimed blessing." Her hair hung limply to chin length, and she never wore makeup. She also had an unnerving habit of gazing too long at a person; with her hawkish nose and thick glasses, she could make a person feel like a naughty two-year-old. But now Wendy had recognized Mariel's discomfort and had the kindness to smooth it away. It was time for Mariel to reassess Wendy.

Vivian was much older, past middle age, with steel-gray hair cut solely for easy care and a nondescript figure that curved in all the wrong places. Mariel knew almost nothing about her. She probably wouldn't gain much during the trip, either, for the older woman drove silently, making no more than an absentminded grunt now and then during the conversation.

As Felicity carried on with her story, Mariel became curious about Vivian and Wendy: How did a woman decide to become a full-time missionary, especially a single woman? She asked Wendy when Felicity finished speaking.

"I come from northern Minnesota," Wendy said, "a small town named Bemidji. I decided to become a missionary when I was very young. I actually intended to become a doctor, but discovered I didn't have the aptitude for it. Teaching was right for me, and a missionary kids' school is a good place to use it."

"But teaching M.K.s—is that really…"

"Authentic missionary work?" Wendy asked dryly.

"Well, yes."

Felicity gave a loud laugh. "Let's hear your answer to that one, Wendy!"

Wendy shrugged. "Hudson teachers do have less contact with Chinese nationals, I admit, but missionary kids need ministry every bit as much as the Chinese people. They can make or break their parents' work. Besides, all missionaries, whatever their role, wonder how much effect they are having. It's a trade hazard, I suppose. I do provide a needed service for the people who are doing church-planting and so forth."

"Don't let Wendy fool you, Mariel," Felicity interjected. "She's *quite* the little missionary. She teaches English once a week at a local Chinese church and has a Bible study in her home for some students from the local Chinese teachers' college, and all of that on top of teaching her little kiddos."

Wendy shrugged diffidently. "Vivian, of course, teaches at the seminary, but you probably knew that, Mariel."

"Real mission work," Felicity announced.

"What do you teach?"

"Christian education, church history, missions, evangelism. Come up to the seminary, sometime."

"Um, yes, thank you. I might do that."

Vivian glanced to her right. "You, too, Felicity, since you've never been." She had spoken gruffly, but the invitation was kindly meant, and Felicity smiled.

58

The conversation turned to what seemed very much like gossip to Mariel. From their discussion of mission concerns, Mariel realized she actually knew very little about the way a missionary society worked.

Mariel was especially curious about a Mr. Jacobs that Vivian was snorting over, who seemed intent on diverting mission funds for what Vivian called "a half-baked, ill-advised, claim-jumping foolishness." Vivian was now animated and vehement, passionately convinced of being in the right, while Wendy was vainly trying to smooth ruffled feathers. *What happened to Christian charity?* Mariel wondered. Vivian's attitude seemed more fitting to a corporate business room than to a mission effort.

They arrived mid-afternoon, so after settling into her cabin, which she would be sharing with her three car-mates, Mariel had a chance to walk around the grounds. The cabin snuggled into the side of a hill above Chengching Lake, actually a reservoir, and by following the path down through the trees and around the water to the other side, Mariel came upon two charming Oriental delights—a nine-corner bridge and a flaming red pagoda trimmed in gold.

The bridge spanned a narrow inlet and turned right and left enough times to form nine corners before reaching the far side. Mariel walked halfway across then paused, facing the water. The afternoon sun reached out friendly fingers to warm her as she leaned against the white railing. Birds sang in the trees around her, and the barest kiss of wind rippled the water toward her. She let out a long sigh and felt peace settle over her. If only she could stay here, away from all the other people, the weekend would be wonderful.

She finally turned toward the pagoda at the end of the bridge. She walked completely around its base, noting the singularly

Oriental beauty of the gold tip-tilted roof, the many tiers, the red arches and pillars. Then she went inside and climbed the circular flight of stairs to the top.

Climbing to heaven, they said. If only it were this easy.

At the top of the stairs, she saw a magnificent view. Across the expanse of water, paths led up into the hill, and the cabins were barely visible in the trees. She stepped forward, intent on looking down at the face of the pagoda and then stopped abruptly.

There on the small balcony stood Adam Lyons.

She had known he was at the retreat somewhere, of course, but had taken refuge in picturing him at a meeting. That he should be here, so close, a mere arm's length away. And that he had been watching her as she progressed across the lake.

She spoke instinctively: "What are you doing here? Don't you have any meetings to attend this afternoon?"

Adam cocked an eyebrow and she realized too late how rude her words sounded. She stepped back from him, gripping the rail and drawing from it some semblance of equilibrium.

"Sorry. I thought you might be organizing something for the weekend."

"Nothing like that here," he said, shaking his head in mock regret. "I'm out of my element—an educator among evangelists!"

"I can't imagine you with nothing to say!"

Mariel thought for a moment that he'd be angry at her bluntness, but he laughed with full and genuine amusement, and she felt an unexpected warmth spread through her cheeks.

"You're right," he said, his amusement lingering. "I'll always have an extra two-bits' worth. However, since I am very well behaved here—I never speak out of turn and absolutely never demand my own way—these good people have been known to welcome my ideas once or twice. It's true," he said, seeing her disbelief grow. "I *can* mind my manners."

She laughed too. "Seeing is believing," she scoffed lightly, keeping her smile.

"Come on," he said, motioning to the stairs. "I have all weekend to prove myself. Right now it's almost time to eat and with this crowd I doubt we'll get much if we're late."

Supper—Mariel carefully sat with Wendy—was a simple affair of sandwiches and side dishes the missionaries had brought with them. Afterwards everyone gathered in the large circular meeting room for an evening of skits and games and a late-night snack. To her surprise, Mariel lost herself in the laughter and competition and sheer silliness, and the evening sped by for her.

Following some short skits, standard ones which Mariel remembered from her own summer camp days, someone who was dressed up in a gorilla suit bounded into the room. He was obviously a familiar favorite for the children immediately squealed and shrieked and jumped up and down. Some of them boldly held their place, but the little ones either ran to hide behind Mama or climbed into Daddy's lap. The enormous figure loped and leaped around the room, lifting giant arms above the children, tweaking their noses, and tickling their tummies. He made most of them go off into gales of giggles by pondering stupidly over a child's pig tail or scratching excitedly under his arms. After making a round or two of the room, he had even Mariel laughing.

When the gorilla removed his mask to take a bow, Mariel was shocked for here stood one of the oldest, most serious missionaries. Mariel had pegged him as the fuddiest of duddies after he gave a long and incredibly hackneyed blessing before supper. Yet here he was, making crazy with the rest. Quite probably the gorilla was an old routine, the year-after-year repetition revealing a lack of creativity, but Mariel was charmed anyway by the pleasure he brought to the children.

During charades, players acted out other missionaries in the room, using habits to identify them—chewing the ends of their glasses, dozing off in a meeting, doodling incessantly, rubbing their knee. This game was new, judging from the fun everyone seemed to have with it.

The skits mostly spoofed mission work itself, and while Mariel couldn't catch all the inside jokes, she could certainly appreciate the extent to which they were all willing to make fools of themselves. One skit, in particular, spoofed the spirituality that Christians in America expected missionaries to demonstrate when they visited churches. Felicity, who Mariel could see really did have dramatic talent, acted the missionary and Wendy the stateside church-goer. Felicity appeared wearing an incredibly dowdy dress which hung unattractively down past her knees, opaque tights, and old-fashioned laced-up hiking boots far too big for her. Over her auburn hair, she had pulled a wig the color of dirty dishwater; it had a tight schoolmarmish bun perched on top. Artful makeup created a pallid complexion. Her collar was buttoned up tightly around her neck and a false bosom hung low to her waist.

"Why, Missionary Dwyer," Wendy greeted her, "how are you today?"

"Oh, *showered* with blessings. Deluged. Flooded." Felicity looked as glum as a child on the way to a dentist's, and yet she boomed out her answer, waving her arms expansively—and taking her false bosom with her. "This is the day the Lord has made and I must rejoice in it."

"So. You're on furlough *again?* Four years of work, and then a whole year off. You missionaries certainly have it easy. And all that traveling you get to do! How many churches are you visiting during your vacation?"

"Thirty-five churches, four summer camps, three missionary conferences, five spiritual emphasis weeks at Christian schools, twelve mission days for children's clubs, twelve trips to see personal supporters, and somewhere in there, I'll take a six-month refresher course at the Bible College."

"Think of that! And all of it paid off your mission account. What a life!"

Felicity turned away from Wendy to hitch up her skirt and made a droll face to the audience.

"What will you be doing at our church today?" Wendy asked, all innocence. "Just a little sharing, I suppose."

"Ah, yes, just a little: I've had a breakfast meeting with the mothers-and-daughters' group, and I'm going now to a prayer interlude. During Sunday school I'll be visiting every opening exercise, then singing in church and giving the testimony. The ladies' group has arranged for me to be a luncheon speaker for the young couples' group, then I'm back here to give devotions to the choir, then primary group, slides and a talk during the evening service, the youth group after evening service, and a late-night devotional for the people with whom I am staying. My Sunday: a day of rest."

When jeers delayed the skit, Felicity glanced toward the crowd and allowed herself the small luxury of rolling her eyes, earning more applause.

"Oh, well, how *nice!*" exclaimed Wendy.

Somehow both women kept a straight face, although this time when Felicity turned away from the audience to hitch up her skirt, Mariel thought she saw her shoulders shaking a little.

"Of course," Wendy continued, "we all know how *much* you missionaries like to give these little talks to churches!"

Wendy had to pause for the hoots and hisses.

"How is the work, may I ask? Many conversions?"

A short pause as Felicity bit her lip. "Thousands," she gasped out. "Every week. Decisions all the time. Barely have time to change the baptismal water. The field is white unto harvest, purely white with harvest."

"That's fine, that's fine," Wendy nodded. "That's what we like to hear. But we want to help you. Tell me, what could we send out to you?"

Felicity hitched up her bosom and thought for a moment. "A bucket, any old, used bucket will do, so I can draw water from my well. And a few candles, for light, you understand. A new washboard—we have to wash everything by hand. And, oh, if you could collect...some used tea bags?"

Here the group, as if waiting for an old joke, let out a collective whoop.

"Oh, and just one thing more," added Felicity. "I could certainly do with a replacement for this."

She smashed a bedraggled pith helmet over her topknot. Turning, she presented herself to the appreciative audience: the quintessential missionary. A wave of applause spread through the room.

❧

After the activities, Mariel took her Russian tea to the corner of the meeting hall and found a quiet place to watch the group. Within minutes, she saw Adam advance from across the room. She hoped he would credit her flushed cheeks to the warmth of the room.

"You look a little thoughtful," he said, as he drew up a chair beside her. "Something bothering you?"

"Not really. It's been a very entertaining evening."

"Then what?"

She shrugged, but his interest was undeniable. "I've had some preconceptions shattered tonight."

"Such as?"

"These people are crazy! Costumes and skits and laughing at each other and themselves. I thought missionaries were more serious than that."

"They like to have fun," Adam said. "No, they *need* to have fun. If the Bible gives an accurate picture, a person's spiritual needs can be more pressing than physical ones. So the way they do their jobs is pretty important. They know it, and it causes a lot of tension and stress, so God gives them this capacity for craziness."

"I'm like the people Wendy represented, I suppose."

"Don't take it too much to heart. Felicity will always have a little acid on her tongue, and laughing at deputation among ourselves makes it a little easier to bear."

"Is it as bad as it sounded?"

He shrugged. "For some of us."

"Thirty-five churches and Bible clubs and camps and all the rest?"

"She exaggerated, but for some missionaries getting up even *once* in front of a church is a nightmare."

"And tea-bags?"

"*Used* tea-bags. Yes, indeed, people have sent them to Taiwan."

Mariel shook her head, still confused. "But missionaries *should* be spiritual giants...shouldn't they?"

"What makes it hard for missionaries is the *way* people expect them to be spiritual. Jesus lampooned the Pharisees' phylacteries, and yet many Christians want to bury missionaries in modern-day equivalents: spiritual talk, clothes, entertainment. It's like Pastor Cartwright has been saying about the Gnostics in his study on Colossians. Some people think the material world and all its pleasures are somehow vaguely sinful. But God wants us to enjoy life. Refusing laughter and good times and fun is like reserving some of God's best gifts for the devil's use."

"I'm sorry."

"Hey, you're learning. Give yourself a chance." He looked at her speculatively, and she detected a friendly glimmer in his eyes. "Besides, haven't these missionaries been guilty of the same attitude toward you?"

"I don't understand."

"You break the mold yourself, Mariel. Such an attractive woman. We aren't used to having someone like you teaching at Hudson—especially unattached ones. Haven't you sensed a little awkwardness?"

He spoke so calmly she wasn't sure how to respond.

"So don't apologize too much for your misconceptions. We have them, too."

His friendly expression altered and something in his eyes made her blush. He savored the long lashes falling over flushed cheeks, her bowed head as she struggled to regain her composure, but when she looked up again her eyes were steady.

"Anyway," he said, leaning back in his chair and stretching his legs comfortably, "wait until tomorrow. They'll seem more like missionaries then when they're thrashing over mission business and spending half the morning in prayer."

"What do they actually do—in their work, I mean?" Mariel asked, sweeping her hand across the scene in front of them.

Adam sorted them all out for her. "Our gorilla man, Fred McManus, runs the seminary, which means taking care of all administrative details and teaching Bible courses. His wife, Hannah, cooks and houses the students. Vivian you met driving down with her. Ron Reston teaches theology and hermeneutics and his wife tends their ever-growing family. Six children so far and another on the way. Ana Gutierrez teaches music and languages.

"Besides the seminary, we have church planters: George Gunderson and his wife; Max Stavos and his wife; Ethan Webster and his. They go into rural areas or unchurched city regions, start a home Bible study, and eventually establish a church. Max and Olivia cover four or five rural towns. Ethan and Beth have recently seen a multi-level church built right in the middle of one of Taipei's most crowded sections. George and Mary Gunderson, you should meet. They are Jessie's parents—Jessie, your yearbook editor and our star female athlete.

"Now, who else? The Hudson teachers you've seen on campus, Wendy and Felicity, and Carrie Stinson, who teaches kindergarten, and Josie Wales, our bookkeeping/business teacher.

Carter Hickman and his wife—she's the other pregnant one over there—are out on a one-year internship for his doctorate in missions. You stayed with Gladys and Chet Carlton when you first came to Taichung. They work with the city youth in clubs and so forth and run a very successful camp all summer. Then we have several single missionaries involved in Christian education efforts: Mary Goudge, Tamara Heath, Elizabeth Griffin."

"Lots of single women."

"Yes. Married couples and single women. It's an old pattern."

He had taken his share of ribbing that evening as the subject of a hilarious series of letters to a Lonely Hearts column, all fun in themselves but with enough barb to make Mariel think perhaps more women than Gladys Carlton begrudged Adam his ability to survive without a spouse. In this traditional setting, marriage was so much the norm for men that any confirmed bachelor understandably upset the group's equilibrium.

"So women can manage on their own, but men can't?"

He frowned. "I beg your pardon."

"Well, all except one man."

To her relief, he laughed. "You're right. Unfortunately a lot of people assume that single women are on the mission field because they couldn't get a husband back home, but that's hardly the case. Take Wendy, over there. She looks meek enough, but she's one of the strongest people I know. Same goes for Tammy and Mary and all the rest."

Mariel looked away across the room, hiding her expression. Did he have to be such a prince? She'd find it so much easier to dismiss him if he were more of a toad!

"So? Does that finish the group?" he asked.

"What about a Mr. Jacobs?"

"Oh, yes, Jacobs. How could I forget him? He's something of a maverick in our mission. He wants to establish an orphanage up in the hills somewhere, for the aborigines."

"An orphanage?"

"You sound surprised."

"Well, yes. On the way down, I heard his work described as 'half-baked, ill-advised, claim-jumping foolishness.'"

Adam grunted knowingly. "Vivian."

"Is an orphanage such a bad idea?"

"I'm afraid so. The project has a lot of glamour and would appeal to the folks back home, but Jacobs hasn't weighed out everything carefully enough—finances, how many workers he would need, government support, and lots more. It's a big undertaking."

"Why did Vivian say 'claim-jumping'?"

"Because other missions already have orphanages, both in the hills and in the cities," he explained. "We tend to divide things up over here on the island to make the best use of resources and avoid overlap. Some mission agencies do prison ministries, some operate Bible colleges, one does radio broadcasts to mainland China, and others run orphanages. That way we can all focus on strengths."

"What is ECM's strength?"

"Not orphanages!"

"Then what?"

"Christian education," he said promptly. "We have our seminary, summer camps, and other youth programs. And church planting, too."

"Not to mention an investment in the administration of Hudson Academy," Mariel said to the ceiling.

He chuckled. "Yes, that, too, although all the missions contribute staff to Hudson." He sat up straighter and turned more completely toward her. "Well, Mariel, how am I doing? I've been on my best behavior—"

"Not that hard, I would think. Once a teacher, always a teacher."

"Is that what I've been doing?"

"Very effectively, thank you."

He paused, his gaze steady and probing. "You still haven't called me Adam," he said. "In front of the students, it's one thing, but here, together? Is it so hard to say my name?"

Mariel looked across the room to where Wendy was gathering her things, obviously preparing to walk across the park to their cabin. "I have to go," she said, standing up and reaching for her jacket.

"'I have to go, *Adam,*'" he prompted her.

Mariel sighed and her eyes met his. The humor in his eyes deepened, mingled with something else. As much to escape from the sudden flush of feeling that swept over her as anything, she gave him what he wanted. "Okay— I have to go, *Adam.*"

"Ah. Thank you." He leaned indolently back in his chair and hooded the triumph that now gleamed in his eyes. "Until tomorrow then, Mariel."

What had she seen in his eyes? Promise? Challenge? Threat? She couldn't decide, as she walked to the cabin, exactly how she should label his last words.

Mariel prepared for bed quickly and tried to sleep, but long after Felicity had come in and gone to sleep herself, Mariel lay awake in her bed. The night sounds around her seemed incredibly loud, the crickets mocking her and the wind in the trees full of sudden, unsettling little gusts, as if wanting to attack her. Her own heart was high-stepping a skitterish rhythm and in danger of bolting. With the memory of Adam sitting beside her and the specter of his smile in her mind, she knew exactly what was causing the tension in her emotions.

She had been frankly flattered to have Adam spend so much time with her, and he apparently planned to prove his good behavior to her over the whole weekend. A tremor ran through her, leaving her warm and slightly winded. It had been so long, so very long, since she had experienced a man's attention, and she couldn't decide which was more unsettling: that Adam was giving that attention to her or that she was actually welcoming it. To herself, here in bed, she had to admit she had purposely asked questions to detain him. She could also admit he had been happy to stay. Both admissions overwhelmed her, and she pressed a pillow over her face.

All fine to feel this sudden, euphoric rush of pleasure, but she had to remember where that same attention had led her in the past: broken promises, walls around her, cold, crushing silence, and then the end. Surely she would not be that foolish again? Better to keep her distance in the first place.

She punched her pillow again and fell back into it. For so long, the memory of David's face as he left had been enough to cultivate her anger and caution with men. Why now was hope pushing so relentlessly upon her?

It was a long time before she slept.

Morning brought the first full day of meetings. Mariel had

nursery duty. As a short-term teacher with no stated commitment to the mission, she was the natural choice for tending the missionaries' small children.

Did it have to be small children? she wondered.

Slipping into the cabin after breakfast, Mariel heard Felicity in the bathroom talking to Wendy. "Did you notice Mariel last night? She kept Adam talking to her the whole time. Do you suppose she's trying to achieve the impossible?"

Mariel's breath stilled.

"How should I know?" Wendy said sharply. "Whatever happens, don't hassle her!"

"Why not? She looks like she could handle it."

"Don't be cruel, Felicity."

Wendy, the tigress, Mariel thought.

"All right, all right, stop fussing. But she did monopolize the man."

Mariel's temper flared and she almost spoke. What a selfish, thoughtless woman!

And not worth a scene, she reminded herself.

She slipped back out of the cabin and came in more loudly, calling out a greeting. She thought she managed to sound almost natural, but her hand shook when she picked up her brush, and she stood looking down at it, scowling. She should have come back to the cabin immediately after the skits last night.

Then, when Mariel emerged from the cabin, there was Adam standing patiently against a tree, like an adolescent suitor waiting to walk his girl to school. Mariel wanted to slap him.

"I'll walk with you to the Restons' cabin where they've put the nursery," he said.

"You don't have to!" Mariel declared and started walking down the path ahead of him.

"I think I do. You're going the wrong way."

She closed her eyes for a moment, took a deep breath, and then turned back toward him. "All right. Which way?"

Adam walked beside her cheerfully, talking about how hectic the nursery would be and some of the issues the missionaries would be discussing. She hardly heard him. As emotionally confused as she felt, when Adam opened the door to the Restons' cabin, Mariel noticed little about the "nursery" or the mothers or children. She was thinking only about getting rid of Adam before everyone in the room started sharing Felicity's suspicions.

Then through all the distractions a little two-year-old girl came toddling toward Mariel. She was unbalanced by a bright red helmet that sat on top of her curly blond hair, and she was laughing. She reached out pudgy little arms to catch herself against Mariel's legs.

The child's arrival struck Mariel like a bolt of lightning. She unclasped the child's arms and sat her down none too gently, then turned abruptly to go outside, pulling hard against Adam's hold on the doorknob to shut it behind her. Her face was chalky with shock, the pain evident in her every movement as she walked away from the doorway. Outside, she leaned wearily against a nearby tree. She felt so dizzy! She thought she might fall.

"Mariel, what is it?" She felt Adam's arm around her, leading her around the cabin where no one was likely to see them. "Tell me," he said. His face was inches from hers. "What is it? Was it the little Reston girl?"

His concern finally penetrated her shock, making her frantic.

She fought off his hold and turned her head away from his, leaning against the cabin wall as if it could hide her.

"Go away, Adam. I'm all right. Just go away."

"I don't understand."

"Of course you have to know *everything* that's going on, don't you? Well, not this time. Just leave me alone."

She felt him step back from her, and when she turned, she saw that his eyes had become analytical, almost cold. She remembered too late that this man was her superintendent, with power over her, and she forced herself to speak calmly.

"I'm fine, Adam. Thank you for your concern. I didn't sleep well last night and seeing the little girl brought back a painful memory, but that's all it was. You don't need to worry."

They stood staring at each other, and she mustered every ounce of pride she had to quench his concern. She lifted her hand in a self-deprecating gesture and laughed. "You must think I'm crazy. But really, I'm fine."

Only a fool would have been deceived by her effort, and Adam was no fool.

He finally said, "All right. As you wish. Shall I suggest they find someone else for the nursery?"

"No, of course not. Give me a minute, and I'll go in."

She knew she had offended him, possibly even hurt him. That thought almost defeated her, but she couldn't bear his knowing. Not that indignity. Anything but that.

"Then you'll need this," he said and held out a handkerchief to her. She realized her face was wet with tears and almost groaned. So much for convincing him everything was all right. He said as much with his cold eyes.

Nevertheless he turned and left without another word.

So there, Miss Felicity Dwyer, Mariel thought bitterly as she struggled to still her breathing. *As if I could achieve the impossible.*

Katy and Luke began their Double Ten trip right after school on Wednesday.

"We have to," Katy said when she convinced Luke and the other two couples who would be going with them. "It'll be a great warm-up for the next day. We'll get about twenty miles out of the way, not to mention a lot of kinks and tight muscles, and we'll have a great place to spend the night."

A fellow missionary kid, a few years older than Katy, had promised them lodging. Clem Johnson had settled with his wife in a small town south of Taichung.

The group pulled out from school after 3:00 P.M. and headed south. As they left town behind them and began to ride side by side down the two-lane highway, Katy stole a glance at Luke. He was wearing loose-fitting khaki pants strapped at the ankle to avoid mangling from the bike and an old burgundy sweatshirt cut ragged at the shoulders to make it sleeveless. He had just had his hair trimmed back to its college cut, and he looked as lean as ever.

Katy sighed. She hadn't seen Luke much since school started other than the shared lunches on the plaza or the few times he had come up in the evening to join her and Mariel on their balcony. From what she did see of him, he seemed preoccupied and distracted, like before a big test in college. *Probably school,* she thought, as she had every other time she had wondered about him. The weeks leading up to Double Ten had proved hectic for her. She had felt once or twice like a bareback rider barely managing to stay on. The lectures and tests and grading had been bad enough. Added to those were the volleyball team, the inevitable faculty meetings, acting as sponsor for the Girls' Athletic Association, and the many tasks the students roped her into. Mariel, of course, handled school with characteristic ease, but then she was more disciplined and had taught before. Luke, in his first year like Katy but with no actual student teaching, was sure to be feeling the pressure.

Even so, she had felt something of their old, easygoing, who-cares-about-life friendship slipping away, and she missed it. She couldn't say exactly what she had expected with them both out here in Taiwan, but she had certainly counted on his friendship.

At Crocker, Luke had been one of many good friends, there for the good times, for the group times, for the campaigns and parties and projects. Of course, he had spoon-fed her through chemistry, but they had also struggled together through Greek and Sanders' Revelation class and Harris's philosophy and a few others. With three or four other friends, Luke had woven a common and prominent thread through her college days.

Katy had dated often in college, always carefree times of fun that left her dates with the memory of a good time and little expectation of anything else from her. As far as Katy knew, Luke had never dated at all, finding in their group all the social life he needed. He had certainly never asked Katy out, not once in all four years. Why would she have wanted him to, anyway? He might have fallen for her and ruined a good friendship. No, thank you! She gave an extra hard pump to her pedal and threw her bike ahead of his.

"Such strong thoughts, Katy Martin!" Luke exclaimed, pulling back up beside her. "Your students cause you trouble today?"

"Just one guy," she answered him. "Just one troublesome guy, but let's not think about that. Let's have fun!"

The road they were biking on seemed deceptively flat, but in fact followed the gentle inclines of broad rolling hills, first up exhaustively long stretches, then down refreshing ones. They biked south along the western side of the island. To their left the emerald green rice fields rose to the mountains that lifted the island's central core, and to their right the scenery faded abruptly as the land met the Formosan Straits. They rode two by two, Katy riding most often with Luke and occasionally with one of the others. They met and passed a lot of traffic. The slower mopeds and motorcycles and three-wheeled putt-putts swerved around them without danger, but when the first low rumble of an approaching car was heard, someone yelled out a warning, and everyone relinquished the asphalt to suffer a jarring few minutes on the rough, stony shoulder of the road. Overhead, trees blocked out the still hot October sunshine.

They passed through towns, the houses and shops tightly packed together to preserve precious farmland, and as always Katy marveled at the constant swirl of people. Students in their uniforms were coming home from school, girls giggling and pointing, the boys hanging arms over each other's shoulders and calling out questions. Women gossiped with each other and chased off ubiquitous stray dogs and scolded children loudly with the harsh and cutting sounds of Chinese. The men on bicycles—seemingly hundreds of men on bicycles—darted through the melee, narrowly eluding the frenetic taxis and the three-wheeled covered motorcycles that often served as the Taiwanese pick-up truck.

Most eye-catching for foreigners, Katy thought, would be the feats of balance and endurance that people achieved on their bicycles. They never said no to carrying anything—four or five cages of chickens, huge baskets of papayas and mangoes, luggage and bedding, and boxes of wares, not to mention the occasional friend in need of a lift.

"Look at that," Katy said to Luke as they stopped at a traffic light. An elderly man on a bike was weaving through the intersection. He had a kitchen table and two chairs strapped to the back of his bicycle.

The noise in the towns precluded much talk. Taxis, without apparent cause, blared so incessantly that the sound was useless as a warning. Bicycle bells, dogs' barks, children's shouts in play and mothers' in anger, merchants' greetings to friends across the busy roads and intersections, hawkers' calls, bikers' tirades against road-hog taxis, and even a firecracker or two thrown in anticipation of Saturday's Double Ten celebration—all added to the cacophony. No circus could equal the drama.

After two hours, they drew up at Katy's friend's house. Katy introduced everyone proudly: "Clem Johnson, Sue Johnson, I want you to meet my friends, Becky and Ned Waters, Nila and Jerry Cook, and my old college friend, Luke Shepard. Aren't we a bedraggled lot?"

"And we're only two hours along the way!" exclaimed Ned.

Nila groaned. "No one will recognize us by Sunday."

"Buck up, Nila," her husband, Jerry, said. "Think of how much extra food you can eat after all this exercise."

Eat well they did that night. After everyone had cleaned up, Clem and Sue led the weary group down the road, through a narrow alley, and then into a tiny Chinese restaurant. It had only four tables, each round and large enough to accommodate six to eight people. Two long fluorescent lights shed a cold and sterile light on the room and a scuffed up terrazzo covered the floor. To Katy, the Ritz couldn't have been more appealing.

"*Jyaudz!*" Katy exclaimed. "Clem, you old weasel! You couldn't have chosen better."

Clem gave the order to the waiter, who shouted it out across the small room to the waiting cook, and within minutes the fat Chinese proprietress set a stack of ten round bamboo trays piled one on top of the other in the center of the table. As quick as a cardsharp, she dealt each person a small saucer, a bowl, a pair of chop sticks, and a glass, then poured out a clear, eruptingly fizzy soft drink. Becky and Ned, newcomers to Taiwan, looked around the table in confusion.

"*Jyaudz?*" Ned said.

"Yes. Say it like this: *jow-dzuh,* equal accent on both syllables. They're small dumplings," Sue explained, placing a tray before the couple and lifting the top to release a billow of steam. Inside sat ten small white packets. "They're filled with a mixture of ground pork, cabbage, ginger, and garlic. Before you eat them, mix vinegar and soy sauce in this little saucer, dot it with sesame oil, then dip the *jyaudz* in, and enjoy."

"They are usually steamed in these bamboo steamers," Katy continued, after Clem said a prayer of thanks for the food. "Each tray has an openwork base in it so when the cook fills the trays with *jyaudz* and stacks them up over boiling water, the steam rises through the stack and cooks all the dumplings."

"Very efficient," Nila said.

"More importantly—very tasty," Luke added.

"I take it Katy's already introduced you to these?" Clem asked.

Over chopsticks raised to their mouths, Katy and Luke exchanged a brief glance and smiled.

"In college," Luke said.

Katy explained. "A group of us got together once a semester or so and made *jyaudz*. We'd keep going for hours, stuffing and cooking, stuffing and cooking. How many do you think we would make, Luke?"

"Who knows? We ate them faster than anyone could count." He took a drink and then turned to Clem. "How many would you missionary kids eat? To hear Katy talk, your record was enormous."

"Well, there are ten *jyaudz* to a tray. Back then, especially during soccer season, we could all eat over five racks at least. Our fullback ate seventy-eight in one sitting."

"That's nothing," Katy retorted. "It's the lean, wiry ones that can pack it in. You know as well as I do that my brother Nick once topped one hundred...well, I admit he didn't feel so great afterwards."

Clem laughed. "Why don't you tell them about some of your own misdeeds, Katy-girl? How about the time your home-ec class made cherry pies for the Christmas banquet but forgot to put in the sugar."

"Who said I was to blame?"

"And the time you dropped everyone's band music right before concert time?"

"Jeff Quarters tackled me from behind. It wasn't my fault!"

"Ha! I heard he was paying you back for sewing his uniform cuffs together."

"Adolescent fun, that's all."

"And the time the cheer leading squad missed a bus after an away basketball game?"

"Well, yes, that *was* my fault, but it was an innocent mistake."

"And then the starting five staying behind to look for you? Was that so innocent?"

Everyone was enjoying the exchange. Everyone except Luke. He had put his arm lightly across the back of her chair and was gazing thoughtfully down at the table.

"Now wipe those smiles off your faces, everyone," Katy warned them, "or I will lead you all astray tomorrow."

"Katy's the only one of us who can speak Chinese," Jerry explained, "so we're at her mercy."

"Katy? Speak Chinese? Now I could tell tales about that, too."

"She's doing fine," Luke said, and Katy realized he was worried about her. Good old Luke! She looked up to smile at him and then changed the subject.

"When's that baby due, Sue? Will Dr. Schwartz be delivering it?"

"Two months and absolutely Dr. Schwartz. Like father, like son—or maybe daughter."

As Katy expected, the mention of babies caught the other two couples' attention and steered the conversation away from herself.

"Thanks," she whispered to Luke, "but you don't have to worry. Clem was Christopher's best friend, next to Nicholas, of course, and he's like another brother to me. He'd be the first to defend my honor."

Turned slightly toward him, she had drawn her shoulder away from the arm he still held carelessly across the back of her chair. He put his hand forward, and for a moment she felt his thumb rubbing gently against her shoulder. Eyes half-closed, he studied her, and she became aware of a sudden tension between them.

He spoke so softly she almost missed his words: "Not the first, Katy. He wouldn't be the first."

Then someone spoke to Katy and the brief moment passed. She wondered later as she got ready for bed if she might have imagined the whole exchange.

They began riding the next morning a little after 9:00 A.M., cycling leisurely through town and country. All along the way people were preparing for the Saturday celebration. Flags of the Republic hung from upstairs windows, across the roads, or on posts along the streets, and firecrackers popped frequently near their bikes, flung by boys leaning over the houses' high enclosing walls.

In the open stretches, Katy rode almost exclusively beside Luke, although the trip hadn't seemed to lessen his brooding any. She struggled to find something to talk about.

"Nila seemed a little blue last night when we started talking about babies," she said to him.

"Jerry told me they've wanted children almost since they were married four years ago."

"That's awful."

"Jerry's beginning to think God has other plans for them. They're out here on a one-year appointment to see if they would like to be missionaries full-time. They're thinking about going back to seminary and coming back as church planters."

"That's great, but...still kind of sad."

"Do you want children so badly, Katy?"

"Well, of course! A big family's great. Besides, kids might help me grow up. Don't you think?" She thought for a minute and then added, "But then I probably need to learn discipline more than my husband will!"

"Why?"

Katy shrugged. "Somewhere around adolescence I realized how much of the childrearing my mother had done in our house, and how often my father drifted away to his study, out of sight and—even more—out of hearing."

"Did that bother you?"

"Oh, I realized if I ever really needed him, he'd be there. I just couldn't count on him noticing that I needed him. My mom has spent her whole life making it possible for him to work."

He was watching her intently. "Will it be like that for you, Katy?"

"Who knows? I hope not. I've always thought my parents had very little time together. Dad worked so hard, and Mom made sure he could. Where's the fun of that? The friendship or

joining? When I marry, I want to enjoy my husband so much—
and have him enjoy me—that I can hardly bear to see him go to
work. I want us to feel half complete when we're apart. Maybe
we could even work together somehow."

Luke looked down and away from her quickly, hoping he
had managed to mask the longing Katy's words had ignited within
him. "Sounds nice," he muttered and gratefully found she was
willing to bike on in silence.

For perhaps the hundredth time Luke wondered what Katy
would say if she knew how he felt. When he had followed her
out to Taiwan, the position so hastily accepted back in
December after he had discovered her plans, he had intended to
sweep her off her feet, get married, and go back to graduate
school with her. He had been blaming lectures and tests, faulty
experiments and soccer games for delaying his plan, but truthfully,
he was terrified. In college she had never seemed ready to get
serious about anyone—if he had thought she was, he'd have been
after her like a shot. Yet here she was, talking about marriage and
children, and he was too scared to do anything. He had cared so
much and for so long, and yet he was choking at the most crucial
time.

The outskirts of a town appeared around them. Again ban-
ners and flags hung everywhere, and at the entrance of the town
a massive arch lifted across the roadway proclaiming the coming
celebration and other patriotic sentiments. Katy must have been
thinking about something else, for Luke looked over just in time
to see her riding her bike straight toward the base of a massive
wooden arch.

"Katy!" he yelled, but he was too late. She smashed her bike
straight into the arch. He slammed on his brakes, and as his bike
skidded out from under him, he jumped off and ran to her. She

lay in a crumpled heap on top of her bike, her eyes shut and body limp. As the crowd gathered and the anxious faces of the rest of the group peered down on them, he smoothed her hair gently back and bent his face close to hers.

"Katy!" he whispered urgently. "Katy, talk to me!"

She groaned and moved her lips close to his ear. "A dragon, a big red dragon. Rise up, fair knight, and deliver me."

A grin broke across his face, his relief mingled now with the heady sensation of feeling her whisper on his cheek. "Katy! You scared me."

For one moment the world contracted to just the two of them, and if the traffic continued to swell around them, if horns blew or dogs barked or their friends spoke, they didn't notice. But a busy street corner in a Taiwanese town, surrounded by curious onlookers, four of whom were colleagues, was no place for a man to declare undying devotion. Luke reluctantly pulled back and gently removed the twisted bike from under her.

"Are you hurt?" he asked. "Did you pass out?"

"No. I was just stunned for a few seconds." She pulled herself to a sitting position. "Klutzy me. Look what I've done to my bike!"

"I'll take it," Jerry said. "There's sure to be a bike shop nearby."

"We'd better all go," Katy said, standing up with Luke's help. "We'll never find each other again if we separate."

They spent the next three hours in the town locating a bike shop and waiting impatiently for the smiling little mechanic to fix it. They finally abandoned the shop and went to eat Chinese noodles in Taiwan's equivalent to a greasy spoon. Katy ate only a little. Luke finally leaned over and asked, "Head hurting, Katy?"

"A little," she whispered, "but don't say anything. I've caused enough trouble."

He smiled and shook his head before turning to the group. "Katy and I are taking a walk," he announced. "We'll meet you back at the bike shop at 2:00 P.M."

He moved her gently out of the restaurant. After stopping briefly to take some aspirin from his bike pack, he walked her slowly down the street toward a small park he had noticed and found a bench for her. She leaned her head gratefully back against his arm.

"Thanks, Luke," and said nothing more for an hour.

On the road, he cycled beside her. "I wish we could have found a doctor. You probably have a concussion."

"No! It was only a headache. I feel fine now."

"Even so…"

"Forget it, Luke. Let's enjoy ourselves."

They were hours late on their schedule, and when evening came, nowhere near the comfortable mission house where they had planned to spend the night. In the gathering darkness, the group collectively turned toward Katy when they drew into a small town.

"We need a Holiday Inn," said Ned.

"Clean sheets," Nila said, "hot shower, the ten o'clock news."

"Dream on," Katy scoffed. "Not only are hotels hard to find, but my Chinese has never included checking into one. I'll have to ask around."

Everyone they asked appeared ready to help but invariably ended the conversation with the characteristic shrug of ignorance. Darkness had fallen completely as the group approached the far end of the town. With significant relief—her head was beginning to throb alarmingly—Katy stopped her bike outside a medium-sized two-story building that had a small banner of characters over its door.

"I'm not exactly sure," she said, "but I think that last character is the one for hotel. I'll go ask."

Inside a counter ran along one wall, and on the opposite side stairs led up to the second floor. A rather plain and overweight, middle-aged Chinese woman in a shapeless white shift sat on top of a stool beside the counter. Two younger Chinese women, also plainly dressed but heavily made up, sat beside a table near the stairs, one flipping through a magazine, the other doing nothing. All three women stared at them when the group entered. The two younger women whispered to each other and tittered, but Katy didn't catch their words.

"We need four rooms," Katy said carefully. "We want to sleep here one night."

An eruption of rapid Chinese came from the middle-aged clerk.

"What did she say?"

"Don't they have any rooms?"

"Quiet, quiet," Katy said. "Let me listen. They seem to be having a disagreement over something, but I can't quite follow it. Oh, now she said, 'Yes, we have rooms. Will we pay $5 a night?'"

"Is she kidding?" Nila countered. "Take them before she changes her mind."

"You won't get much for your money," Katy warned them as she paid. "*Tatami* beds, most likely—bamboo mats, in other words—and cotton comforters."

One of the younger women threw out a question and looked pointedly at Luke.

"She wants to know who sleeps where," Katy interpreted, and explained that the two couples would sleep together and she and Luke would sleep separately.

Again one of the younger women said something so softly Katy couldn't hear. The two younger women were still eyeing Luke. A rapid-fire scolding came from the clerk, which sent the other two back to their languid boredom. The older woman led them all upstairs and down a narrow hall to a row of four rooms at one end.

Later, having eaten, Luke settled himself for the night on the firm *tatami* and pulled the puffy quilt over him. As he began to fall asleep, however, he heard a couple enter the room next to his. The minutes passed, and Luke became uncomfortably certain about the activity in the adjoining room. The scene downstairs made sudden sense: the two languid women, their lackluster expression, the older woman treating the younger ones as employees, the general giggling and speculation directed toward him, and the listlessness that reclaimed the younger women as the group mounted the stairs.

So, Luke thought, as he tried to cover his ears more completely with the quilt, *Katy's done it again.* Well, he'd keep this story to himself. After all, he grinned, would Katy ever consent to marry a man who had knowingly spent the night in a Chinese bordello?

The Monday after the bike trip down-island, John Guthrie Rutherford III, entered Katy's classroom just as her last class ended. He was able to hover unseen near the door as the students filed out. Such was his habit: scout out the landscape, reconnoiter the opposition, and plot his strategy. John Guthrie Rutherford was a man who knew how to gain an advantage.

To believe his brother Malcolm, only an all-out attack would have any effect on this teacher, but looking across the room, Guthrie wondered. Could this be the tyrant Malcolm had railed against, this creature? Curly black hair, rosy cheeks, and deep brown eyes, dancing with life. He realized with a start that those eyes were watching him.

"Mr. Rutherford?" Katy said, rising from her chair. She offered her hand.

If I held her in my arms, he thought, *those curls would tickle my chin.* Then amusement flickered in his eyes. That he, at thirty-five, should be so immediately bewitched by black curls.

"Yes, I am Guthrie Rutherford. At your service."

She was shaking those curls now in confusion. "You're not Malcolm's father, are you?"

"Hardly. I'm his brother, or half-brother actually. My father worked for the State Department here in Taiwan, but he reached sixty last year and mandatory retirement. He and my stepmother retired to Massachusetts. Malcolm, however, wanted to graduate from Hudson after being here three years. It was a small thing to move my base of operations from Hong Kong to Taipei. I do business fairly often in Taichung, anyway, so I see him often. In the meantime, he's in the boarding school."

"I see," Katy said, pulling out a chair for him and one for herself as well. "You wanted to talk about Malcolm, I suppose."

Guthrie wondered what her name was—something lively, no doubt. She moved with the darting grace of a gazelle.

"Of course," he said. "Specifically, his last test grade in English. Though I hate to be a nuisance, I do feel obligated to play my father's part this year, and I believe he would seek you out as I am doing to inquire about how we could lift Malcolm's grades. Rutherfords have always gone to Harvard, but even my father's connections cannot coax him in if he fails English."

Katy was disappointed. Malcolm had talked about his famous brother more than once: most famous linguist on the island, incredibly successful in his business dealings with the astute Chinese, widely traveled throughout the Orient, rumored to be a future ambassador. In his suave, European-cut suit and barely conservative haircut, he looked straight out of a novel, vaguely unconventional, clearly accomplished, and oh so far above the concerns of a high school English teacher.

So much for glamour and mystery. All this man wanted was to have her raise his brother's grades. Well, he could think again.

"First of all, Mr. Rutherford, nothing you, his parents, or even I can do will lift Malcolm's grades. Only Malcolm himself can do that by studying and working a good deal harder than he has been. Believe me, he *earned* that F. If you have looked over his essay, you must know he didn't read the assigned book. How else could he have called Rochester a 'confirmed bachelor, determined never to marry'?"

Her tone left him no room to interrupt—and, in fact, he was enjoying her tirade too much to even consider it. Her eyes had become even more animated and a delightful flush was coloring her cheeks.

"Furthermore, Malcolm would do better at Harvard if you and your father allowed him to get in on his own—or fail to get in, if that's what he wants. He is bright, I'll grant you that. But a boy whose shoes are always tied for him will eventually go to college stumbling over his shoelaces."

Katy saw amusement glittering in his eyes and too late realized how ridiculous her last statement sounded. She always went a little bit too far!

"Yes, I suppose so," he drawled, and mercifully kept a straight face. "But if Malcolm is stumbling now, perhaps it's because he doesn't know how to schedule his time or study properly. I'm not in the least interested in tying his shoelaces or force-feeding him *Jane Eyre*. His failings, however, extend beyond Victorian melodramas to several other classes. I'm wondering if you could possibly recommend someone to tutor him? I would, of course, pay well."

"Oh!" Katy exclaimed. So he wasn't trying to get her to raise Malcolm's grade. Then she realized what he had said. *Victorian melodrama? How could he? Nabokov or Vonnegut were probably more to his liking. Ugh. What made him think sheer laziness wasn't Malcolm's problem? Study skills, indeed.*

In her brown eyes, flecks of gold glittered with **anger**, but Guthrie was only more enchanted. What a challenge to prospect that gold!

"All right, Mr. Rutherford," Katy said, sighing. "I'll look into finding a tutor. I will also propose a workshop on study skills to Mr. Lyons and see how he reacts. Will that suffice?"

As she changed later for volleyball practice, she lamented again her lack of sophistication. When would she ever learn to handle men like that? Mariel could have met him head on, going one colder and haughtier with each exchange, until finally the great John Guthrie Rutherford III, would have turned tail and run. Ha! That would be fun to see.

But not little Katy. Oh, no. She only earned his amusement.

She banged her locker door a little more vigorously and vowed to forget him.

"There's a call for you, Katy," one of the girls yelled out from the office. "Coach Wilson didn't say who."

Guthrie's voice over the telephone sounded even more sophisticated than in the classroom, and for a moment she let the slight Massachusetts accent lull her. Then his words sank in.

"Miss Martin, I have a rather big favor to ask you, and as late as it is, you may be unable to help me. Would you come to dinner with me tonight? One of my clients here in Taichung has sprung a rather fancy affair on me, and I would so much prefer to have your charming presence beside me than to face the banquet alone. Could you come?"

"Tonight? A fancy banquet? This evening?"

"Ah," he said knowingly. "Much too short notice, as I was afraid. Then perhaps, if I gave you a little more warning, you would allow me to take you to dinner the next time I'm in town?"

"Oh, no, Mr. Rutherford—I mean, I could come tonight, if you like. I think I could get ready. What time?"

"I'll pick you up at 7:00 P.M. Do you live in the teacher apartments at the edge of the school compound? Excellent. And Miss Martin?"

"Yes, Mr. Rutherford?"

"We'd have a more pleasant evening, I believe, if you called me Guthrie."

"Oh! Katy. My name's Katy."

"For Kathleen?"

"Katherine, actually."

"Then I shall call you Katherine. Watch for me."

After practice, at which the girls couldn't help but notice how distracted she was, Katy raced home with Mariel, chattering the whole way about what she could wear and what she could talk about and how she'd ever survive without sounding like an idiot.

At the bottom of the stairs leading up to their apartment, Mariel asked, "Why so nervous, Katy? You dated in college."

Katy stopped and stared at Mariel. "Oh, sure, but they were only college boys, hardly shaving yet. This is a real man! At least thirty and rich, rich, rich. And so smooth. Did you know he has a chauffeur-driven Cadillac? And wears designer suits? Someday he's going to be an ambassador."

Katy started climbing the stairs. "Just think," she added, turning back to Mariel at the head of the stairs. "This is a real dinner date, to a banquet."

Katy couldn't see Luke rising from a chair on their porch, couldn't see the apprehension on his face or the pale color of his cheeks, and to his immense credit by the time she turned again and saw him he had composed himself.

"Luke! You'll never guess! I have a date tonight with Malcolm Rutherford's brother. Get this: his name's Guthrie. It reeks of the upper crust, doesn't it? He's taking me out to a fancy dinner with some clients of his. What do you think?"

"Wonderful," he strangled out and stood still and unmoving as she unlocked her door.

"Well, I've got to get dressed. You guys take care."

Katy disappeared into her apartment, but if she was too excited to notice Luke's frown, Mariel wasn't. "Come inside, Luke. You look like you could use some iced tea."

"That obvious, huh?"

"To me. I don't think she noticed."

"Why should she?" he said, scowling. "I'm a fixture in her life, like an old armchair or something."

"Um, and that's not exactly what you want, I suppose." She held out a glass of tea to him and got him to sit down. "You're crazy about her, aren't you?"

"Can you blame me?" He was gripping his glass so tightly she was afraid it would break.

"Then why haven't you told her?"

"And become another of those 'college boys'? Get real, Mariel."

Katy bounded in wearing a simple green dress that hugged her curves and made her look far more attractive than Mariel suspected she realized. "How does it look?"

"*You* look wonderful," Mariel said.

From his sudden vantage staring out the window, Luke grunted out a compliment. Mariel quickly grabbed Katy and pulled her into her bedroom. "Let's see if we can find some jewelry to match that."

She delayed Katy as long as possible, and then to her relief, Luke called out that Guthrie had driven up.

"Wish me luck!" Katy exclaimed before bouncing back out.

Luke stayed frozen until the big black car had driven away.

"Come on back to the couch," Mariel said, pulling him away from the window. "You'll feel better after telling me all about it."

"How'd you know I was in love with her?"

"Both showing up here? A little too coincidental, I thought. No man pays as much attention as you have to Katy without intending something more than friendship."

"So why hasn't she realized that?"

"She will."

"Ha!" He lapsed back into silence.

"Luke! Tell me. I really care."

He leaned back and visibly tried to relax. "I fell in love with her right away in that freshman chemistry lab she talked about, but it was obvious she wasn't ready for anything serious. I decided to wait it out. She had lots of male attention, someone like Katy always would, but I wasn't worried. They weren't any of them what she needed. In fact, I think she purposely chose guys that wouldn't really interest her that way. But this guy, Guthrie. He's different. *She's* different. I was planning to take her out this week-end, as a sort of warm-up, then take her to the Veteran's Day Banquet they have here at Hudson each year, with flowers and a romantic walk and maybe even a ring. Big plans from the big man."

Mariel cringed at the mocking tone in his voice. "You could still do that."

"No." Luke shook his head. "I've waited this long. This fascination with Guthrie will burn itself out. He's not what she needs either. She just doesn't realize it yet."

He stood up wearily and smiled down at Mariel. "Thanks. I've thought once or twice this fall that I might be able to give you someone to talk to, and instead you've done all the listening. Someday, maybe I can return the favor?"

"Maybe."

"Well, thanks again." He leaned over and kissed her on the cheek. "You're a good friend, Mariel."

Out in the night, Katy sat comfortably ensconced in Guthrie's Cadillac. Excitement, anxiety, nerves, anticipation, they caught her up in a swirling vapor of emotions. What in the world would she talk about to this man of the world? He'd prob-ably gone to Harvard, too, she thought, even more dismayed somehow at the thought, for she'd never known anyone who had gone to an Ivy League school. Beside her, he was talking rather pleasantly about the evening ahead, and she wondered if he felt the need to instruct her.

"We'll be only two of many guests," he said, "and will actually be unplanned-for guests. I had a meeting with the president of a large clothing company here in Taichung, and as I was leaving his assistant let fall something about the dinner tonight. Of course, good manners dictated that Mr. Wang invite me, and those same good manners required me to accept. You won't know from their behavior tonight that we weren't expected, however."

"You had business here? What exactly is your business?"

"I own a firm of trade consultants with branches in Hong Kong, Seoul, Tokyo, and Taipei. We help clients establish a smooth transition of goods from the Orient to the United States and back again."

"Sounds challenging."

"Of course, but worthwhile."

With the diplomacy he must have to practice, no wonder someone thought he'd make a good ambassador, she thought, as he helped her from the car.

A few minutes later, Katy entered one of Taichung's fancier restaurants. Large round tables filled the room, decorated in the bright Chinese red used so often to signify happiness. Waitresses met them with appetizers of sunflower seeds and tea. Within minutes, she found herself seated next to Guthrie at one of the large tables, surrounded by the typical formality of a Chinese gathering. She often wondered if Chinese children cut their eyeteeth on a manual written by a Chinese Miss Manners.

The dinner passed far more quickly than Katy had anticipated, and within in an hour-and-a-half they were on the way home. "I won't keep you tonight," Guthrie said at her door, "since you must teach tomorrow. May I call you the next time I am in town?"

Goodness, Katy thought, and nodded.

Seven

Two weeks after Katy's first date with Guthrie, on a Friday evening, Mariel entered Katy's apartment just as Katy was beginning to frost a chocolate cake.

"Double-rich, devil's food cake," Katy said. "For Luke. Tomorrow's the anniversary of Dragon Day. Four years ago today, he helped me return the letters of the Crocker College sign. I bake a cake every year for him."

She lifted an icing-laden knife from the bowl and stopped, frowning. "You know, I've hardly seen him since I went out that Monday night with Guthrie. We talked so often in college about the away games Hudson plays that I thought we'd have a great time together at the Taipei School soccer game last weekend. But we ended up on separate buses going and coming, and I hardly saw him the whole time we were there. It's all kind of strange."

The soccer game with Hudson's arch rival, the Taipei School, was one of Hudson's biggest fall events. All three school teams had games, the girls' volleyball team and the varsity and junior varsity soccer teams. Mariel had gone with Katy to do stats for the volleyball team. She had seen firsthand how Luke had eluded Katy—ironically similar to the way Mariel herself had avoided Adam. Luke carefully noticed which bus Katy entered and rode on the other one. At Katy's volleyball game and the varsity soccer game, he found a seat far up in the stands. For the JV game, of course, he had been helping to coach. He again avoided Katy and Mariel at dinner. But Mariel had seen him watching Katy, and he hadn't looked happy.

Was Luke giving up on Katy? He never visited them in the evenings and for all his attention eating lunch on the plaza, he might as well have been eating in his classroom. It seemed a little dangerous to ignore Katy so thoroughly.

"Have you seen Guthrie since that evening?"

"Yes," Katy said, smiling a little secretively. "Once for dinner, and he came by last weekend. We drove up into the mountains and shared a big picnic lunch. He's awfully sweet, you know. He makes me feel...well, don't laugh, but he makes me feel grown up." With a tone that sounded suspiciously smug, she added, "He's taking me to the Veteran's Day Banquet."

"Guthrie?"

"Yes. Don't sound so surprised, Mariel!"

"I'm not surprised he asked you. I thought...well, Luke..."

"Luke! Luke didn't ask me."

Mariel couldn't help smiling. Maybe Luke had better prospects than he hoped.

"Who's that?" Katy said, responding to a sound at her door. When she opened it, she exclaimed, "Jessie!"

She sounded so horrified that Mariel moved quickly to follow her. Over Katy's shoulder, Mariel saw Jessie Gunderson balancing shakily against the doorpost. She looked awful.

Mud spattered the front of her T-shirt, and a raw scratch blazed over most of one elbow and the side of her leg. Worse, in her other hand she cradled her shoeless right foot. Bits of gravel and pieces of glass were embedded deep in the sole, and blood was dripping from a particularly deep cut. Poor Jessie looked white and too shocked to even cry.

"Into the bedroom," Katy said.

As she and Mariel laid her gently down, Jessie struggled up, panic tapping her reserves of strength. "No! Let me go! Please, I can't stay here."

Mariel glanced at Katy in surprise. She could smell alcohol on Jessie's breath.

Katy caught Mariel's eye and shook her head sadly, but didn't look too surprised. "Lie down, Jessie!" she said firmly and bent over to hold Jessie's shoulders steady against the bed. "You're at my house now, Jessie. You're absolutely safe. We're going to take care of you."

Once Jessie stopped struggling, Katy gently took out the one barrette dangling forlornly across Jessie's face and smoothed her hair back from her forehead. "It will be okay, Jessie. Close your eyes now, if you can, while I fix the bed. I'm just going to put something under your foot and then cover you."

From the door, Mariel watched Jessie's panic subside. Whether from Katy's work at the shelter for battered women or her innate kindness, Katy was dealing well with Jessie's crisis. Unlike Mariel, Katy seemed able to completely ignore questions about what had happened. No criticism, no investigation, only firm command and comfort.

As Katy put a light cover over Jessie, she continued speaking.

"I will leave a small light here by the bed and ask Miss Forrest to stay with you. I need to call Dr. Schwartz. She'll have to clean your foot up before it gets infected."

Panic flared again. Struggling frantically to sit up, Jessie gripped Katy's arm and wailed: "Don't tell Judge, Katy. Oh, please, don't tell Judge. I'm so ashamed and..." her voice trailed off in a reedy whimper.

Katy put her hands on either side of Jessie's face and gazed straight down into her eyes. "Jessie. I won't call Judge. I won't. Trust me."

Jessie fell back exhausted onto the pillow, and Katy beckoned Mariel. "Stay with her, Mariel, and if you touch her or hold her hand, do so firmly. Keep talking, so she'll know you're here, but keep it low."

"Talking?"

"About anything. Pray if you want. Just keep talking so she'll know you're here."

Unwilling to pray, Mariel finally told Jessie about the cake Katy was making and what good friends Katy and Luke had been in college and how much Mariel enjoyed Luke, especially his stories about Katy in college. Jessie's eyes stayed open, gazing directly into Mariel's, but from her glazed expression, Mariel knew her thoughts were far away, still frantic and ashamed.

So she should be, Mariel thought. *She had obviously been drinking. She had only herself to blame for this mess.*

Jessie let a high, short moan escape and Mariel reached out gingerly to hold Jessie's good hand, the one unscratched from the fall. Without thinking, she began to make circles on Jessie's palm with her thumb. As she did so, she remembered that other night three years earlier, when she had been the one lying on the bed stiff from shock and someone had held her hand in the same way. With the remembering came compassion and empathy, and her words softened. The girl heard, her eyes focused momentarily, and then finally closed into a light sleep.

When Mariel looked up to meet Katy's eyes, she discovered tears in her own and was surprised. Katy beckoned her from the bedroom, pulling the door to without shutting it completely.

"I called Adam. He has to know about this kind of thing. Besides, then it will be up to him to decide what to do…about everything."

At the mention of Adam's name, dismay pulsed through Mariel. Adam? Here? So unexpectedly? Then sanity returned. Of course he had to come. This was his calling, he would even call it his ministry, and Jessie was under his care. If he remembered that disastrous scene at the retreat, he certainly wouldn't mention it now.

A rueful smile crossed her lips. *If* he remembered?

Mariel nodded toward the bedroom. "What do you think happened to Jessie?"

Katy's lips set in a firm line before she answered. "I bet it was Jack. She's been going out with him this fall. He must have taken her drinking, the turkey."

"But how did she get hurt?"

Katy shrugged and began to fill the coffee pot. "Jack has a motorcycle. He lives way across town and rides it everywhere. Maybe he took her out on that, got a little drunk, and lost control. She sure couldn't go back to the dorm looking like that."

"She's not going to be too thrilled about seeing Adam. Is he the judge she talked about?"

"No. Why postpone the inevitable? As painful as it'll be for her, she'll be better off in the end."

"I didn't think missionary kids acted like this."

"You mean getting drunk and doing stupid things like riding a motorcycle out of control?" Katy's mouth twisted. "Why ever not?"

"Isn't Jack a Christian?"

"Maybe. It would be hard *not* to make some kind of commitment in this environment. But at some point, God has to make a difference, a difference that shows. That's when you can tell if the faith is real. How does it go…it's not the profession of faith that saves you, but the possession of faith. It's hard to tell with Jack how he stands."

"And Jessie?"

"She's a Christian, I'm sure of it, so this is really going to hurt her. Once a person knows Jesus, really knows him and loves him even in an immature way, it's never easy to mess up like this." She lifted her head toward the door. "Oh, that's probably Dr. Schwartz."

It was Adam, with a stony look in his eyes. His gaze swept the room, registering Mariel's presence, and their eyes met for a sensitive moment, his own shadowed with concern and hers overcome with an unexpected empathy. He nodded his head briefly, though whether to acknowledge her support or merely her presence, her wary heart wouldn't let her decide.

Then he turned abruptly to Katy. "How is Jessie? Is the doctor here yet?"

"She is now," rang out a voice behind him, and the doctor herself pushed in past him.

She was a middle-aged woman, never married, and rather gruff in her manner. In her own domain, even Adam would have to answer to her. She was given to embarrassing the missionary kids, most of whom she had delivered and cared for throughout their childhood, but the relief on Katy's face now as she pulled the woman into the bedroom told Mariel all she needed to know about the community's confidence in Dr. Schwartz's medical skill. Under the gruffness and command was the sure and gentle hand of a healer.

In the bedroom, Dr. Schwartz spoke quietly to Jessie, who had woken with her entrance. She checked Jessie's scrapes and then examined her foot. Adam stood at the bedroom door to see the damage himself, and Mariel waited beside the table, listening.

"So he took the corner too fast, did he? Not surprised the cycle went out from under you. Pesky things, they are. Far more dangerous than you young ones give 'em credit for." Dr. Schwartz finished her examination and then sat beside Jessie on the bed. She spoke even more gently. "Been drinking, too, I suppose. Both of you?"

Jessie's head was buried in the pillow, but a murmur emerged. Dr. Schwartz continued. "Well, I'm glad you didn't climb back on the thing. Took guts to walk away. You hold onto that, child. We'll all get into trouble now and then. Can't be stopped, more's the regret. What we *do* in the trouble, now that's what counts. Don't forget, girl—it's what you do from now on that counts!

"Now. Got to clean y' up, and that arm'll hurt bad, but I'll put something in that foot so you won't feel it while I stitch you up. Got that? We'll get these muddy clothes off first and clean you up. Kate, shut that door and lend me a hand."

Adam turned abruptly and faced Mariel. They were inches

apart, so close she could feel his breath, and yet she couldn't turn away. Her senses were charged with a sudden tension, and it seemed to her that time had mysteriously altered. It was waiting, delaying, until she discovered something. Then she had it: He wore the same expression he had worn outside the Restons' cabin; in his eyes she saw the same strength and patience that had carried her through that shock. She reluctantly required of herself the small admission: Katy had been wise to call him. This man would always be a very present help in need.

She stepped back from him gingerly and motioned toward the kitchen. "May I get you some coffee, Adam?"

He pushed his hand through his hair and took a deep breath. Mariel could almost see him forcing his tension away. But probably out of sight, not out of mind. Jessie's own father couldn't have been more concerned.

"Yes, coffee, please. Then, if you don't mind, you can tell me what happened."

Sitting across the table from him, she told him as succinctly as possible what she knew. He listened throughout, tightening his face at her description of Jessie at the door, nodding at Katy's sure management, and grunting compassionately at Jessie's panic over the unknown "Judge."

"Too late for that," Adam said. "He's outside now, sitting over on the wall by the volleyball courts. My guess is Jack called him already to taunt him. Poor guy."

"I don't know who 'Judge' is, Adam."

"Oh. Yes, you do. 'Judge' is Steven Williams. A grade school nickname. Steven and Jessie have been sweethearts since fifth grade, I think, or maybe sixth. They broke up last spring, and too bad, since that led to Jessie dating Jack."

Here the frustration flickered again, and with his guard down, Mariel could see it was partly self-directed. He said, "Jack's a puzzle, one of those bright kids intent on getting into trouble. Maybe I should have expelled him for past problems, but I can't see that it would have helped. I'll probably have to suspend him now, for a while. As bad as he acts, he still needs help."

He took his glasses off and rubbed his eyes, the action making him appear oddly vulnerable. By revealing his doubts and indecision, he was granting Mariel a rare confidence, and her heart warmed to him. In her few discussions with him, he had overwhelmed her with his competence and control; now here he was needing support himself. He leaned back in his chair and smiled ruefully at her, and she sought desperately for some way to help him, some way to comfort him. In the stress of that desire, she instinctively offered the best strength she had—she directed him toward God.

"I read somewhere," she said slowly, "that we should never doubt in the dark what God has told us in the light. I mean, you had reasons for working with Jack, reasons you believed were correct before God. Shouldn't you remember those reasons now and, well, trust him?"

He looked up at her thoughtfully, his head tilted, assessing her, and too late Mariel realized how uncharacteristic that comment must sound to him. She had, after all, made no secret of her unwillingness to talk about spiritual matters. Was he going to say something? Not him, please!

Sensing her sudden withdrawal, Adam merely nodded and said, "Maybe."

Then to Mariel's relief, Katy emerged, and Adam abruptly reverted to the matter at hand. "How is Jessie?"

"Oh, Adam, I'm so glad you're here," Katy said, holding her hand out to him. The old disorganized Katy had returned and the questions spilled out. "Have you called her parents or should I? Shouldn't she stay the night here instead of going back to the dorm? Oh, goodness, Adam, I feel so confused."

Mariel stayed until she was certain she couldn't do anything else to help and then escaped. Once home, she slumped weakly onto her couch.

Her words of advice to Adam had slipped out instinctively, but thinking back to them now, she was stunned.

Bad enough to hear Dr. Schwartz telling Jessie that what counted was how she reacted to trouble. Even worse that Mariel herself would counsel against questioning God in the dark. She had certainly done that. *More* than doubted. She had turned and denounced God, fleeing the one she had felt betrayed by. Tonight God had used words out of her own mouth to chastise her. Trust God, indeed.

Left on her own, she had chosen a form of hedonism first—a mind-numbing, empty pursuit of pleasure and entertainment. Promiscuous sex had never appealed to her, and she insisted on too much control in her life to indulge in alcohol. But food and movies and hours and hours of sleep quickly became as much of a drug to her, and she loved being alone.

Eventually, however, those had ceased to appeal. The message of secular movies finally sank in—life in itself has no meaning. Invent the meaning yourself, through romance, through sex, through excitement. Pretend love and truth are possible, even as you head toward the cliff's certain death. In the end, she had known she had to find God again or go crazy.

There was also the mystery of why she couldn't get away from

Christians. How strange: She had been bitterly angry, obstinately rebellious, determined to cut off fellowship with God himself, yet she had nevertheless been drawn to his followers. Through the whole dreadful process of Annie's accident and David's death, the care and concern of a few faithful Christian friends had been the only bright spot in her life.

Why? Because Katy was right; being a Christian did make a difference. Mariel had never achieved more than a superficial relationship with the non-Christians she met at work. Those without any deep convictions somehow found a purpose for their lives—being happy, making money, looking after themselves and their families—but without any noticeable context for their choices, which puzzled and disturbed Mariel so that she felt compelled to keep her distance.

Those who did have compelling convictions were almost too predictable. They saw Mariel as a potential convert to their pet causes, and she hated it. One day a group of eco-conscious vegetarians had taken the table next to hers at a health bar. Listening to them criticize people who didn't share their views, she had a moment of personal epiphany: Why was their particular concern in life so singularly important? Why had protecting animals become the deciding virtue for them? Why not taking care of the homeless? Why not something less worthy, like amassing wealth and possessions? Who was to say one was better than the other?

To each his own, she supposed, but if all were equally significant, well, then, all were just as equally insignificant.

In the end, desperate to believe that life counted for something beyond her own experience, she went back to spending time with her Christian friends, grateful to find a few who didn't constantly try to counsel her or get her back to church.

Now she was teaching missionaries' children, for Heaven's sake.

For Heaven's sake. The words rang in her mind like a church bell. She saw it all now: he was getting his way, in spite of all her efforts to the contrary.

Mariel had long insisted that he, even more than David, had betrayed her, he who had so much power and yet refused to help. He could have protected Annie, strengthened David, stopped her. He could have made the difference. Yet here he was tonight, revealing that his grip on her was as tight as a shark's. He gave the slightest pull and she helplessly betrayed his hold over her, spouting spiritual advice to Adam.

Never doubt in the dark. Good grief.

The shadows in the room pressed in on her. Why bother trying? Whether you want to or not, he'll keep you longing for him. Break free, quench every desire you have, but he'll only make you thirsty again and always, every time, inevitably, for him.

She rose, prepared some warm milk, and curiously, in defiance of her habits of biblical abstinence, found her Bible and looked up Colossians.

Pastor Cartwright had said something about this hold of God's in his last sermon. If Christians continue in their faith, he said, they will be holy, perfect, free from accusation. Mariel would have claimed this "continuing in the faith" impossible to achieve, like a mother's repeated admonition to be good. But Paul seemed to consider it done already, for his "if" held no possibility of failure. It was unconditional. And why was it possible? Because it was God himself who would persist, God who would hold on, God—in spite of the Colossians' sin—who would not fail.

In spite of *my* sin, Mariel thought. If she had continued in her faith, and she saw now that she had, it was God's doing, not her own. In the past three years she would have abandoned God completely if she could have. *He* had held firm and *would* hold firm, forever.

And yet...

As cruel as his grip upon her had seemed, allowing sickness and death and betrayal, could it be his release would have been far more painful? Could it be, in fact, during all those months of denial and anger, that he had been holding on to her as to a child too close to the edge, at risk of slipping into a great abyss: held on not for destruction, but against destruction; not with a whip, but a lifeline; not as a shark, but a savior?

Could it be that in spite of the promises she imagined he had broken to her, in spite of the betrayal she accused him of, in spite of his tight, painful, unrelenting grip, could it be that all along she had been clinging just as tightly in return?

Her head fell forward onto weary hands. Oh, Hopkins, she thought. You knew: *The mind has mountains; cliffs of fall frightful, sheer, no-man-fathomed. Hold them cheap may who ne'er hung there.*

I admit it, she finally cried out to God. *I need you forever.*

What now? she wondered. *You, God, I can't escape—oh, pain—you, God, I must cling to?*

It was horribly late, but for fear she would change her mind by morning, now so few hours away, she rose, slowly picked up the phone, stared at it for a long moment, and then dialed Pastor Cartwright's number.

His voice, when he answered, rasped with sleep. "Hello? Who is it?... Is someone there?"

She finally spoke, confused somehow that the God who could so easily rule her, would not simply speak for her across wires of his own making. "Pastor Cartwright, it's me," she mumbled, wretchedly. "Mariel Forrest. Could you…may I come see you sometime? I…I think I'm ready now to talk about things."

"Mariel. Of course you may come." He was fully awake now, his voice so close and firm. "Tomorrow? What time shall we meet?"

"Anytime, really. Whenever."

"Okay." He took over, sensing her weariness. "Let's say 3:30 tomorrow afternoon. Rachel always brings me some coffee then. How about coming over for a cup with me?"

"Yes, yes," she mumbled wearily, and then hung up before he could say good-bye.

She was sorry in the morning that she had called him and wished she could cancel. She did go late.

When she arrived at the pastor's house, however, he greeted her as company, and his manner forced an unwanted courtesy from her. He led her into his study and over coffee and snacks talked about food and his wife's pleasure in having a cook and stories of teaching the cook how to make Western food.

"There was more than a little irony in having a woman who hated to cook and had avoided it all her life trying to teach someone else to do the very thing she couldn't do."

Irony indeed, Mariel thought. She knew that irony well.

Something of her thoughts must have crossed her face, for Thomas grew quiet, watching her with a steady regard.

"Mariel," he finally prompted, so gently.

She cleared her throat. "Now?"

"As you wish."

She closed her eyes and turned away from him, the tears suddenly close. He waited.

"All right," she finally blurted out. "You're here, and I agreed to talk, so I might as well. If you want to know, the real trouble is that I'm tired of being a Christian. I wish I could stop."

Inwardly she groaned. After all her carefully rehearsed words, *these* had to come out?

"Go on."

"He has an unfair advantage, Pastor Cartwright. Becoming a Christian gives God the right to have his own way."

Such sudden and complete silence descended that she wondered if he was holding his breath. Well, if she had offended him, fine! The thought unleashed the dam.

"God does what he wants and so unfairly! Non-Christians, they do fine, never even realizing how badly off they are. A lot of them are rich and indulgent and undisciplined, and terribly, terribly selfish. Life goes on for them without a hitch. I can't see a single advantage to being a Christian."

In her sudden eagerness to extend the offense, she knew she was exaggerating immaturely. She forced a slow, even breath and spoke again, holding her hands out before her as if trying to mold her words into some semblance of order.

"This is what I mean. It seems like God is no good to us here on earth. We tell children that he watches over them, that he'll protect them, but we know the words are risky. There are no guarantees. How many Christian children get sick and suffer miserably, are abused, abducted, used brutally. They get abandoned and starve and live through incredible pain. Where's God in all that?"

She gave up order and flung her hands out in hopeless entreaty. "He's not fair even among Christians! Some Christians live shallow, thoughtless, uncommitted lives, and does God touch them? No! They bear children, raise them, live to see their grandchildren and sometimes even their great-grandchildren. Others, dedicated to God, wanting nothing more than to please him, as faithful as they know how to be, those Christians lose everything to him."

He leaned forward. "Mariel?"

"So I wish I could get out, be like a non-Christian, live for myself, however I want, without any expectations of fairness or justice or love. If it's all a gamble, I want to *live* that way. I'm tired of pretending that it's anything more than random."

She jumped up from her seat and strode to the window, twisting the drapes around and around as dry, silent sobs racked her shoulders. She felt his hand on her shoulder and jerked away, huddling again in the armchair. Tissues appeared on the table beside her, and he sat down again.

"You should tell me what happened, Mariel."

"Why? If you know what happened to Rebecca and Spence Martin and their two sons, then you know what I'm talking about!"

"I know the Martins' story." His voice was firm. "I need yours."

She stood up again and moved blindly toward the door this time, turned the doorknob and flung it open, and then couldn't go further. He watched from his chair, prayer on fast forward, and the door shut again. A dry sob racked her shoulders again, but she was wept out.

Slumped in her chair again, she continued. "I had a daughter, a beautiful little girl, and she died almost before she had a chance to live."

Now their expressions were reversed, hers so blank and his so full of dismay.

"How?" Then, "Mariel, tell me everything, please."

"She died in a car accident, a drunk driver."

Again the silence, this time tinged with shame, and he knew he could do nothing except wait.

She finally spoke again. "My husband was driving. The drunk driver swerved over into their lane and hit our car head-on. I wasn't with them. Annie was in the front seat, a special treat for her, wearing a seat belt but not in her car seat. It was too loose. It didn't hold her. She was killed instantly."

After a moment, Thomas said, "And your husband?"

She kept her eyes unfocused, gazing blindly across the room.

"Your husband died as well, Mariel?"

A muscle twitched in her jaw, evidence of her great control, but she couldn't hold her bitterness back. "Not then. He survived. How fortunate! He survived to discover, lucky man, that he might have prevented Annie's death. No one had to tell him that in her car seat, safely strapped in, she would have come through with minor injuries. But I told him anyway, more than once, believe me."

She flinched and turned her head away, closing her eyes as if that could hide the memories from her. "I wish I could believe it was all chance! Chance that we exist, that earth itself exists. A cosmic crapshoot and no one's fault when things go wrong. The luck of the toss: Annie got snake eyes, and David got worse. But somehow I'm supposed to believe that a loving God is behind this."

Outside the shadows gathered, the thickening twilight finding a home within her. She felt trapped, sinking, slipping, something pulling her down and under and into a great darkness. Into her despair came the touch of the pastor's hand, and she remembered again her image of God holding her above the great abyss.

"Help me, Pastor Cartwright! I can't keep this up. Annie's gone, and David too, and I find that losing God would be too much. How can I trust him?"

"What happened to David?"

She turned away from him, her expression closed off again, and sat looking at the floor.

A moment more of frozen distance, and then she leaned back into the armchair, tipped her head up, and sighed. "Moved away. That's what we did. Both of us. Moved away and away and then found ourselves lost. Imagine it, Pastor Cartwright," she said, challenging him with narrowed eyes. "Your child has died, but you can't express any grief because if you do you increase your husband's. Even though you try to hide all your own pain, he believes that you blame him. Of *course* he believes it, because it's true. A little bit. I couldn't help it."

"It's always hard for couples to work through death of any kind."

Her lips twisted contemptuously, and she looked away again. "Bland words to describe what happened to us."

"Which is—?"

The answer was so slow in coming that he almost repeated

the question. Then she turned back to him, and he realized that silent tears were falling down her cheeks. "We tried. We really did. We went to counseling, but nothing helped. We couldn't bear to be together, but we couldn't bear to be apart. It was one of those really horrible situations where nothing seems good, no option seems preferable—no, not even possible. The day Annie died, our marriage did too."

She grew quiet and stayed silent for so long that he began to wonder if she ever intended to go on.

"Mariel?"

She jerked her head toward him as if surprised to find him sitting across the room. Her eyes swept the room, and he saw her shoulders fall in resignation as she realized where she was. She saw Thomas waiting and sighed.

"God took so much, but it wasn't enough. He had to take David, too, and in a way that made me realize I had never really known David at all."

She stood up and went to the window again, looking out far beyond the scene outside. She spoke so softly he had to strain to hear. "The counselor insisted we sleep together. It was a terrible mistake, but I discovered I was pregnant. I did hope, when I found out, for a change—how stupid! David didn't want the baby. He said he couldn't bear the pain of losing another one. I had to either get an abortion or he was leaving."

She turned to confront the pastor, throwing her hand out in dismissal. "What did he think? That I would kill my second child, too? I told him to leave, right then. I didn't want to see him again. I said—" her voice cracked. "I said—"

Her pain was suddenly too intense even for him to bear, and he moved quickly to the door and called his wife.

"No! Don't!" she exclaimed, so that when Rachel appeared at the door, he whispered something and then shut the door again. Mariel remained where she stood, a twisted grimace on her face.

"Don't tell me, Mariel," Thomas said. "You don't have to."

"Because you can guess," she said, "but I will anyway. I said, 'Isn't it enough that Annie died? Do you have to kill this child, too?' He left, of course. The police came later that night. He had driven his car into a tree."

She spoke calmly, in such a flat monotone that she frightened him. "I'll never know—well, this side of eternity—whether he did it on purpose or by accident. Either way, it was my fault. The baby died anyway." A high, thin laugh escaped. "Isn't that the ultimate irony. God must have known I wasn't fit for it, because I miscarried later that week."

"Mariel—"

She shook her head. "Don't tell me what everyone else has, ever since it happened. I know all the words, believe me. 'It wasn't my fault. The shock was too much for me physically.' On and on and on. The same thing over and over again, but I *know* things don't happen by accident. God's somewhere back there, controlling things. Since the day I miscarried, I have wanted to escape his puppet strings, but I can't, and that's what is tearing me apart.

"Help me, Pastor Cartwright! I can't keep this up. David's gone, and I can't do anything to atone, and I can't bear this anger any more. God won't leave me alone anyway, and he won't let me leave, but I'm living in ashes, and I can't bear it."

Thomas reached out to grip her hand, stroking it gently again and again for endless moments, just as she had the night before with Jessie, as if coaxing away her anxiety and restlessness and heartache. He finally said, "Will you believe this one thing, Mariel? If he won't let you go, he's keeping you for more than despair? Can we discover him again together, Mariel? Will you work with me toward that?"

Dumbly she nodded, unwilling to give voice to her fears, her lack of faith, her absence of hope.

"Trust *me* at least, child, if you can't trust him completely yet. In the end you'll be trusting him in spite of yourself because I'm here for him...and for you."

After a brief moment looking at her, during which she felt certain he was casting a benediction over her, he led her to the door. "You've taken a big step today, Mariel, a hard step and alone; we'll go together from here on if you're willing." At her nod, he patted her arm. "Come back next Saturday? Good. Take care."

The next evening after church, as she so often did, Mariel went out onto the balcony to sit quietly in the gathering darkness. The evenings were getting too cool to be comfortable. The moon was barely out, and most of the stars hid behind the clouds. She was too weary to think about much and too frightened to consider if speaking to Pastor Cartwright would make any difference to her. When Katy appeared beside her and spoke, she sounded abnormally loud to Mariel.

"Jessie's parents came yesterday to take her home. She'll probably miss a week of school, but she'll recuperate better there."

Turning toward Katy, Mariel said, "I wanted to ask you: How did Steven Williams get his nickname?"

"His nickname?" Katy smiled wistfully. "Oh, he's had that for

119

a long time. Steven was always a weakling. Really! He may not seem like it now, but back then, in grade school, he was puny and asthmatic. He got so tired of being chosen last for teams that he finally stopped lining up all together. What the boy lacked in muscle, however, he more than made up in brains. He took to watching the kids. That way if he couldn't play all their four square and soccer and kickball, he could at least reminisce with them afterwards. It's no wonder he's so good at journalism and writing. He's has a long time to practice his observation skills. He became a sort of group arbitrator and basically earned status that way instead of through sports the way most kids do.

"Anyway, his name. One day when the kids were playing street soccer, Steven was on the sideline watching as usual. Someone pulled a foul, maybe kicked a kid or tripped him, I don't know. Everyone automatically turned to Steven for the final word, and when he ruled against the one who had done the foul, the kid planted himself squarely in front of Steven and said, 'Who made you the judge?' The name stuck. Everyone called him Judge from then on."

"And Jessie?"

"They've been buddies forever. She was probably the first to jump to Steven's defense. They were named King and Queen of our Valentine's Banquet when they were freshmen, no less. That hadn't ever happened before."

"But not anymore?"

Katy sighed. "We certainly can do ourselves in, can't we? Jessie had been going with him so long, she probably wanted a change. Besides, in high school, brains sometimes take on a less appealing aspect—"

"Nerds and geeks, you mean?"

"You have to admit Steven has a great academic future, but he also doesn't exactly have a lean, mean, athletic body. I suppose Jessie decided she could do better."

"Freedom can be another prison," Mariel said bleakly.

"Well, yes," Katy said. "I think Jessie knows that now. Maybe she can put her pride away long enough to realize that Steven still cares about her."

"You know he was here last night?"

Katy nodded. "I went out and talked to him after you left and told him how Jessie was doing. Once he knew she'd be all right he went on home."

Into the silence that followed a few drops began to fall on the porch roof, and Mariel felt unbearably weary. Was pride keeping her from opening her heart's door again? "If with all your heart you truly seek me—" Would God respond to less than *all* of her, less than even half a heart?

"Mariel?"

Katy's voice drew Mariel back, and she felt tears on her face.

"Katy," she said slowly, considering. Could she bear to do this again? Was it worth getting it over with? She leaned back and took a deep breath. "There's something I need to tell you."

"What is it? You sound so serious!"

Of course, after hearing Mariel's story, Katy could well understand why Mariel had spoken so solemnly. Whatever Mariel had expected from Katy, she had forgotten Katy's experiences with battered women. Mariel found Katy's response to her story gentle and tolerant and very, very kind.

Getting ready for bed later, the question occurred to Mariel—was that what she was, a battered woman? If so, by whom or what? Circumstances? Sin? Her own willful, immature nature?

For once, she didn't allow herself to add God to that list, however much she was tempted to. Not this time.

K aty caught up with Mariel walking home from school the next day. "Hey, we need a break! A group of us are going to the shacks tonight to eat *jyaudzs*—the Withers and the Cooks. Why don't you call Luke, and we can all rehash the bike trip for you? Have you ever eaten *jyaudz?* I know the *shacks* sounds awful, but the food's great, really!"

Glancing sideways at Katy, Mariel couldn't decide whether Katy was babbling because she wasn't sure Mariel would be willing to come, given last night's tears, or whether she was thinking of Luke. Probably Luke. Should she tease Katy and ask her why she couldn't call Luke herself? She supposed for Katy's sake, she'd have to go along.

To Mariel's surprise, somehow Luke agreed to come. Only as their taxi pulled up outside the flimsy restaurant did Mariel realize Katy had called the other two couples first so Luke would have to accept. The evening was a merry one in spite of Luke's dour expression and Katy's occasional thoughtful glances toward him. Mariel was curious, of course, but as reticent as she was about her own deepest emotions, she hesitated to ask Katy what was going on between them.

Later as Katy went out with the others to catch a taxi, Mariel pulled Luke back. "Guthrie's taking her to the banquet, Luke. Did you know that?"

Luke pulled a scowl. "I figured as much. To make things worse, I have to go. I'm one of the chaperones. Would you like to go with me, Mariel?"

"Second best?"

"Very best in a different way," Luke said gallantly. "Besides, I have an idea that my date will be the most beautiful one there."

"Oh, you charmer," she said, laughing. "All right. Count me in. Just for you, I'll come."

Luke turned to lead her out, then stopped. "Maybe you can distract Guthrie. Now there's a thought!"

Katy, standing outside in the gathering October darkness, wondered why Luke and Mariel had stayed behind. *Really, she was becoming obsessed with Luke!* During the past weeks she had often sat on the balcony in the gathering chill, hoping to hear his footsteps on the stairs. Not once since the bike trip had he come. Though he still ate lunch with Mariel and Katy, during their lunches he often seemed oblivious to them, staring vacantly across the plaza. More than once he'd risen abruptly and wandered off with his lunch only half-finished.

"Luke's acting awfully strange, isn't he?" she asked Mariel later that week.

"Strange?"

"Distant."

"Maybe he's lonely out here," Mariel suggested. "The holidays are coming up. Thanksgiving and Christmas make people think about home."

Katy shook her head. "That doesn't sound like the Luke I know. Are you feeling lonely, Mariel?"

"I'm fine. Too old now with too many years alone. I won't let myself—well, I'm fine." Mariel stood abruptly. "It's getting too cold out here. I'm going in. As for Luke, Katy, why don't you ask him if something's wrong?"

Katy stayed outside. She didn't notice the cold. Images from the Double Ten trip flooded over her: Luke's protectiveness at the *jyaudz* table, his nearness a few minutes later and his murmured comment to her, the sweetness of waking on the park bench after she had hurt her head to find his eyes upon her.

She didn't need *Dear Abby* to tell her the reason for her depression now. In fact, she'd felt that same depression each time she had begun hoping for any interest on Luke's part. That hope always led to the same conclusion: Why, after so many years of knowing each other, would he suddenly fall in love with her now? How embarrassing for them both if she were to try to encourage something that wasn't there! Surely it would be the end of their easygoing friendship. How dreadful that would be!

No. Better to settle for friendship than to risk something more and lose all. Through four years of college she had smothered any desire for Luke that had flickered within her. What had been wisdom in college had now become self-preservation, her very survival.

At least she had Guthrie for the banquet. That was a coup!

On Saturday Mariel met with Pastor Cartwright again. This time he began immediately even as he poured the coffee.

"Tell me how you came to know God, Mariel. How did you become a Christian?"

"You're so sure I am a Christian?"

He studied her a moment before answering. "Yes, Mariel. The Hound has you, for sure. So tell me how."

She recognized the allusion. The Hound of Heaven. She felt cornered and panic gripped her, and if anyone else had been sitting before her, she would have risen and fled the scene. Something about Pastor Cartwright held her to her chair, though whether it was a desire to please him or to shock him, she couldn't say.

She mumbled through her testimony, telling him about her family, that she accepted Christ early, that she'd learned quickly the wisdom of obedience.

She somehow got off track and began to speak about the churches she had attended. "We always went to a certain kind of church. The pastors gave salvation messages almost every Sunday morning. We did study the Bible, but mostly only in Sunday school. The whole thing was a system of rules, I think—giving a certain amount of money, bringing people to church, coming to all the services, no drinking, no smoking, no dancing—know what I mean.

"I don't know how old I was, but I began to think perhaps the people were missing something. They'd give their ten percent but couldn't spare a penny more. They'd be there whenever the church doors were open, but they'd swear and act like pigs at softball games—the church softball league, no less." She frowned. "Am I wrong? I suppose I'm too judgmental?"

"You thought they deserved judgment?"

"Only because they were so pompous. I couldn't keep the

rules either, but at least I tried. I decided to succeed where they failed, and I think I almost did. I read my Bible *every* day. And praying! I prayed. I really did. And I did ministries and witnessed and was an all-around, really good kid. I was sure God thought so, too, when I met David."

The words stopped abruptly, and she felt the memory of her confidence recede. They sat in a silent tableau, she with her shoulders curved forward, her head bowed, he leaning toward her, almost reaching out.

He touched her with a word: "David?"

She swung her head back and forth, mindlessly, as if somehow it helped to ease the pain.

"I've thought again and again about why God punished us so horribly. If it had been only David, maybe I could understand. He wasn't perfect. But our little Annie! She was so patient, so gracious to everyone she met. Goodness seemed to shine out of her. Why would God punish her?"

She hadn't been able to look at Pastor Cartwright, but now, stealing a small glance at him, she saw in his eyes something of her own pain, and also a deep regret. So, her guilt was found out.

"I know what you're thinking. God *wasn't* punishing Annie. Things happen, God allows them, suffering builds our character—I've heard it *all*, believe me! But it doesn't feel right to me. It was *me*, I know it! I didn't deserve her. I wasn't a good enough mother—and don't tell me I shouldn't feel that way, that no mother is 'good enough.' Those things you want to say are only words, and they've never changed what I know inside. If she had stayed with me, I would have ruined her, and so God took her away. Then I *did* ruin David. That was the proof."

She moved wearily to the window and leaned her head

against the pane. "I wasn't fit for either of them, so God took them away. That's the truth, and I can't ever change it."

After a few moments, she felt his hand upon her head. "Mariel, we'll work this out, you and I and God. Come sit down, now; I'll pour you some fresh coffee, and we'll leave this and move on."

Once seated, he said, "I understand what you're saying about how you feel, but I'm convinced that the way to resolve your problems is in God, not in you. To understand your feelings and deal with your fears, you need to know God and understand his character. John tells us that knowing God leads to eternal life. Daniel says strength and great energy come from knowing God, and Jeremiah says knowing God allows us to serve and obey him. Best of all, Job says we can have peace from knowing God, and you need that peace.

"Where do your feelings come from? I'm not a psychoanalyst, Mariel. I can't take you through the labyrinth of your past. But I can help you know God, and knowing Him can make all the difference. Will you work with me?"

It sounded awful. Knowing herself, she had to believe that knowing God would serve only to highlight even more her failings. As his perfection rose before her, her own imperfections would bury her deeper into guilt. Then how could she count on his hand continuing to hold her safe?

Yet this man, so unlike any minister of God she had ever met, made her helpless to refuse. She would come back.

As Mariel waited for Luke to pick her up for the banquet, she stood near the door looking down at his orchid. Incredibly, she could have been holding Adam Lyons's orchid. It might have been Adam who was coming for her. Even now she couldn't believe he had asked her.

For the first few moments of his phone conversation, Mariel didn't even listen to what he was saying, concentrating instead on hearing his voice so close against her ear, a novelty that briefly drew away all of her attention. Then his actual words broke through her trance, and she almost dropped the phone.

Go to the banquet with him?

"No, I couldn't possibly," she sputtered and gratefully gave her excuse of going with Luke.

Adam paused and then said, "Actually, I expected Luke to ask *Katy.*"

His voice was calm, almost dispassionate, and Mariel wondered why he had asked at all if it made so little difference to him when she refused! Feeling a little bit rebuffed, Mariel explained about Guthrie.

Adam chuckled and said, "Obstacles in the course...of true love, I mean. Poor Luke! They'll work it out eventually, I'm sure. At any rate, it's good that he has you. I'll see you there then."

Now she wondered, if it *were* Adam who was coming, what would she be feeling? Concern, anxiety, apprehension? Yes, certainly, all those. An evening with Adam, especially at such a public function, would be dreadfully intimidating.

Then why was she feeling just a little disappointed?

And who would Adam take instead?

Adam was standing in the lobby of the hotel where the banquet would be held, talking to some of the students. Periodically his eyes wandered to the entrance, though he didn't actually admit to himself whom he was watching for. Then he saw Mariel and all pretense vanished. She had come! She wore a soft, slim-fitting, knitted dress, which wrapped her in a violet haze. From among the curls of her upswept hair twinkled tiny amethysts, matched by her earrings, and on her wrist she wore Luke's orchid. For Adam, her elegant beauty transformed the faded and slightly tawdry hotel lobby, and he almost stepped involuntarily toward her. Instead, he tried to get her attention. Unfortunately, no matter how vehemently Adam willed her to look his way, Mariel's gaze stayed fixed on the students waiting to have their pictures taken.

She was certainly beautiful, Adam thought, *but she was incredibly difficult, too.*

Patience, he told himself. He had time.

Smiling ruefully at Mariel's recalcitrance, Adam caught Luke's attention. Luke had been standing by the door, anxiously surveying the room; his tension noticeably decreased when he realized Katy had not yet arrived. Adam motioned for Luke to come over.

Ah, finally Mariel looked up. A smile. Not with her eyes, but still a smile. Adam could start with that.

Luke held out his hand in greeting. "What's up, Adam? Tell us the routine here. We're both novices, you know."

"Your picture first," Adam said, motioning toward the line of students. "The photo's an essential memento of the big event. Then we stand around and wait here in the lobby until the hotel's ready for us. We go in and eat, listen to some jokes, some special music from the girls' sextet and I think this year a barbershop quartet. After that we all go back to campus to watch a movie. *Star Wars* tonight, to go with the outer space theme."

"What, no dance?" Mariel said. Her eyes were open just a little too widely for the question to be as innocent as it sounded.

"Now, now, Miss Forrest, you know we don't do that at Hudson!" Adam said, in his most disparaging tone. Then he smiled and continued normally. "That's not to say some missionary kids' schools don't allow dancing, just not Hudson. That's how it started and how it will continue, I'm sure. Video tapes are readily available now, but at one time the movie was a real treat. We gave our order months in advance and then waited in suspense to find out what they actually sent us. One year they sent us *Cool Hand Luke* by mistake. The kids wouldn't eat eggs for weeks!"

Luke laughed, but it sounded painfully hollow to both Adam and Mariel, who shared a look of shared sympathy as Luke glanced toward the door again. Still no sign of Katy.

Luke looked back at Adam. "The students tell me you're the MC tonight, Adam. Is this like the photographs—another essential tradition?"

"Only at the Veteran's Day Banquet. By the Valentine's Day Banquet they've seen enough of me." Adam watched as Luke went through the same painful routine of checking the entrance again. "Look," he said kindly, "you two go get your picture taken. The line's getting short and dinner's sure to start now."

Luke shrugged and stepped back for Mariel to lead the way. As she did so, she slipped a doleful smile up at Adam, amusement glittering in her eyes, and shook her head slightly. He winked back and briefly saw her face shine with genuine mirth before she passed him. As Luke and Mariel threaded their way across the room, Adam had to forcibly restrain himself from punching the air in triumph. That intimate exchange of humor was small, but still a definite advance. This time she had given him a real smile.

Difficult—yes, she was that—but not impossible.

When dinner was called and Katy still hadn't arrived, Luke began to hope perversely that she wouldn't come at all. Perhaps her "real man" had been too busy. Then, as he was helping Mariel to be seated at their table, he glanced up again and there she was. She wore a dress of blue silk, the material so stiff that her sleeves stood out from her in shimmering puffs and the skirt flared out from her waist like a school girl's. Any other similarity to a school girl was erased completely by the neckline, which dipped quite radically for a Hudson banquet; nestled above the faint swell of Katy's breasts lay Mariel's sapphire pendant, winking scorn across the room at Luke. Standing with Guthrie in the doorway, her hair a commotion of curls, cheeks blooming with excitement, she was suddenly not his friend and longed-for lover, but Katherine the woman, poised and beautiful, and suitably worthy to hold the arm of a future ambassador.

Hope left Luke on a sigh.

The four sat down to dinner, and Mariel quickly found herself in the role of hostess. Luke seemed suddenly sunk in a slough of gloom. Katy appeared oblivious to anything but the surrounding students' curiosity over her mysterious date, and Guthrie merely sat silently beside Katy, smiling indulgently. It would be a long night if Mariel didn't take charge.

"You're in business here in Taiwan, Guthrie?"

"The trade business."

"He has offices all over the Orient," said Katy.

"With such far-flung offices, where exactly do you call home?"

"Until my father retired from the State Department last year, I operated out of Hong Kong. My parents have now returned to Massachusetts permanently, leaving Malcolm to finish his last year at Hudson. So I now operate out of Taipei, to keep an eye on him. I have a condo there."

Luke forced himself to imagine Katy there—curled up in a deep leather armchair, gazing out on a panoramic view of the city. She would be sipping coffee from a gold-trimmed china tea cup, brought to her by a well-mannered butler.

Katy's voice interrupted him, asking Guthrie to recount a story from his travels, and that became the pattern for the dinner. Unless he was speaking, Guthrie wore a slightly bored expression, but he came alive with his stories and they were entertaining—tales of traveling the Orient, college pranks, memories of Hudson in the sixties when Guthrie had attended the school.

With each story Luke sank deeper into gloom.

He had never imagined he could fail. Winning Katy had seemed as certain to him as his As in chemistry, having fun with friends, some benefit from studying God's Word. He had dreamed so long of marriage to Katy and yet, across the table sat Guthrie, the perfection of his silk tie mocking Luke, the magic of his gaze enthralling Katy, the wit in his speech entertaining them all. A very suave NO to all Luke's dreams.

As the dinner ended, just before Adam stood up to do his jokes, Mariel leaned a little closer to Luke and said, "Adam didn't bring a date tonight."

"Oh, he never does," Katy announced from across the table.

"In all the years since his wife died, Adam has never brought a date to a Hudson function."

"I can't believe it!" Mariel exclaimed. Her jaw dropped for a moment in stunned surprise, and then she quickly tried to cover up her reaction. "Why not, for goodness' sake?"

Katy shrugged. "Who knows? Except that the poor woman would probably get the wrong idea. I mean, he hasn't been in any hurry to remarry, has he? It would be like that apple Aphrodite threw out."

"Excuse me, that was Eris who threw the apple—the goddess of strife," Guthrie said. "Aphrodite ended up winning it."

Katy's hand fluttered briefly. "Right, right, whatever. The thing is, if he asked someone, it would be so easily misunderstood."

"I suppose so," Mariel said.

"Especially if he started doing it after all these years," Luke drawled, and grinned lazily when Mariel cast him a sharp glance.

Did Luke know about Adam's invitation? What did that mean? She stole a glance at Adam, but he was talking to some students. What did any of it mean? Mariel had no answers. The man was an annoying enigma, and she wasn't going to waste any more time trying to figure him out. Even so…She glanced at Adam again and this time caught a smile. Oh, he was so frustrating!

At the movie, Luke managed to steer himself and Mariel clear of Katy and Guthrie, though his finely tuned ear could still hear Katy's laughter across the room, sending him further into despondency.

Later at Mariel's apartment, over a cup of tea, Mariel touched Luke's arm in sympathy. "Pretty tough on you, Luke. I'm sorry. Thank you for taking me, though. Katy must not realize what she's missing."

He nodded glumly, caught between his desire to respond and his fear of over-responding. Finally he turned to her, throwing his words out with abandon. "I suppose you think he's perfect for her, don't you? He's so smooth, so accomplished, so—perfect! All right. But so what? How long can it last? How long can she feel so good about a man who cares only about himself?"

In his passion he had risen from his chair. "Did you notice how often he asked Katy questions? How often he asked anyone questions? The man spent the whole meal talking about himself! He probably couldn't tell me one thing about Katy, about her dreams or ambitions, her fears or worries—not one thing!"

He sounded so intense that Mariel had to hide a smile.

"I agree!" she said, holding her hands up in surrender. "He's a self-centered, supercilious, conceited, egotistical snob, but hey, he's also tall, dark, and handsome, and rich to boot!"

At Luke's stunned expression, Mariel could no longer hide her amusement. "Oh, Luke, he's not right for Katy, and she's too smart to think so for long." She gave him a push toward the door. "Go home, you coward, and lay some battle plans. What have you got to lose anyway? Put up a fight!"

"Do you really think I should speak to her, Mariel? Do you really think I have a chance?"

"Yes! Tell her you're going crazy and get it over with. But for now go home and rest up. You'll need your energy."

The Monday after the banquet, Katy was a little surprised to find Luke waiting on her balcony when she returned home from school. It was late, 8:30 P.M., for she'd eaten supper with Bridget in the cafeteria.

Luke watched her climb the stairs and felt a spasm of doubt. She seemed so reluctant to greet him. Even so, he remained determined to speak his piece. After this evening, the choice would be hers.

At the top of the stairs, she said, too brightly, "Luke! How are you? It's been so long since you've been up to see us. Where's Mariel?"

"I don't know. I came to see you."

"Oh. That's nice. Do you want to talk out here?"

"Inside, I think. It'll be warmer."

She went to the kitchen to get him a hot drink and upon her return, launched immediately into a story she had heard at supper about Bridget's boyfriend, Leo.

Luke didn't listen. He sensed only her nearness, so necessary to his happiness, and the pleasure of hearing her voice, and his desire to hold her in his arms. He would return to graduate school with or without her, but his love would continue, like a deep-rooted tree that didn't need rain to bloom.

"Katy," he said abruptly, halting her in mid-phrase. "Katy! About Guthrie. I...I don't really know how to say this."

Her expression gave no encouragement.

"I really don't think you should see him," Luke blundered on. "I think he's—"

"Stop it, Luke," she exclaimed. "I already know you don't like him. I saw that at the banquet, you frowning at him, frowning at me, frowning at both of us. Do you think I'm blind? I think I should be allowed to make up my own mind about Guthrie!"

"I only want what's best—"

"Sure you do. You're speaking as a friend. Well, I don't think that gives you permission to interfere in my love life!"

Luke's expression froze. *There you are, chum,* he thought. *If you had any doubts where you stood, now you know.*

"Fine," he said and stood up. "Then I'll go. Say hi to Mariel."

It was as if the lights had suddenly gone out for Katy, his departure was so sudden and complete.

Telling Mariel about it later, Katy had to admit Luke was right about Guthrie. "He likes himself more than I do, I think."

"Then why bother with him?"

"Oh, he brings me flowers and takes me to dinner and certainly ups my status with the students. What girl could turn all that down?"

Mariel didn't look impressed. "You'll have to call Guthrie after this, you know, the next time you encounter one of your little dragons. Better be careful!"

As fate or luck or God himself would unkindly have it, a new dragon, this time in the form of a small monkey, arrived in Katy's life not seven days later.

At first, she had hoped Luke would simply ignore their conversation. No chance. He didn't actually avoid her. He just didn't seem to realize she was near. When they were together, unconsciously wanting to share something with him, she would quite irresistibly bring her eyes up to his—only to discover he was looking elsewhere.

She went over to Mariel's once to find Luke there. But when she sat down, he got up to leave.

She saw him occasionally on her way home from volleyball

practice, standing across the soccer field with the boys. He'd be wearing his old gray sweat suit, suddenly so dear to her, his face grimy with sweat, hair pushed back, stance so casual.

Wasn't he worried at all? Didn't it bother him that they weren't friends?

You fool, Katy, she scolded herself. *He'll come apologize soon. He never stays upset for long.*

But she couldn't stop thinking about him.

So when her youngest brother, Billy, asked her to take care of his monkey—*monkey?*—she surprised him by agreeing almost immediately.

"It'll be fun!" she told him, not bothering to explain why she needed a diversion so badly.

Billy had found the little thing, a female he said, downtown somewhere, undernourished and dying, her carnival owner ready to give her up for lost. Billy had seen himself as the monkey's savior. For two nights he had hidden her in the dorm storage room, safely caged and too sick to do more than barely whimper. She was healthier now, thanks to some antibiotics Billy had purchased from a cooperative vet and the food he'd pilfered from the dining hall, and she was making too much noise to be safely hidden. With discovery imminent, Billy had turned to Katy.

Katy quickly discovered how much healthier the monkey had become. She returned from school the next afternoon to find the cage empty, the wire mesh torn from its side, havoc all around. Following the sound of its chatter, Katy found the monkey swinging gleefully around the shower curtain rod.

She flung herself forward immediately to try to grab the monkey's leg, but landed with an unladylike thud on the bathroom floor. Well, food probably wouldn't work as bait, she decided ruefully, removing the empty banana peel from the bottom of her shoe. This monkey had obviously found something to eat.

Nor would speed, she decided a few minutes later. Trying three times to grab the monkey she succeeded only in ripping the shower curtain, side-swiping a lamp, and falling head over hassock in the living room. What sound effects!!! Deciding numbers might help, and remembering Mariel's advice about dragons, she decided to call Guthrie. He was coming over later for dinner. Perhaps he could come a few minutes early.

When Guthrie arrived, she was laughing, absolutely enchanted by the little imp's cleverness. Katy quickly stifled her giggle when she saw Guthrie's face. "My word, Katherine," he said, taking in Katy's tattered stockings, shoeless foot and the blouse that had come out from her skirt.

Katy quickly explained about the monkey.

"Well, call one of the servants!" he said. "They should be able to round it up quickly enough."

"I couldn't do that, Guthrie. I promised to keep her absolutely secret until next weekend when I can take her home for Thanksgiving."

Overhead, the monkey clung to the main stem of the light fixture, swinging it ever so gently to and fro, and chuckling incessantly. No question whom she considered the sideshow.

"Don't tell me your parents will decide to keep it?"

"Her, Guthrie. She's a her. And no, I'm sure they won't, but they've had much more practice than I have in dissuading Billy, so I thought I'd hold her in safety until then and let them deal with him." She giggled. "Though I didn't hold her safely enough, did I?"

Guthrie didn't laugh.

"Come on, Guthrie. You're here now. Help me catch her."

He scowled. "Very well. What shall I do?"

He was obviously more resigned than resourceful, Katy thought, as she fought off comparisons. Unfortunately, plotting strategy had always been Luke's role.

"I guess the easiest place to corner her is the bathroom, at least now that I've removed the banana peels! Let's herd her in there. Then you chase her toward the door, and when she gets by you, I'll catch her on the way out. That way, I'll be the one who has to grab her. Okay?"

From his glowering expression, her plan was far from okay, but he did take off his expensive suit jacket, roll up his sleeves and set forth, muttering under his breath.

As the monkey tried to swing past Guthrie, however, because Guthrie was stronger or faster or had longer arms, he succeeded where Katy had failed, snagging a leg and holding on. He let out an astonished "Katherine!" as much in triumph as surprise. She jammed the cage over the monkey, strapped the wire firmly in place and wrapped extra cords around it to keep it doubly secure. As she worked she involuntarily pictured Luke's amusement, but finding Guthrie beside her instead, her smile vanished.

Guthrie's spirits rose as hers fell. He grabbed her by the waist and swung her down beside him onto the couch. "Well, that was a change of pace!" he exclaimed, grinning broadly.

"Would you still like some dinner?"

He heard the tentative hope in her voice, paused, then misunderstood completely and instead of refusing responded, "Of course, but I'll take you out. Is the monkey snug now? Then I'll be back in an hour to pick you up. Do you know—that was actually fun!"

After Guthrie had gone, Katy stayed in the armchair, reluctant to move, unable to plan, longing most of all to escape the next few hours. Visions swept through her mind like a whirlpool, and try as she might, she couldn't slow them down—visions of Guthrie and Christopher—dear Christopher—and dragons and dreams of the future, and her thoughts drew her deeper and deeper until only Luke's brooding gaze remained.

How often in the past she and Luke had laughed together. How full their book of memories and how prominent his role! To have deprived him of this latest misadventure seemed so wrong, a party without the guest of honor, Laurel without Hardy, Ginger without Fred.

Luke had always been a friend. To dream that his care could be the fruit of an emotion deeper than friendship, that he could know her so well and yet want her, that he could do so forever— to dream this seemed indulgent, to believe it, impossible. Between them stood the deep pool of her doubts, her inadequacies and fears, yet there he stood, incredibly, all that she wanted, and she dared to imagine him beckoning.

In the end, no doubt, however demoralizing, could eclipse the power of his pull; no risk, however great, could diminish her desire to have him love her.

She was too frightened to think further, too anxious to pray. She would get ready for dinner; shower, dress, then deliver her regrets to Guthrie after the meal. And then? Her heart quickened. For as unpleasant as dinner would be—and she never could remember afterwards what she ate—dessert would be sweet. She was sure of it!

Later, she watched Guthrie's car disappear around the bend,

gathered her courage, and ran all the way from her apartment to Luke's. Outside his door she paused to catch her breath, then knocked, her heart keeping time with her hand, pounding out a beat of fear and anticipation so intense she still breathed with difficulty.

When Luke opened the door, he looked down with eyes narrower and harder than she had ever remembered.

"Katy," he said. "It's late. What's up?"

She couldn't draw her eyes away, though at his expression tentacles of fear began to grow around her heart, pulling her down. Why hadn't she realized before how stern he could look? When had his jaw ever been so set? She longed to smooth his hair back, to see his mouth soften, to catch a flicker of warmth. She rubbed sweaty palms against her slacks.

"May I come in, Luke?" Her gaze wavered. "Please? I have to talk to you. I ran all the way here. I couldn't wait."

He sighed, then stepped back resignedly. She moved across the room to sit gingerly on the couch, right on its edge, then stare across the room at him. Here with him she found she couldn't speak after all. The last seven days loomed large before her; she should leave.

She jumped up. "You're right. It is late. I'll come back, tomorrow maybe. I'm sorry, Luke."

She would have pushed past him to escape, but he blocked her way. "Sit down, Katy. You might as well tell me what's wrong."

She returned to the couch and watched him. He sat still as a statue. At her silence he glanced quizzically across at her, and she spoke in a rush.

"You were right about Guthrie, Luke. I knew you were.

142

At dinner tonight, he kept calling me Katherine. 'Katherine...Katherine,' almost on purpose to torment me. I finally asked him, please, to stop, to call me Katy. He put down his fork, looked at me so solemnly, and declared in his serious voice that of course he would not. To him I *was* Katherine and certainly not Katy."

Katy's hands shook. "Oh, Luke, it was awful! I've been so foolish!"

He raised his brows, but whether he was incredulous or questioning, she couldn't be sure.

"*Why* couldn't I be Katy, I wondered? Katy is past, he said; I was now a gracious and dignified young woman, a woman he could be proud to love."

Luke's face tightened, and Katy pressed on. "It became very important somehow to convince him that I wasn't gracious or dignified; I really *am* Katy. Life isn't and won't ever be the series of banquets and concerts and refined picnics he has taken me to. I suddenly became frightened by the way he was holding my hand and sitting so still and waiting for me to finish my chatter, suddenly worried he would do something really dumb that we'd both regret, like ask me to marry him."

Luke's eyes narrowed beyond reading, and she gave up trying to figure out what he was thinking and concentrated instead on her hands, holding them tightly to stop their shaking.

"So I kept it up. You see, I knew that for every vacation he'd program and pre-schedule and format, I'd want to be the Gypsy, wandering from place to place at will. And when he would come home expecting dinner set out, candles and linen and all, as often as not I'd be weeping over some old movie on TV, my meat still thawing in the sink. It all became clear how terribly, utterly different Guthrie and I are. It was then I thought of you."

Somehow she had crossed the room to stand stiffly before him and stare mesmerized at the shirt collar poking above his sweater. She could see from his throat he was having trouble swallowing. The color had drained from his face, and he held his arms crossed, his jaw still clenched. Try as she would, she couldn't meet his eyes.

"Why, Katy? Why did you think of me?"

He sounded nothing like her old friend, Luke the dragon killer, Luke the defender. Fear claimed her, paralyzing her.

Some of the terror must have reached him, for he said again, "Why, Katy?" but this time his tone coaxed her. He reached down to fold her shaking hands in his, their warmth compelling her gaze upward, and when he drew her to him and put his arms around her, she buried her face against his chest and spoke again at last.

"Oh, Luke," she cried. "I thought about everything I want with my husband, the dreams and the friendship and fun, and in my mind, when I opened the door to welcome him home, when I drew him into our home, it was you, Luke, only you, it had to be you! I knew then how much I love you! I have for so very long and I will forever."

She shrugged off his arms, now holding hers painfully tight, and looked up to meet his eyes. "Oh, *please*, Luke, say you love me! Tell me I'm not dreaming."

Then he was her own Luke again, laughter back in his eyes, his smile broad, his arms drawing her to him. The tenderness that glowed in his eyes was mixed with joy, his relief all the greater for having been so long in coming.

"If I say no?" he asked, plainly teasing her. "What would you do then?"

144

She lifted hands to claim him, molding his shoulders, palm to cheek, fingers through hair, all with a sculptor's loving, languorous study. For so long, sitting with him, talking, watching him, she had longed for this freedom. Somehow during her foray Luke held back, though his breath became increasingly ragged.

"What would I do?" she said at last, letting her lashes drift slowly down and up again. "Only this—" and she stretched up to brush his lips with a light, tantalizing kiss.

With a short gasp of stunned pleasure, Luke gave the kiss back with fire and urgency, desire and depth. From her he drew assurance, drawing deeply on her embrace, and when the kiss started, if he still doubted her love, Katy's passion and yearning more than convinced him that her love was finally his.

Some time later when they were sitting on the couch, she described the monkey episode to Luke. "Really, the monkey convinced me to come see you tonight. I've wondered ever since that night you came up to talk about Guthrie why you cared so much. Eventually I stopped wondering *why* you cared so much and started thinking about *how much* you cared. It was seeing Guthrie so upset about the monkey that made me realize how faithfully you've helped me, how...how selflessly you've watched over me, and suddenly it seemed like you must be in love with me!"

Luke said, "I have a confession," then laughed at her expression. "Nothing bad, silly goose, just something I couldn't tell you before. Our both being here was more than an accident. All those friends with their knowing looks were absolutely right—I followed you out here like a moonstruck sleepwalker. I couldn't go to graduate school without you, Katy, and if loving you meant following you out here, I was willing. I found out you were coming to Hudson before I went home for Christmas last year. Your parents told me. They coaxed Adam into offering me the science job out here, then called me long distance."

"My parents did that?"

"Your mom knew how I felt way back after our sophomore year when they came to visit you. We had that party for all the missionary kids, remember, and I went, and you told all the stories about my helping you. That got your mom watching me, and then it didn't take long. She cornered me afterwards, and—well, basically approved, I guess."

"My mother?" Katy said. "Three years ago? She figured it out in one night?"

He chuckled. "No one else did. Mothers have a way of noticing when young men follow around after their daughters, abject devotion tending to warm their hearts."

"Well, for goodness' sake, why didn't you ask me out?"

"Because you were Katy, wonderfully uncomplicated. You weren't serious about guys. Lots of dates, some good friends, and you had everything you wanted. I thought once we came out here, I could monopolize your social life. Enter Guthrie...."

"Oh, no, not Guthrie," she exclaimed. "Enough about him. Go on."

"The plan was to get your attention and then say, well, something like this." He stopped, held her hands against his chest, and took a deep breath. "Katy, I love you with all the depth my soul offers. I will forever. I'll seek always for your good and want nothing more than to love you better and better. Will you marry me?"

"Oh, Luke, of course I will!"

He held off her kiss, his request not yet finished. He said: "At Christmas?"

"You mean, this Christmas?"

"Yes, this Christmas!" he repeated. "I've wanted to marry you for all these years, Katy, ever since you sprayed me with the water hose back in freshman chemistry. So *I'm* not rushing into anything. Now you say you love me, so why wait? Say yes and we could have part of our honeymoon in Hong Kong; we'll be over there anyway for the basketball tournament."

How very difficult it would be ever to refuse him anything! "Okay," she conceded. "I'll talk to my parents. If they think it's possible, then yes, Christmas!"

He grinned, satisfied, for he knew her mother. "Now, why don't we go tell Mariel?"

"Oh, Mariel," Katy scowled. "She's been all on your side, you know!"

"More than you know." His eyes glimmered. "She's been giving me progress reports all week!"

Nine

When Mariel opened her door to find Luke and Katy on her doorstep, she knew immediately what had happened. Luke was unable to mask his pride, and Katy clung to his hand as though it was the only thing keeping her feet on the ground. During the previous weeks, Mariel had wondered how she would react when she finally saw them together, whether jealousy would rise unwanted within her or whether her selfish regrets would overpower her. To her great relief she laughed, spontaneously, genuinely and joyously, and gathered them both into a giant hug.

"Oh, Luke, congratulations! And Katy, you crazy girl! Come in and tell me everything. Don't hide a single detail—I deserve the whole romantic story."

With much laughter and some still-stunned glances between them, Katy and Luke proceeded. Sitting in the armchair opposite them, Mariel felt at last the twinges of regret and longing she had dreaded. She imagined another hand reaching for hers, other eyes just as tender, the same overwhelming, driving need to touch and claim and hold, and as the images receded, a great weariness and immobility came over her. She found it impossible to believe those pleasures would ever be hers again; Adam might be showing some small interest, but how long could it last when he knew her failings?

So, later, when Katy suggested that Mariel come south to spend Thanksgiving with the Martins, she refused. "This will be your and Luke's big weekend, Katy, introducing him to your family, making plans, finding time for each other. I don't think I should go."

"The holiday will be dreadful here all by yourself!" Katy exclaimed, perching on Mariel's armchair. "Actually it was my mother's idea. Of course she doesn't know that Luke's coming. But believe me, she would still want you to come."

"Besides," Luke said, "with you there, maybe they won't notice when Katy and I make ourselves scarce."

A few days before Thanksgiving, Holly Lyons sought Mariel out at lunch time.

"Are you going somewhere for Thanksgiving, Miss Forrest?"

Mariel, grateful beyond words that she had accepted Katy's invitation, struggled to hide her surprise. Was Holly issuing Adam's invitations now? "Yes, actually," she said. "I'm going down to Tainan with Katy and Luke."

Disappointment clouded Holly's face momentarily and then new hope broke through. "But will you be gone *all* weekend? When are you coming home?"

This time she spoke reluctantly: "Friday afternoon."

"Oh, great, Miss Forrest! Could you come—I mean, do you

think—" Holly took a deep breath and started again. "Dad says it's time for me to get some new clothes, and he just *hates* shopping, and he doesn't know a *thing* about clothes. Really! So I was wondering, would you come to Taipei with me on Saturday? *Please?*"

Holly looked so ardent that Mariel couldn't stop from smiling, and seeing the smile, Holly jumped to her own conclusions.

"Oh, you *will!* Thank you, Miss Forrest! Oh, this is so great!" Holly gave Mariel a big hug and before Mariel could raise any objections began to suggest arrangements. "We could go up on Saturday morning by train and shop during the day and then come home in the evening. Will that be okay?"

Mariel stepped back from Holly, taking in shining eyes and an eager expression. Without knowing, Holly had answered Mariel's most pressing question: would Adam be there? Presumably not. A warm smile spread across Mariel's face. This might actually be a lot of fun.

"What time on Saturday morning, Holly?"

"Eight o'clock. I'll bring a taxi by." After another hug, Holly ran across the plaza to meet her friends. Mariel shook her head, wondering if she was being wise, and then shrugged. She could use some new clothes herself, since Taiwan's winter was going to be colder than she had realized.

At Thanksgiving, Katy sent her brothers and sister on an earlier train (the monkey secured in baggage), so intent was she on springing Luke unexpectedly upon the entire family. Mariel went with Luke and Katy on a later train. Accordingly, when the trio arrived at her parents' house, Katy made Luke stay in the taxi while she and Mariel went in, and then after gathering the family into the living room, she announced, "I have a surprise."

The siblings looked at her expectantly and her father said, "Oh?" but Rebecca, a sudden excitement shining in her eyes, clasped her hands together and sighed.

"Oh, Mom, you're hopeless!" Katy exclaimed, and then called out toward the gate. "Okay! Everyone, let me introduce you to your future in-law, the man who will be taking me off your hands, the one, the only, Luke Shepard!"

Everyone whooped and whistled and shouted except Rebecca, who immediately reached out to give Luke a big hug. "So you did it, Luke!" she laughed.

"Excellent! Excellent!" Spence grabbed Luke's hand over his wife's back and the three boys clustered around Luke.

"Good luck!" shouted Peter above the confusion. "You're going to need it!"

"You've got to be crazy," added Troy.

Billy just jumped up and down trying to climb onto Luke's back.

Somehow Katy pushed through the crowd. "Wait a minute! Don't I get any of these good wishes?"

"What for?" Peter asked.

"You won't need any luck with Luke," Billy declared, revealing an advanced case of hero worship.

Even Bridget said, "All you should get, Katy, is a big congratulations!"

Katy's scold dissolved into a dreamy smile. She leaned back against Luke and pulled his arms more tightly around her. She said, "I agree, Bridget. Believe me, I agree."

Mariel spent the next morning helping Rebecca prepare the Thanksgiving dinner. To Mariel's surprise, before dinner the next day, Katy brought out a guitar to Luke and asked him to sing the grace. "Sing the one from *Godspell*," she said. "It's perfect for Thanksgiving."

So, in a rough, yet moving baritone, he sang of the good gifts that God had sent, ending with a call to thank the Lord.

Looking over at Katy with an expression dimmed only by his slightly lowered lids, Luke murmured, "I certainly thank him."

"I thank him," Rebecca added.

"I thank him," Billy chimed in.

Each in turned echoed Luke's praise, except Mariel, who managed only a nod. At last they gathered hands and Spence prayed.

That afternoon the family went to a nearby middle school to play soccer, and though Billy tried to coax Rebecca into playing, she said only, "No, Billy, I want to talk to Mariel."

They watched for a while from the bleachers, and then Rebecca finally asked, "How is your friend, Mariel?"

Mariel half-smiled, realizing Rebecca was giving her the option of silence, but she had thought so frequently about her last visit, and there had developed within her such a spirit of kinship with Rebecca that she found herself unwilling to maintain even this veneer of deception. Mariel said, "You knew I was talking about myself. I'm the one who's so angry at God."

"Yet you came out here to Taiwan?"

Mariel shrugged. "I was pretty desperate."

"How have things gone this fall?"

"Not that well. Everything seems so different from what I was raised with." Mariel went on to describe her childhood religious experiences as she had with Pastor Cartwright.

Rebecca nodded her head slowly in regret. "This legalism is an old problem with the church. Paul certainly saw it."

The sounds of the soccer skirmish drifted across the field to them, and Rebecca sat silently watching the game. Mariel knew Rebecca was giving her a chance to change the subject, but she found that she couldn't.

"What I remember from the past months," she told Rebecca, "is isolated things, flashes of insight, I suppose, and many new questions. For example, Pastor Cartwright is preaching through Colossians and spoke about Christ canceling our bonds and nailing our regulations to the Cross. That was a new idea—that because of the way we are, rules become useless, except to show us how sinful we are. But I'm not sure Paul really believed it. At one point, he says something like, 'Don't let anyone tell you what to do and what not to do,' and then a few verses later he turns around and starts telling us what to do himself. When he talks about God's impending judgment, well, that's the picture of God I've always had. I've been very confused—first saying rules are useless and then saying God will judge us for breaking them. Do you know about Colossians? Do you know the part I'm speaking about?"

"Yes." Rebecca nodded slowly. "What you need to remember is that in one place Paul is talking about the Mosaic law. In the other place, he's talking about the law written on our hearts—the completed law that God instituted on the Cross."

"You're way beyond me."

"The law in the Old Testament became the people's primary way of knowing God and becoming like him—not the only way, but the main way. The law declares the glory of God because it shows his justice and order. In the end, though, no matter how much the Israelites wanted to obey the Mosaic law, they inevitably ended up breaking it. It showed them they were sinners, and it made them discouraged and angry—much as you are right now."

Rebecca paused as if waiting for Mariel to indicate her understanding. Instead, Mariel shook her head in confusion. "I've never attempted to keep the Old Testament law! Did you think that was my problem? The New Testament has enough rules on its own."

"But our motivation is so different!" Rebecca exclaimed. "Now we know God from within ourselves, through his Spirit. We obey him because we want to please him, not to avoid punishment or earn blessings. That is the new glory he offers us. Isn't that true?"

Mariel shrugged.

"It seems—" Rebecca hesitated, and then went on. "You seem to want to earn something from God—if not his salvation, then at least his approval or blessing. So you've tried to meet requirements through your behavior, but you can't. You fail again and again. No wonder you're so angry. His system seems stacked against you, impossible and unfair.

"But he knows that a system that depends in any way on our being good won't work. In the Old Testament, he set up a contract with the Israelites: If my people will humble themselves and turn from their wicked ways and not worship idols and depend on God, then God will respond by blessing them and their crops and their land. It was conditional. The Israelites do their part, and God does his part."

"I suppose now we don't have a contract like that?" Mariel said.

"Oh, we have a contract with God. Don't let anyone tell you we don't! But what a contract. These are the conditions now. If God is faithful, then he will bless us; if God is just, he will bless us; if God is honest and holy and—well, if God is God, then he will bless us and love us and care for us and make us more and more like his Son. Don't you see? The conditions are all on him now. At great cost to himself, he set up a new system."

"You can't be saying that we can sit back, do what we want, and we'll end up perfect?"

Rebecca smiled sadly. "Mariel, you've been trying to sit back and do what you want. Are you happy? Is your life easy? We *can't* sit back. He won't let us, will he?"

Mariel looked away. How truly Rebecca had spoken.

Rebecca continued: "One day you'll see that the system of rules and accomplishments you think so unfair and intolerable is all of your own making. He died to set you free from it, Mariel! He knows it's stacked against you.

"One day you'll discover God's infinite, incredible, precious patience with us. He wants you to love him, Mariel, to enjoy him, to talk with him and trust his work in your life, as a friend and a father and as your God."

"As part of the process he took Annie and David away?"

"Annie was your little girl?"

"Yes, and only two when she died."

Rebecca clasped Mariel's hand. "He was there, Mariel, still good, still God. Death came from our sin, our collective sin. Happy children and loving marriages—now *those* come from

God. They were his idea, and he does bless most of his children with them. He may still bless you."

Mariel grunted and looked away. After a moment, she asked, "And all those rules in the Bible?"

"Obey them to please God and to be as holy in fact as he declares us to be in position. He sees Jesus in your place, you are declared to be as right with God as Jesus himself is. Not bad. But that doesn't mean you can't become as holy as he declares you to be. That's his plan. To grow into the obedience and holiness that Jesus has.

"But, Mariel, that growing into His holiness—you can do that without being afraid of condemnation. 'Therefore there is now *no* condemnation for those who are in Christ Jesus.' 'You did not receive a spirit that makes you a slave again to fear, but you received a Spirit of sonship.' When we sin—and of course we will—we don't need to be afraid. We should feel remorse and regret because we've failed the one who holds us so dear. But not dread, and no condemnation."

At the far end of the field the game was breaking up. As her family walked toward them, Rebecca squeezed Mariel's hand again. "Give it time, Mariel. Give it time."

Rebecca stood to meet her approaching family, but Mariel stayed up on the bleachers for a moment trying to collect her thoughts. She would have to ask Rebecca where those verses about condemnation were. No condemnation. Made perfect. Could it be this simple? Not foster children after all, but sons, real children of the King?

☙

Down on the field, Peter complained loudly to Rebecca about the game.

"I told you we should have put Katy and Luke on the same team," Troy muttered.

They both threw a disgusted look toward Luke, who was helping Katy on with her coat. Peter explained: "Every time Katy tried to take the ball away from Luke, he let her!"

"That's love for you!" Spence laughed, swinging Rebecca down off the bleachers and hugging her. "Count Luke fortunate! He only lost the ball. Samson gave up his hair, his strength, his sight, and in the end, everything else as well!"

"*Delilah*, Dad? You're comparing me to Delilah? Luke, don't listen to him."

Luke closed one eye as if sizing her up. "Whoa. He's known you a lot longer than I have. Maybe I need to reconsider."

"Oh, no," Troy said, jumping behind Katy to push her toward Luke. "This is a top of the line model, guaranteed to satisfy. A number-one, okay wife. But, hey, you got second thoughts? Peter, show him another model."

On cue, Peter pushed Bridget forward: "Kind sir, another sister right here! What do you think?"

Luke laughed. He pulled Katy to him and grinned at Bridget. "No thanks, boys. This one feels just right!"

After talking with her parents that night, Luke and Katy announced their wedding date the next morning: "The day after classes end at Christmas," Luke said.

"Bridget will be my maid of honor, and will you be a bridesmaid, Mariel?"

"Of course. Thank you."

"Harry Doyle, my roommate from college, is flying out to be my best man," Luke said.

"For the wedding?" Peter exclaimed. "Wow. That'll set him back."

"It almost set *us* back, actually," Luke said, a little sheepishly. "Harry and I had a little bet: If I managed to marry Katy *before* Christmas, he would pay his way out. If after, I would have to pay."

"Luke Shepard!" Katy exclaimed. "You made a bet like that— about our wedding?"

"You must have had some anxious moments," Spence said.

"Oh, believe me, I did. I really did, but not only about that ticket!"

Katy went to drape her arms around Luke. "Well, stop your worrying now, Luke. I'm all yours!"

Troy made a face. "Oh, mush," he said.

"Wait until school," Peter said, knowingly. "When the girls hear Luke's taken, I predict sackcloth and ashes all around."

"You better lie low, Kates."

"They'll put a contract out on you."

"That or they'll try the job out themselves."

Katy stuck her nose up. "Well, tough luck on all of them. Luke's mine now, and they'll have to find their own hunk."

Mariel returned to Taichung on Friday as planned and on Saturday discovered why Adam had abdicated going shopping with Holly. Untiring, unhasting, and just plain obstinate summed up Holly's shopping habits—with a quirky, adventurous taste thrown in. Before beginning, Mariel thought Holly liked bland basics like jeans and T-shirts, spiced up with colorful vests and hats and earrings. An hour into the morning, Mariel was wondering desperately how Adam had ever managed the bland basics. By mid-afternoon, having advanced through countless smaller boutiques to end up at Taipei's biggest department store, Mariel was beyond desperation and trying for simple survival.

"No, Holly, not the white leather mini-skirt. Not the platform shoes either."

"But they go with this bell-bottom pantsuit!"

"Not on my shopping trip they don't!"

"Did my dad tell you all these rules?" Holly finally objected, throwing the last of her pile into the air.

Mariel laughed, enjoying Holly's vivacious antics. "I promise: I never even spoke to him about this." (Obviously a serious oversight, which she would correct when she saw him next!)

"Then how come you and he have such similar taste?"

"*Taste,*" Mariel said dolefully. "That's the key word here."

Hands on her hips, Holly glared across the scattered clothes at Mariel. "He *knew* you'd back him up. I should have asked Katy to come with me!"

Mariel laughed again. Fortunately, Adam's daughter was too cheerful to hold Mariel's supposed betrayal against her for long. "Let's compromise, Holly. Like you probably do with your dad."

Holly smoothed her hand over the jeans she was wearing. Covered with silk-screened dinosaurs, they fit Holly like a second skin. "Can I keep these dinosaur jeans?"

Mariel winced at the neon colors, but nodded anyway. "Okay, in a bigger size."

Holly smiled and shrugged sheepishly. "You're right. I'm not sure I could sit down in this pair, and I'd feel pretty silly standing through all my classes! And the boots? Can I keep them?"

"If you can afford them."

"And the vests?"

"All except the one with the battery-operated flashing fireflies. That's a little too wild!"

"Spoilsport," Holly scowled, then grinned and gave Mariel a hug. "Thanks anyway, and I adore the dresses you picked out for me."

A voice came from behind them. "Dresses? When have you ever worn dresses?"

Mariel swung around sharply. Adam. Standing against a pillar beside some clothes racks. Watching her reaction closely and apparently amused.

"Daddy!" Holly exclaimed, throwing herself into his arms. "I wasn't sure you'd make it. We were almost finished here."

"Meeting's all done, honey, right on time. I didn't want to miss a chance for dinner at the Grand Hotel."

"Um, wait a minute," Mariel said. "Grand Hotel?"

Holly twisted toward Mariel. "Dad says as a thank-you, he's taking us all to the Grand Hotel for dinner."

Mariel's gaze shifted from Holly to Adam, her face a study in consternation.

"What's the matter, Mariel?" Adam said, his eyes glinting with humor. "Don't you think you've earned it?"

"Oh, Holly is certainly…" Mariel bit her bottom lip, searching for a word. "Certainly…"

"Oh, Miss Forrest, just say it," Holly exclaimed, laughing.

160

"I'm a challenge and a bother, and I tend to push as far as I can to get my own way."

"Where could you *possibly* have picked up those traits?" Mariel wondered aloud, and was rewarded with a warm chuckle from Adam.

"Let's see what you've chosen," Adam said to Holly, walking over to the pile of bags.

"You can't take anything back!" cried out Holly.

"Better not," muttered Mariel under her breath, and Adam laughed again.

When Holly took the last purchases to the register, Adam stepped closer to Mariel. "A long day, Miss Forrest?" he murmured.

She turned an incredulous expression on him, saw the humor in his eyes, and almost stamped her foot. "I'm glad you're having such a good time! Why didn't you warn me?"

"And risk having you change your mind? I may be many things, Mariel, but when it comes to Holly and clothes, most of all, I'm desperate!"

"I know why now!" Mariel's eyes narrowed. "I wonder…"

"Yes?"

"Could this promised dinner possibly be good enough to get you back into my good graces?"

Adam looked at her sharply, and somehow the noises around them receded and the surrounding racks of clothes and shoppers faded into a blur. His words were slow and deliberate: "I didn't realize I *was* in your good graces, Mariel. Could I be?"

In the suddenly charged atmosphere, Adam's hooded eyes watched Mariel gravely, waiting for her answer to a question that asked far more than the words alone implied. She swallowed slowly and blinked, her heart pounding.

"Mariel?" he murmured.

"I can't, Adam," she blurted out. "Please try to understand."

"How *can* I understand when everything about you is such a mystery?" He touched her hand briefly, the contact electric, and when she drew back stiffly, he sighed. "Okay. Time out. But I won't stop trying. In the meantime, for tonight at least, can we just have a good time? After all, a major headache is behind us." As an afterthought, he added, "You'll have Holly along as protection."

Mariel held his gaze for a frozen moment, and then took a deep breath and tried to relax. She made a valiant attempt to sound normal: "Behind *us,* he says," and lifted her hands in silent entreaty. "How did this become *my* headache, I ask you?"

"Because the poor male of the species takes help wherever he can find it."

"Well, you're a lot poorer this afternoon, that's for sure!"

"Oh, really? At least what she's buying looks good. I thought it might help her to hear from someone else that her typical choices aren't appropriate. Perhaps it's wishful thinking, but I don't think she'd actually wear most of her choices."

"A white leather mini-skirt?"

Adam groaned. "Please! Don't give me an entire catalog. I am very grateful."

Mariel smiled. "Once again, I've received an education from you. I should say thank you."

"Come eat with us, then," Adam said, then laughed. "You see, I'm ready to press any advantage. Think about it, anyway."

With that instruction, Adam advanced toward the cash register where Holly was getting her change. "Holly, did you spend more than I said?"

Left behind among the racks of clothes, Mariel took another moment to collect herself. Did she dare run off? She could leave them here and catch her own train back. She looked at father and daughter collecting their parcels. She could also go with them and enjoy what would certainly be an entertaining and delicious dinner.

Over his packages, Adam's eyes sought hers out, a question clearly evident in his, and she finally nodded, her decision made. His smile was like the sun at the end of a long day, and she went toward him to help carry the packages, an answering smile on her own lips. For tonight, at least, peace.

After bundling Holly's packages into the back of the van, Adam drove Mariel and Holly through Taipei, around the sweeping road leading to the Grand Hotel, and up the hill to the front door. An imposing, distinctly Oriental structure standing above the city, the hotel was a classic Taipei landmark, renowned for decades of service and quality.

After turning his keys over for valet parking, Adam stepped around the van to take Mariel's arm, politely cupping her elbow as he led her into the hotel lobby. Wearing a new dress, Holly walked beside him, some of her playfulness giving way to a more mature poise in the face of such an impressive setting. Noticing it, Adam caught Mariel's eye and winked.

"Way cool!" Holly enthused inside.

"Everything's so ornate!" Mariel agreed.

Holly shook her head, leaning closer to Mariel. "No, I mean look at those guys over by the desk. They must be college students!"

"I can see the local sights are lost on you, my little Philistine!" Adam declared. He grabbed Holly's hand and led her toward the restaurant. "Let's go eat!"

The large, almost cavernous dining room was brightly lit and sumptuously decorated. Round tables crowded the floor, many filled even at 6:00 P.M., a relatively early hour. Looking around, Mariel decided no one could ever accuse Taiwanese people of being somber. Everywhere she looked, people were showing their emotions, cheerfully laughing or boisterously reacting to some comment.

After being led to one of the smaller tables, Mariel began watching a nearby family. Around the table sat an older father, two couples in their thirties, and three children, carefully primped for the outing. One of the mothers caught Mariel watching the chubby toddler, and the two women exchanged smiles, children forming a universal bond. Mariel loved the way the older family members hovered over the children, obviously cherished and loved.

Two or three discussions seemed to be going on at once around the table, although members seemed to switch from one to the other at will. Perhaps it was the language, with its sensational swoops and staccato syllables that made the conversation so dramatic.

"Any preferences on what to order?" Adam asked, interrupting her reverie.

"Anything you absolutely *hate* to eat?" Holly added.

Mariel shook her head, content to let Adam choose, but

Holly launched immediately into her own requests, and as they carried on their own spirited discussion, Mariel took pleasure in watching Adam and his daughter interact. Unabashedly fond of each other, they obviously enjoyed each other's company, Adam laughing at Holly's attempts to manage him, Holly confident that Adam would hold to the boundaries he thought best for her. Looking back at the day's activities, Mariel had to admit that while Holly had certainly pushed to the limits of what Mariel would go along with, she had never pouted or whined when she didn't get her way.

Some agreement between father and daughter reached, Adam turned to Mariel. "How does this sound? We'll order Peking duck, of course, and Steamed Ham in Honey Sauce—"

"That is *so* good!" Holly exclaimed.

"And a lobster dish that we like—"

"Sliced Lobster Sauté and Curry Lobster," Holly elaborated. "It sounds like two dishes, but it's only one. You'll like it!"

"For dessert, we'll order a Grand Hotel specialty: Glazed Bananas."

"And Bird's Nest Soup, too!" Holly objected. "She *has* to try Bird's Nest Soup!"

"Does that sound okay?" Adam asked.

Mariel laughed. "Wow! Isn't that too much food?"

"Um. Well, perhaps," Adam admitted, "but there are too many dishes we want you to try! We'll have to take the extra home."

Mariel looked from Adam to Holly. So they had been negotiating with Mariel in mind? "Thank you. I'm sure it will all be delicious."

The order complete, Mariel leaned closer to Adam and asked,

"Which language is the family at that table over there speaking—Mandarin or Taiwanese?"

He listened for a moment, then nodded. "Taiwanese."

"How can you tell?"

"Mandarin has only four tones; certain syllables go down, others go up, some stay high and stable, and others dip low. Taiwanese sounds even more theatrical—it has seven tones."

"Which language is more common?"

"Oh, Taiwanese by far. When people from the mainland came to Taiwan during the Communist takeover, they brought Mandarin with them. It became the lingua franca, the language of business and government. But in everyday life, most people speak Taiwanese." Adam cocked his head momentarily. "This family over here, on your other side, is speaking Mandarin. Maybe you can hear the difference."

In this way, talk flowed easily over the delicious dishes, the soup, and dessert. Much of the time, Holly dominated the discussion, catching Adam up on some of the treasures she passed up during the day. Mariel found herself laughing repeatedly at Holly's animated descriptions, her own spirits buoyed by the way Adam's gaze lingered on her, lazily savoring her laughter.

In the restroom after the meal, Holly stood in front of the mirror, swirling her long skirts around her. Catching her eye, Mariel said, "You look so grown up, Holly!" and the younger girl smiled, her own assessment affirmed.

When Holly left the room a few minutes later, Mariel eyed her own reflection much more warily. Thank goodness Holly *wasn't* as old as she looked. A few added years, a little more perception, and she wouldn't have missed the interplay of emotions between Mariel and Adam. Mariel tore a strip of toweling off and wet it, holding it to cheeks that had no need for rouge or blusher.

This was insane. She had no business feeling this way about a man. Mariel stiffened her back, took a deep, determined breath, and thrust out her chin. She would walk out there in control again.

Adam Lyons, don't think this evening changes anything!

The long ride home down the multi-laned highway from Taipei to Taichung took place in relative silence. Holly soon dozed off in the back seat, and Mariel was more than happy to give Adam the impression that she had as well. For a few minutes, Mariel watched Adam thoughtfully from under lowered lids, her gaze playing over his hands competently holding the steering wheel and his arms, relaxed but alert. For the students and faculty in his care, Adam's confident, self-contained manner must be immensely comforting, and it was no wonder that Holly was so consistently cheerful and fun loving. Mariel let her perusal drift up to his face, taking in a strong jaw, his nicely rounded head, and the composed bearing of his neck and shoulders, and then she firmly closed her eyes. All fine to make resolutions; much harder to keep them.

Peter and Troy proved to be right in their prediction of fun. On Monday as the students were rising to leave chapel, the president of the choir stood up and announced a special presentation. "Come on up here, Luke!"

None too eager, Luke arrived in time for the stage curtains to open and reveal a giant paper heart stuck to the backdrop with "Luke + Katy" painted sloppily across it. As a sickle moon slowly rose and fell behind a makeshift door frame, four boys from the choir crooned about "K-K-K-Katy!" and the moon shining over the cowshed. At the end, the choir president said, "Now that you're going to be at Katy's beck and call, we thought we'd make it easier for her to find you," and hung a huge cowbell around Luke's neck.

Later that same week Katy and Mariel arrived at the school one morning to find pictures of Katy from when she was in high school plastered all over campus. Every one of them caught Katy at a disadvantage: off balance while cheer leading, with pie all over her face, hit in the stomach by a basketball, and cleaning up after a typhoon, drenched and bedraggled.

Each picture sported the question: "You really want to marry *her*, Luke?"

"I can't believe it!" Katy exclaimed. "They're from the old journalism files. These pictures were embarrassing enough in high school, but now...Oh, NO! They wouldn't have ...I hope they didn't...."

She started walking rapidly down the halls checking each picture; Mariel had to run to keep up.

"What are you looking for?" Mariel asked.

Giggling students began to follow them.

"Oh, there was one awful picture of me by the swimming pool, roughhousing with the guys. They're sure to have used it, but where?"

Mariel chuckled. "I'd try the science classroom door."

Katy grabbed Mariel's arm and started to run through the crowd of students. "I've got to get it, Mariel. The picture makes me look like a vamp! You distract Luke if you see him coming."

But Luke was already at the door, beginning carefully to take the photograph down. On this sign the students had written: "Are you sure you can handle her?"

"Luke!" Katy exclaimed. "You can't mean to keep that picture!"

Luke laughed, reached around to hug her and whispered something into her ear. Katy blushed and drew back wide-eyed—and uncharacteristically silent. Luke laughed again and kissed her.

The bell rang, and the crowd scattered, but the pranks continued.

The Friday before finals began, with the wedding a week

away and the mad flurry of arrangements almost complete, Luke arrived at Katy's door, looking forward to a quiet evening with her. On her door he found this note:

Fair suitor, wouldst thou find thy maid? Look first then where the public masses are weighed!

With a groan, Luke put a hand dramatically to his forehead. "Fiends! Disaster and desperation. Someone's kidnapped Katy!"

Mariel emerged from her apartment, and a dozen students strained for a look over the railing.

Luke growled at them threateningly, and they giggled.

"Look at it this way," Mariel whispered. "You've only got one more week of this to look forward to."

She held a paper bag out to him. "Here's supper, Luke. I doubt you'll get a chance for anything else tonight. Let's go; I'm coming with you."

The evening became a long, hectic, laughter-filled one for Luke, alternately scowling and tussling and cajoling his ever-present student guides. The first clue led to the pay scales in a big downtown department store, the second to Katy's *jyaudz* shack, and so on.

At long last Luke found Katy peacefully playing Scrabble with Adam at his house. After satisfying the expectant students with a lengthy kiss for Katy, Luke scolded Adam. "So you were in on this? You're one of my groomsmen!"

"Who better?" Adam said, grinning. "Come on in, kids. There are hot drinks in the kitchen."

Mariel went to help Holly pour. As she sat and listened to

Luke and Katy share their respective adventures, a feeling of awe crept over her. She couldn't believe that in her given circumstances God would allow her any greater happiness than this. The warmth in the room was much more than physical, the pleasure so much from the heart. That God was allowing her to share in Katy and Luke's joy, to find in them friendship, enjoy her job, to receive care and concern from Pastor Cartwright and Rebecca. She caught Adam watching her from across the room and blushed. Perhaps even to sense this strange interest from Adam! All this she could accept as God's allowance to her. She had, after all, come to the mission field and was weekly revealing her heart to Pastor Cartwright.

Then her mind caught. If Rebecca were right, God wasn't in the business of balancing accounts—her good deeds on one side and his gifts on the other. Rebecca had been adamant: God wanted to give her, freely, more than she could ever deserve. Could Rebecca be right? Did God really intend her to take pleasure in life, to find happiness in knowing him? No requirements for his love, no measuring up, just accepting and enjoying?

She looked around the room, at Luke and Katy, at Adam and the students. Did these people ever wonder about God? Was it all as simple for them as it seemed?

Sunday evening Mariel went alone to the special Christmas service. Luke and Katy had gone to Taipei to meet Luke's parents.

At first it seemed a typical school service: The band played a rousing prelude, and then the lights dimmed so the choir could march in to candlelight, singing "O Little Town of Bethlehem."

When they blew their candles out, a spotlight fell on Victor Imoto, a sophomore with a lyrical first tenor voice. With only flute accompaniment, he sang "O Holy Night."

Even before his last note faded, before anyone could begin to clap, Victor's spotlight dimmed, and another appeared to reveal Pastor Cartwright standing at a podium at the right side of the stage.

He began immediately:

"A divine night, unlike any other, for on this night the Father gave his son into the keeping of mere mortals. For us the night has always caused wonder and joy, and so it should, for on this night we received the greatest gift the world has ever known. But what was the night like for the Father in Heaven; what was it like for the triune God?

"He is wealthy beyond belief, this God we worship, and in his hands are strength and power to exalt and give strength to all. God is power.

"And he is perfect. He who made all and knows all and sustains all—of what could he possibly have lack? He desires our worship, yet he never needs it. He may want our prayers, yet he never needs our counsel. And friends, though he covets our love, he wants not even for this.

"Wealthy, powerful, peerless, perfect: He is God, complete before he made us, complete without us, complete even were he to cast us away from himself forever.

"Yet one dark night, one Christmas night, the father of all creation watched the birth of his son. Seeing the baby asleep, I believe he knew the same desire to protect that child from harm that I have felt looking upon my own children. Seeing the baby awake, perhaps he felt, too, the same shock of joyful recognition that every earthly father feels. Here was his Son!

"To have felt all that and to have known already the child's painful end! Perhaps the angels could see as we still can't the price

God paid at Christmas. Perhaps he knew as we still don't how crucial his choice and how desperate our need. On that Christmas Eve they sang: 'Glory to God! Glory to God in the Highest!'

"Why did he choose this for us, we who deny him, turn against him, accuse him, and spurn him? Why would he turn his wrath upon his own son to give us instead his mercy and grace?"

Behind the pastor the stage curtains opened to reveal a nativity in the shadows. Even Mary's face was hidden by her headpiece. A gentle spotlight illuminated the baby's face, a real baby, downy head shining in the light, cheeks rosy, face gentle and vulnerable in sleep.

"The angels sang, the shepherds praised, that night in Bethlehem. Joseph looked on with wonder as Mary cradled the child. But what of the Father as he looked down from Heaven, what did he feel that night? How could he not feel some grief and pain? Why would he love us so?"

As he finished speaking, an oboe began to play the song, "Why Should He Love Me So?" and as the notes, so sad and sweet, hung over the auditorium, Mariel began to cry.

After a moment of lingering silence, first a trumpet and then the rest of the band played an introduction, and then everyone sang, "Come, Thou Long-Expected Jesus."

At home Mariel read through the words to the last hymn again, marveling how closely they aligned with Rebecca's words: Jesus came to set people free from their sins and fears; they can find rest in him. He came to deliver them and will rule within them graciously through his spirit. Only by his merit—not theirs—will he raise them to his standard.

It's all there, she thought. *It's not only Rebecca who believes this.*

Israel's strength and consolation, hope of all the world. Could Jesus be such for her? Could she really *rest* in him? On that night, so dreadful for the Father, when he sent Jesus down the long road toward his death, had God really intended this—her own deliverance?

The next morning, as so often happens after a deeply emotional experience, she was vaguely embarrassed by her tears and skeptical about her reactions. The fact of God's sacrifice remained fast, however, and the words of the last carol continued to drift through her consciousness, so that long after the emotion had faded a hope in Christ's merit continued, taking root within her.

Perhaps because of the emotional impact of the Christmas service, or perhaps because of the end-of-semester rush, by Friday night, standing in place at Katy and Luke's wedding rehearsal, Mariel had a splitting headache. She had been fighting her feelings all day, trying desperately to contain a rising tide of frustration and hostility. Left to herself, she would probably have overcome it with a good book and an early evening. Instead here she was, taking part in what felt like a nightmare to her. Behind Luke, Adam kept trying to get her attention; between them Pastor Cartwright's voice droned on, the mere sound of it a reminder to Mariel of unpleasant admissions; and the final galling injury, Luke and Katy looked so naively happy.

Only one other person in the sanctuary seemed to be sharing space in Mariel's pit. In the back row, three pews back from the other ushers, sat Jessie, stolid, withdrawn, and mutinous. *Maybe Jessie and I could sit together at the rehearsal dinner,* Mariel thought. *We'd make tremendous company for each other.*

As the rehearsal proceeded, Mariel continued to watch Jessie, becoming concerned about her obvious unhappiness, an attitude that had become habitual since that horrible night at the end of October. It had been impossible to keep the affair secret in so small a community, so that everyone knew, and Jessie had felt terribly humiliated. The nine days' wonder had passed, but Jessie hadn't recovered yet. One night after Thanksgiving, Mariel had gone over to Wendy's house specifically to ask about how the Gundersons would be likely to handle their daughter's problems.

Wendy had considered for a moment, then said, "They're strict, I'll admit that. Jessie's their only daughter and much younger than their four boys, so it must have been a blow to them. But they're good people, Mariel. They do love her."

To her own sorrow, Mariel herself had known the shackling love of a too-strict parent.

After the rehearsal ended, while Thomas was giving Luke and Katy a few last instructions, Mariel sought Jessie out. She was standing against the wall, watching everything, enjoying nothing.

"Hi, Jessie," Mariel said. "This is quite an event, isn't it?"

Jessie shrugged.

"Do you think this close to Christmas people might be too busy to come?"

Still no response.

"Are you going to Hong Kong, Jessie?"

Finally, a flicker of interest from the all-around athlete. "Maybe."

"Don't you want to go?"

"I suppose. I'm on the team, but—" She bit her lip. "I haven't actually asked my parents yet."

"Afraid to?"

Jessie nodded dumbly.

"Because of Jack."

She hung her head this time.

"Jessie, that could have happened to anyone."

"It hasn't happened to many kids at Hudson, Miss Forrest. I feel like a complete idiot! That Friday night—well, anyway, I was stupid," she spoke with total disgust.

"What about Hong Kong, though? You're not on probation anymore. Everyone probably expects you to go."

"That's just it, Miss Forrest. My parents haven't said anything. I think they don't trust me. It would be different—" Jessie stopped, her eyes drawn irresistibly to where Steven was talking to the other student ushers.

"If you were still going out with Steven?"

"He asked me out after Thanksgiving," Jessie blurted. "Did you know that?"

"You turned him down?"

"Yeah, well, it's just this, Miss Forrest—he's being nice, you know?"

What could Mariel say? No one liked being the one to blame, the one who needed forgiveness.

"I know it's hard facing up to a mistake, Jessie, but sometimes it's only for a minute and then it's over." Mariel touched the girl's hand gently. "You've trusted him in the past, Jessie. Judge hasn't changed."

At the sound of the old nickname, Jessie's head swung around toward Steven. This time he was watching her from across the room, his eyes vaguely questioning. Had he heard something?

Jessie gulped back a sob and bolted out a side door.

Mariel's spirits closed further in on her. What right had she to counsel someone, she who found trust so elusive?

As she might have expected, given Katy's perverse sense of humor, Mariel was seated beside Adam at the rehearsal dinner and near Thomas Cartwright and his wife. Fortunately they spent most of the dinner discussing Chinese wedding customs, mostly for the benefit of Luke's parents. After dinner, Adam served as MC for a series of comedy sketches about Luke and Katy's future struggles and triumphs in married life. As the evening ended, Mariel gratefully gathered up her coat. She needed only a taxi to make her escape complete.

Hands gripped her coat from behind and helped her into it. "I'll take you home," Adam said, and his voice allowed no refusal.

They were silent as he led her to his car on a side street, but once inside, he turned to her in concern. "You seem very quiet, Mariel. Everything okay?"

"Yes. Thank you. Just take me home."

"I'd like to listen."

She glared out of the windshield, struggling to swallow her objections and let the moment pass so she would not expose her feelings to Adam. The silence lengthened until finally he started the car.

"Okay."

Somehow the sound of the ignition loosened something inside Mariel, and as the car began to move through downtown Taichung, Mariel's frustration spilled out.

"I'm worried about Katy and Luke. From what I've seen of

marriage, it's not exactly heaven on earth."

"What *have* you seen of marriage?"

"Two humans, both fallen, putting themselves in close contact, wanting something the other person can't give, both bound to be disappointed. Even in the best marriages, the raw material is flawed, seconds or thirds. Isn't that true?"

At a light, Adam turned and looked at her. "How did you become such a cynic, Mariel?"

"I'm thirty-two years old. I've seen enough. What's in my description to disagree with?"

The car moved forward before he spoke again. "Is there no room for redemption—the belief that step by step God will bring us closer to what we lost, our ability to truly love?"

"What does that mean, Adam—truly *love?*"

He shrugged. "Love is…layered, and takes different forms, but at its core, love is wanting what is best for the other person, regardless of personal cost."

Wanting what is best. Mariel let her thoughts wander to her last months with David. Would love like Adam described have delivered them from the silence and shame that poisoned their world? She was so lost in this question that it was a few moments before she realized the car had stopped. They were outside her apartment. "What's the likelihood of that happening? Face it, we humans work out an intricate contract in our relationships, meeting needs as our own are met. That's what really happens!"

"Mariel," he said, his voice full of pain.

"I'm too tired to talk about this!" She groped in the dark for the door handle, but his words drew her back.

"I suppose it was your parents' marriage that hurt you so badly."

"If that's what you want to believe."

"Well, you're wrong. We do need each other—men and women, I mean. Think of creation. Why did God create Adam alone, except to emphasize that Adam needed Eve? The family is God's arena for godliness to grow. We begin with marriage to an equal, a friend, and then have children, whom we serve even more selflessly. That is God's blessing for most of us." He reached across the seat to grip her hand. "Mariel, don't worry about Luke and Katy."

Almost against her will, she felt herself respond to his touch, and some of her anxiety dissipated. "I'm tired, Adam. I'll feel better in the morning, really. Thank you for bringing me home."

Inside, she leaned weakly against her closed front door, thinking over the exchange. Slowly a smile grew as she remembered Adam's last comments.

If God didn't want the first Adam to be alone, why had he left this Adam single for so long? The poor guy—he'd probably heard teasing like that all his life, but it sure lifted her spirits!

Forever afterwards, Mariel remembered Katy's wedding as a series of vivid pictures, each bright and brimming with joy. The wedding was held the day after school ended. Mariel went over to Katy's apartment in the morning to help her get ready.

When Mariel arrived, she found Katy laughing, the singularly infectious laugh of a person who is truly happy. The laughter bubbled all day as old friends came by to wish her well.

"If only Sammy could be here now!" exclaimed Mrs. Rizzo, one of the missionaries who came by. "He'd be wondering how

Luke's nose has escaped intact!"

Rebecca laughed. "You don't remember, Katy, but one day when you were both three, Sam asked you to marry him. You promptly bit him on the nose!"

"I'm glad you abandoned bigamy!" Mrs. Carlton declared.

"Oh, I do remember that," Katy said, giggling. "In your backyard, Mrs. Carlton, when I was about eight. Both Graham Elliott and Sam Rizzo wanted to marry me. I couldn't decide, so I married both!"

Just before getting into the cars, Katy grabbed Mariel's hand. "Is this really happening?" she whispered, her eyes shining. "It isn't just a dream?"

"All real," Mariel assured her, squeezing her hand back. "You'll see."

Katy had told Mariel that every missionary who could possibly make it to the wedding would be there, and when Mariel walked down the aisle of the church auditorium later that afternoon, she believed it.

"It's not that often we have weddings here," Katy had explained, "so when we do it's like the romantic highlight of the decade."

Judging from the sighs and tears that flowed during the wedding, everyone had been saving those up for quite a while as well.

So the pictures multiplied.

But of all the day's memories, one in particular would linger the longest. After the service, as Luke and Katy swept down the aisle to the rousing notes of a trumpet voluntary, Mariel turned to find Adam's hand held out toward her. She swept her eyes up irresistibly to meet his. They stood there, man and woman, a hand-clasp apart, his warm gaze splashing color on her cheeks and stealing her breath away. Something passed between them in that moment, something of purpose and demand, of heartfelt tension and promise, and then his strong hand took hers and his mouth softened into a smile. Certain that everyone had seen his resolve, Mariel barely negotiated the aisle. In the lobby she escaped quickly into the restroom.

Afterwards, in the crowded dorm cafeteria decorated with flowers and candles, Mariel stood in the reception line between Adam and Harry Doyle.

"Aren't they a romantic couple?" Mrs. Carlton enthused when she came through the line, then leaned closer to Mariel. "Though between you and me, it's a good thing that Luke's married now. It's not good for girls to have such an attractive unattached teacher—if you know what I mean."

Behind Mrs. Carlton, his face clearly visible to Mariel, Adam looked to the ceiling in mock despair. Mariel struggled to keep her face straight and turned with gratitude as Louise Carmody approached with her parents.

As the reception line broke up, Mariel kissed Katy and whispered, "You look like an angel in that wedding dress, Katy!"

"A very light-headed angel, Mariel!"

"Get something to eat," she advised, "and lots of rest on the honeymoon!"

Luke grinned and would have said something, but Katy punched him and said, "Hush, Luke!" so he winked at Mariel instead and whispered something to Katy that made her blush.

"Where *are* you going for your honeymoon?" Mariel asked after the reception line ended.

"We only have a week until Christmas," Luke began. "We'll

be at Sun-Moon Lake tonight and tomorrow night—"

"And then we're going to Olanpi, a little beach on the southern tip of the island."

"A beach in December?" Mariel asked. "I know Taiwan is tropical, but it's still cold."

Katy thrust her hand through Luke's arm. "Olanpi will be perfect for snuggling together on the beach—"

"Or somewhere else…" responded Mariel.

"Mariel!" Katy said with mock severity. "I can see I'll have to separate you two! Come on, Luke, let's go cut the cake."

Mariel lingered at the wedding until Luke and Katy finally swept off for their honeymoon in a shower of birdseed. She looked up from throwing her handful to find Adam beside her.

"You seem much happier today, Mariel."

"Oh, they're so much in love, Adam. Who could not expect the best for them?"

"Not me!" he responded, holding his hands up in surrender.

She laughed and pulled his hands down. "Cut that out. There are too many people watching."

"Not true. They've all gone inside. It's just you and me, all alone." Adam looked around again to check and then took her hand in his. Challenging her with his eyes, he said, "Will you come to dinner with me tonight, Mariel?"

Mariel just as deliberately extracted her hand from his. "No, I can't. Rebecca's expecting me."

"Oh, really? Shall I go ask her if I can have you instead?" His eyes glittered with amusement, for they both knew Rebecca would side with romance every time.

Mariel glared back at him. "Don't you dare!"

"Have it your way," Adam said softly, then leaned a little closer so she could hear his whisper. "Maybe not tonight, Mariel; maybe not even next week, but one of these days you'll have to say yes."

Mariel tilted her head back and raised skeptical eyebrows. "Will I? Why?"

"Because of the way you blush when I smile at you. There, see? You're doing it now." He leaned even closer, so close she could feel his breath on her cheeks. "I feel it, too, you know, Mariel—this attraction. Someday you'll let me prove it."

He vanished back into the church, leaving Mariel standing alone in the parking lot feeling oddly excited and warm.

He had already proved something: Her emotions were like clay in his hands.

That evening, Spence took the boys downtown to do Christmas shopping and play video games, but Rebecca stayed behind with Mariel in her apartment. "I want to stay and chat with Mariel," Rebecca told Spence.

Moodily munching leftovers from the reception, the two women relaxed in Mariel's living room. After a few moments, Rebecca asked, "Have I ever told you how Spence and I decided to get married?"

Mariel shook her head lazily, and Rebecca began.

"Spence and I went to Crocker College, the same as Katy and Luke. In my junior year, I had two boys in love with me: Spence Martin and James MacGregor. Spence, you know. He was quiet and scholarly even back then. James, you'll have to imagine.

Handsome, for one thing. Roguish brown eyes that sent shivers up my spine and a smile that looked like a laugh. James did well in school, though probably due more to his charm than his brains. James always got his own way, but no one minded because he always made people believe in him.

"Life was so exciting that fall. Having James in love with me was like being on the beach in a storm—tangy and tumultuous with a delicious threat of power and danger each time he came near me. Out of all the girls in the school that fall, James chose me. I could have died happy the first time James asked me out, except for one thing—my understanding with Spence.

"Such an old-fashioned word, isn't it? An 'understanding.' He had never said anything, but I knew. Every time he brought me hand-picked flowers he told me. Every time he found a used book by a favorite author. Each time he read my papers, so horribly inadequate next to his, or helped me study for a test, or read the novels I had to read for my literature classes so he could discuss them with me, even when he wasn't taking the course. He told me in so many precious ways: He meant to marry me as soon as we both finished school, and up until James asked me out, I wanted nothing else.

"For a while I thought I could date both of them. Other girls dated around. Why not me? I had that answered very quickly. Spence would have none of it. He saw me one night with James and didn't ask me out again all fall. I missed him now and then, but I'm sorry to say that James knew how to banish a girl's better judgment.

"At Christmas, James convinced me to go to Disneyland with him. Three other couples were going, he told me. I figured that by sharing a room with the other three girls, I'd have enough money for a good time. I was twenty-one by then, would be spending my own money, and going with seven other people. What could go wrong? My parents reluctantly agreed.

"Not so, Spence. Don't ask me why he thought I'd want his approval, but he came over to my dorm one night in early December to assure me that I didn't have it! He laid his opinion out for me: I was crazy to trust James. 'Why,' I wanted to scream at him, 'was he wasting so much time on me, then, if I was so crazy?' I didn't say anything though, just sat there glaring at Spence and getting angrier and angrier. Poor Spence left, convinced that we had no future."

"One of the boys drove. We started out mid-day, crowded into his van, all eight of us. Around dinner time, we reached Anaheim, and James and I got out. Not the others, you understand. Only James and I.

"'Where are they going?' I asked.

"'On down to San Diego,' he said. 'That's where they all live.'

"'But what are we doing here?' I asked. You see, I was still too stunned to think clearly.

"'We're going to Disneyland!' he exclaimed, and then laughed.

"The laugh should have told me. 'But I can't afford a room on my own,' I said.

"'Who said anything about alone?' he said. 'And don't worry about paying for the room. It's the least a man can do!'

"I was furious! I stalked into the hotel, checked into a single room, marched upstairs, slammed the door in his face, and promptly broke into tears. You see, my little display of pique exhausted my entire supply of cash.

"I could have called my parents. I could have called a friend who lived in Los Angeles.

"I wanted only Spence. When I finally stopped crying enough to make myself understood over the phone, he promised to drive down the next day in his mother's car, pick me up, and take me home to Sacramento. He never once chided me, only smothered me with one of his wonderful hugs. We got married that summer."

"What happened to James?" Mariel asked.

"Who knows? He went into some kind of business, I think. Selling used cars, probably, or hoaxing old ladies out of their money."

"Selling tainted securities on Wall Street," Mariel suggested.

"Or filling out fraudulent income tax returns." Rebecca sighed. "Thank goodness I married Spence. He is good at a lot of things, Heaven knows, but most of all he's good, and that has made all the difference in our marriage."

"Katy will be happy, too," Mariel assured her.

"Even when she was a baby, she laughed more than she cried. In the mornings when I went into her room to get her she'd always greet me with a laugh. I remember it was almost impossible to change her diapers because she'd be giggling so much. God must get a lot of pleasure from her."

"Because she laughs?" Mariel said hesitantly. "Do you really think of God that way, laughing like that?"

"Of course God is funny. He invented humor. If you doubt me, look at creation. Isn't a cow funny? Or fish! Visit an aquarium. I picture God sitting there during creation, wondering, 'Well, what wild and crazy thing can I do with this one' and out comes a blowfish or a goonie bird. What a kick!

"Not only funny, but fun. Just think what he gives us to make our lives happier. Chocolate, to begin with. Chocolate sundaes and fudge and chocolate cheesecake."

Mariel grinned but shook her head anyway.

Rebecca continued: "He could have made everything so black and white and boring, but he gave us the smell of baking bread and the sound of Christmas music and the infinitely inviting comfort of a warm bed in winter!"

Mariel laughed now. "Raindrops on roses and whiskers on kittens?"

"Exactly!" Rebecca exclaimed, joining Mariel's laughter.

Could it be? All planned by God? "Warm beds and kittens are nice, Rebecca, but it means much more to me that God has let me know you."

"Oh, Mariel, I feel the same way. So what are your plans for Christmas? Will you come to us?"

"The Cartwrights have asked me over. After all of his help this fall—he's been so patient with me—I couldn't refuse. Besides, aren't Luke's parents coming home with you?"

"In a rather roundabout route. We're touring the island with them." Rebecca looked a little more closely at Mariel. "Do you find the holidays particularly difficult?"

"Yes, I do," Mariel admitted. "But a few quiet days after this semester will be good. Besides I'm off to Hong Kong, too, after Christmas. My cousin, who manages my finances, and his wife are meeting me. He's there for a convention and suggested that I join them."

In truth, Mariel had rather dreaded Katy and Luke's absence

during the first days of vacation, but the time proved uneventful and refreshing. She wrote a few letters, made cookies and sweet breads for her neighbors, and went to dinner and a movie with Wendy—an outing they both enjoyed and promised to repeat.

Late one afternoon Adam called. "Holly and I have been working our way through our vast puzzle collection and the only one left is a stained glass affair that we've never been able to finish. How about coming over to help?"

At the sound of his voice, Mariel's throat tightened. An evening with Adam, music, a fire, and perhaps later, after Holly had gone to bed, shadows and a chance to talk. In a sudden panic, in reflex, she heard herself refusing. Adam took her choice easily enough, going on to wish her a merry Christmas.

So you don't have to think he minded, she told herself sternly. *It was just a passing thought!*

A chilling wind blew in over the ocean, building up the waves crashing onto the beach and bringing gray clouds overhead. Standing near the large rocks lining the sand, Katy felt the wind swirl around her. She pushed herself closer into Luke's arms and burrowed her face into his neck.

"If you're cold, we can go back in," he said, softly.

"How could I be cold? I'm too happy to be cold!"

Laughing softly, Luke opened his coat and drew her in against him, letting his lips linger on hers for a long and satisfying kiss.

"Oh, Luke, I love you!" she exclaimed.

His smiled deepened. "I sure hope so!"

He turned her slightly to shield her from the wind, and they stood looking out across the beach at the approaching waves, each thinking their own thoughts. Then, more sensitive than ever to his feelings, Katy felt a change in him.

"What is it, Luke?" she asked.

"Do you remember that day on the bike trip, when you talked about the kind of marriage you wanted?"

"What did I say?" Katy asked, pulling back slightly to look up into Luke's face.

"You said you wanted to be so close to your husband you couldn't bear to see him go to work—that perhaps you could even work together. Do you remember that?"

"Oh, Luke!" she exclaimed, raising a hand to touch his face. The wind had tousled his hair and given his cheeks more color. He looked endearingly young. "Just think, I didn't know then it would be you! Sometimes I want to grab you and hold on tight, I'm so afraid this will turn into a dream!"

He kissed her again, but briefly this time. His mind was still on his question. "Do you remember saying that, Katy? About working together?"

She frowned up at him. "I can't become a chemist, Luke, but I don't mind. We'll work together on our family. You're not like my father, and I hope we never have to send our kids away to boarding school. We'll have more time together."

"That's what I want to talk about. I've decided to go into college teaching, if you agree. University teaching is a killer. Professors have to work themselves to death the first few years to get tenure. Jobs in industry are almost as bad. My dad worked for an oil company, you know. We knew very little about what he was doing. I never saw the lab where he worked. But as a college teacher, we could work together. You could meet my students. I could do a lot of work at home. Our kids could spend time in my office. I'd have a lot more time with you."

"It sounds wonderful," Katy said. "What's the problem?"

"A lot less money."

Katy laughed and threw her arms around him. "My family's never had a lot of money, Luke. I don't mind. Having more of you will make up for cutting corners."

His arm tightened around her. "Thank you, Katy. That's what I needed to hear. I love you, too, you know."

"Let's go back in," she said, kissing him again. "I've had enough wind and surf for today."

The pattern of Mariel's meetings with the pastor seemed so habitual that when she went to the Cartwrights' house on Christmas Day, she felt the usual tensions and hesitancies come over her. As though by common resolve, however, neither of the Cartwrights made any reference to Mariel's previous visits.

Martha Cartwright was a small, plump woman, friendly and cheerful and unabashedly undomesticated.

"If the food's good," she informed Mariel during the dinner, "thank Thomas. I hate to cook. Thomas learned by default, I'm sorry to say, but has become very good, don't you think? We try to keep my lack of housewifely skills a secret, dear. You won't tell anyone, will you?"

Then Thomas and Martha both laughed, since Martha's habits were a long-standing scandal in the mission community. She loved to read and do puzzles and spend time with people.

She had a reputation for selfless and unfailing kindness, and she loved to entertain—as long as she didn't have to do any of the preparation and little of the clean-up.

"The food is delicious. Thank you, Pastor. And the hospitality gracious. Thank you, Martha."

Later that evening, after an afternoon of Scrabble, as they sat in friendly silence before the fire and listened to Christmas music, Mariel realized almost with surprise that she felt very much at peace. She couldn't point to any resolution God had given her. Her failings still daunted her. She still couldn't pray very well and never with anyone else. On her bad days, her low days, she remained obstinately distant from God.

Yet here she was on Christmas Day feeling none of the old bitterness, only a sweet engulfing gratitude for many blessings: Luke's easy smile, so openly affectionate and welcoming. And Katy—would either of them ever know how great a salvation God had provided through Katy? Rebecca, too, was a kindred spirit. The drama and excitement of the school around her and the students so responsive to her teaching. The pastor, so patient with her. And Wendy and Adam and so many others in this caring community.

Yes, she thought—for the first time in three years—*God is good. Gracious and good and generous. Thank you.*

He deserved more, much more, she knew, but gave this as her best: Thank you.

Eleven

※

Every year after Christmas, the International Educators of the Orient met for a conference in Hong Kong. Also each year, a small informal offshoot of the organization met for cocktails on the Sunday evening before the meetings began. How Adam had ever become part of this rowdy group, he couldn't say, although he suspected his single status earned the first invitation. Presumably, when so many professionals overseas were women, even a bachelor missionary was seen as an asset. It might also originally have been a joke. Perhaps whoever first asked Adam expected a missionary to be a stuffy, uptight prude who would never set foot into a bar. Whatever the reason, he liked these people, however raucous their humor or absent their inhibitions, and while he never stayed for long—or joined them in drinking—they kept asking him year after year, so presumably the feeling was mutual.

They called themselves the "Pen Mentors" because they always met in the lounge of the Peninsula Hotel.

After years of service, the Peninsula Hotel remained one of the most select and quietly luxurious hotels in Kowloon, a remnant of the day when Britannia's rule spread English elegance and service worldwide. Adam had brought Jenny here once for high tea—scones, double-whipped cream, cucumber sandwiches, and scalding hot tea. He'd felt like an interloper, a pauper sharing floor space with princes, but his discomfort had been worth it just to see Jenny smile. The crown jewels had nothing on the sparkle in her eyes.

As he made his way out of the bar and through the ornate lobby now, Adam looked around again at the vaulted arches and gilded cupids overhead. A place to see and be seen, he had heard said of the lobby. He had always considered it a fascinating place.

The person he saw now stopped him in his tracks.

She was there, Mariel, in the Peninsula lobby.

He had been toying with the fantasy of having her with him, back there with the Mentors, wishing he could show off her wit and beauty. What a shock she would have been to them! He almost decided even now that she was merely the product of wishful thinking.

To find her in Hong Kong at all. To find her here at the Peninsula, alone. Then to find her looking like this! Her eyes were half shut and her hand toyed lazily with a mixed drink. She leaned back languidly in a low-slung chair, the picture of decadence. Her floor-length black silk dress was cut slim to hug her waist and hips, her beautiful face, delicate but definitely made up, and her hair, artlessly piled in a shower of curls, the shine of gold there competing with the pearls around her neck. He felt his jaw tighten when he realized what she reminded him of: She had over her the aura of a liquor advertisement.

As if to confirm the image, she moved her drink to both hands, turning it slowly and gazing into it.

The easy elegance in which she wrapped herself made him realize again how beautiful she was. Hers was a beauty completely foreign to him, one he had seen only second-hand in movies or on the cover of fashion magazines. She belonged to this palace, where even now he felt like a pauper in disguise.

Well, he was no longer an impressionable youth.

"Mariel?"

At the sound of his voice, she stood up in surprise. "Adam, what are you doing here?"

He lifted his eyebrows. "You were expecting someone else?"

She pushed away her own surprise at seeing him, realized he was less than pleased with her, and frowned. "Does Hong Kong always put you in a bad mood, Adam?"

"No, it doesn't, but walking into a busy hotel lounge and discovering one of my teachers dressed like you are—that would put me in a bad mood wherever it happened!"

Her voice became as silky as the material she wore. "Dressed as I am, Adam? Exactly what are you thinking?"

"What any man coming into this lobby would think. Have you no sense?"

In his face, behind the coldness, she thought she detected concern so she almost admitted he was right and she should be leaving. Then the humor in the situation took her fancy. "Lucky me," she drawled, looking provocatively at him. "The first man who noticed me was you!"

She knew he didn't drink, so knew the glass in her hand had probably annoyed him as much as her dress. What fun!

She sat back down and motioned to a nearby chair. "Come on, Adam, have a seat." She let her eyelashes sweep down in a deliberately provocative motion and slanted a limpid look back up at him. "Can I buy you a drink, sailor?"

His eyes narrowed, and she braced herself for an explosion. He surprised her instead. "Okay, Mariel!" he said, sitting down in the adjacent chair. "I'll have whatever you're drinking."

Within moments a waiter set a glass before him. Frosty, pink, probably steeped with vodka or gin. He grimaced. He hadn't tasted alcohol for many years, since he was in graduate school. Alcohol and the mission field simply didn't mix—in fact, there was an unwritten but clearly understood prohibition against it for Hudson personnel. On the few occasions stateside when he had been offered a drink, the reason to take it had eluded him. Yet here he was, principles cornered and cowering, and all as a challenge to this creature before him.

"Oh, drink it!" she exclaimed, laughing. "It's only a virgin daiquiri. Too sweet for your liking, I would think, but harmless, I assure you!"

"Virgin? No alcohol at all?" He looked chagrined. "I've been taken!"

"You deserved it, with all your scurrilous accusations!" She batted her eyelashes at him again.

He laughed, and she thought whisky straight could not have produced so warm a glow within her. It scared her. She stood up and said, "You're right, of course, Adam. This is no place to linger, and I was lucky you were the first man to approach me. I should go."

He stood as well. "Don't, Mariel. I didn't mean to chase you away."

"Now that you're here, I don't need to worry about the vultures?"

He grinned. "If that means you no longer consider me one of them, I'm glad! Would you come to dinner with me?"

He issued the invitation almost negligently: Come or no, he didn't seem worried either way.

She held her breath for a moment and then sighed. Why not?

"Okay, but I'll go up and change first," she said.

At her unexpected acceptance his guard momentarily slipped, and she saw what he had been hiding each time she refused—how much he wanted her to go out with him, how anxiously he had waited for her company. His eyes shone briefly like gold at the end of the rainbow. Flustered, she motioned toward the stairs. "Come up if you'd like. I have a suite; you won't be in the way."

"A suite? These rooms are booked up months in advance, and they're terribly expensive. How—" He stopped, looked at the floor and shook his head. "Never mind. Silly question."

"I'll explain. A few years ago I inherited some money from my father, so that explains how I can afford the room. As to how I was able to get the room, my lawyer booked the suite months ago, when he first learned that I'd taken the job in Taiwan. We're related, and I suspect he thought I'd be lonely over the holidays. He's a mother hen."

Adam was a few steps behind her. "Your lawyer?"

"Tax lawyer, investment counselor, all-purpose guardian of my bankable assets. He had other business here in Hong Kong and suggested that I join him."

"Well! You're a woman of many surprises. Where is this lawyer now?"

"Oh, Paul and his wife are at a fancy dinner, but I couldn't face it. They haven't been married very long, and I was getting rather tired of being 'three's a crowd.' So after meeting downstairs, I sent them on alone."

"I can't agree that he's much of a mother hen, not if he left you alone dressed like this."

She shook her head despairingly. "You still want to go out to eat?"

He laughed. "Sure. I'll take you up to your suite."

Later, in a classically styled woolen dress edged in antique lace, Mariel seemed once again the woman he knew, but he was becoming more and more convinced that any knowledge he had of her was an illusion. Add wealth to beauty and he really felt out of his league.

They took the Star Ferry across the bay to Hong Kong Island. The lights on the island rose from the waters, their ascending lines beginning at the bay and continuing upward in the towering apartment and office buildings built on the island's steep, rocky hills. She pulled her coat closer around her; the bay breeze in December was chilly.

She turned to Adam. "What were you doing in the Peninsula lounge tonight?"

He explained.

"You're not here for the basketball tournament?"

"No. I usually miss most of it, attending the conference instead."

"And Holly? Is she in Hong Kong yet?"

"No. She's on her way over with the rest of the students. They arrive by boat the day after tomorrow."

From the ferry, they took a taxi to Jimmy's Kitchen. "Ever

197

had *borscht?*" he asked. "Beet soup may not sound good, but your taste buds will prove you wrong! I come back for it every time I'm in Hong Kong."

Their dinner ordered, he wanted to know how she had passed the time.

"I now know that Hong Kong has more shops than people could ever count," she answered, "but I think Samantha, Paul's wife, has taken me to at least half of them! We've shopped in Ocean Terminal, Ocean Centre, Harbour City, The Landmark, the Jade Market; we've shopped in hotel shops, floating shops, alley shops, and portable shops; we've shopped in morning markets, noon markets, evening markets, even an all-night one. I have shopped for things I didn't even know existed. Samantha can bargain with the best back-alley vendor. I hope Paul never wants a divorce from her; she'd probably win his law degree from him!"

"You've been here four days, and you've spent the whole time shopping?"

"And eating. The two greatest pleasures Hong Kong offers, so they say."

A chuckle. "So where have you eaten?"

"At the big floating restaurant."

"The Aberdeen? Did you like it?"

"I got seasick on the sampan ride out. Don't laugh! We also ate at the Man Wah Restaurant where Paul insisted on ordering Snake Soup. He offered me a bite, but I figured he bought it, let him eat it. Then, of course, Gaddi's at the Peninsula, and the Plume in the Regent.

"No complaints there?"

"Oh, Adam..." She sighed. "Have you ever eaten at the Plume?"

"Afraid not," he said. "There are parts of Hong Kong that are as remote to me as, well, as Broadway or Paris."

"I'm sorry. That was thoughtless."

"It's all right." After a few moments, he said, "If you got seasick on a sampan, be glad you didn't come over on the boat with the students!"

"Is it bad?" she asked. "Katy has convinced me to go back with them."

His eyes twinkled. "That ship is a bad news/good news proposition. The bad news is that the food tastes so terrible you can hardly eat it. The good news is—"

"You're too seasick to try! Great!"

"It won't seem like it on the trip, but you'll survive!"

After dinner, they took the tram up to Victoria Peak, climbing so steeply that Mariel had a sudden, crazy impulse to catch the buildings before they fell from their impossible perches. Adam looked down in surprise as she turned her head into his shoulder.

"Heights," she muttered, her face buried now in the warmth of his chest, and then she refused further thought, letting herself savor instead the comfort of his arms around her.

The air at the top, cooler even than the bay breeze, revived her. The lights that had so charmed from the ferry seemed to have multiplied a thousandfold: neon lights, bobbing ship lights, skyscraper squares against the dark night, the hazy, faltering lights of the sampans, and headlights curving around the hill beneath her. They all threw their reflection onto the bay in answer to the stars. On such a magical night, when Adam reached an arm around her, it seemed entirely natural for her to bend toward him and invite his embrace, and later on the tram down and the ferry back, she told herself it was the chill in the air that caused him to keep his arm around her.

Outside her hotel room, however, she kept a sedate distance, almost as if all her fears about a relationship with Adam had suddenly escaped from the place in her mind where she had hidden them that evening. Key in hand, she prepared to disappear quickly.

"Wait!" he said, taking her hand. "Can't you have dinner with me again tomorrow night? I promise: No shopping and no snake soup."

"I couldn't," she said and carefully extracted her hand. "It will be my last evening with Paul and Samantha before they go back to the States. I'm sorry."

"Then perhaps I'll see you at one of the basketball games. I usually make it to the finals."

"Perhaps," but she almost hoped not. She gave a word, finally, to what he was offering: romance, and among all that she hoped to gain at Hudson, romance wasn't even on the list. Adam Lyons could go back to surviving without women!

Stepping from the crowded hallway into the cavernous gymnasium, Mariel leaned her head back and shut her eyes briefly, breathing deeply. Was there a basketball court anywhere, anytime that couldn't immediately surround her with contentment, move her to excitement? The bright lights so high overhead lifted her spirits with them, and the creak of the bleachers and low hum of spectators filled her with assurance. Here it was: one of the few constants that had never failed her, never disappointed her.

She didn't need a psychology degree to explain her response. In a childhood marked indelibly with her attempts to win her father's interest and approval, she'd won the prize only once, and then through basketball. At first when she had begun watching games on TV with him, she had been so quiet he hadn't noticed her presence, her silence a hedge against his possible anger and impatience. With little more than a mental turn of a knob, those Sunday afternoons flickered like a TV image in her mind: he in his armchair, engrossed in the game; she at the far end of the couch, watching him watching the game.

She had learned the game, guarding her interest carefully until one night at supper she had hazarded a question on some minor point of strategy and discovered her father willing to explain. Thus had begun a brief period of shared interest, the one time she could look back to when he spoke with enthusiasm to her. She had received from him, then, the spark of pleasure and enjoyment she had coveted so long. Her knowledge of the game had grown, its intricacies becoming familiar to her, its strategies predictable, so that by her junior year in high school, she had won a statewide journalism award for her courtside reporting. Too bad that by then her father's interest had waned. What had pleased him at first had annoyed him when she surpassed him.

When she had later entered another basketball court, climbed another set of bleachers, this time following David to her seat on one of their early dates, she had wondered how she should act during the game—truthfully, or like the typically uninterested female she felt sure that David expected?

She never had to decide that night. When the referee lofted the ball, her interest was immediately captured. At half-time, she caught a strange look in David's eye—not exactly critical, but certainly curious and calculating—and she had blushed self-consciously.

"I suppose you can tell I like basketball," she said.

"That's great," he had grinned, "because I do, too."

She glanced now at Adam, climbing the bleachers in front of her. What would he say to a woman who disappeared so completely into the game? She shrugged. Adam could think what he liked, she told herself defiantly. Katy had arranged this double date. If she expected Mariel to spend the game making idle chit-chat, she would have to be disappointed.

Especially this game.

"I didn't actually think we'd make it to the finals," Adam said. "After our center, Byron Jones, graduated last year, I figured we'd be eliminated rather quickly this year."

"A star player can sometimes hurt a team," Mariel countered, keeping her eye on the players as they warmed up, "especially in high school. The team depends too heavily on that one player, and their game goes bad. This year our greatest strength is teamwork."

"You've gone to some of the games at Hudson?"

"Every one."

"So you're a real fan?"

"I guess so." She laughed. "But as much of the game as the team. I've loved basketball since a long-ago Sunday afternoon when I first saw the Celtics play. My greatest ambition through all of high school and most of college was to be the first female play-by-play sportscaster for a major network."

"What happened?"

She shrugged. "Things change."

"Well, you can give me a play-by-play, if you'd like. I haven't made it to any of the games this fall."

"Sure," she answered, and began explaining how each player warming up contributed to the team.

He barely listened, finding pleasure in merely watching her. For four months he had tried to know her, and yet still she remained an enigma to him. He felt like he was searching blind, gaining clues to her past one by one, hints to who she was; yet he was unable to advance any closer to the heart of her. He wasn't about to quit trying, though.

After Jenny had died, though most of his friends and family had encouraged him to marry again, he hadn't felt any need to. Whether that was because of his own perverse selectiveness or God's own leading, he didn't know. Either way, as year followed year, as opportunity rose only to be ignored, he felt himself always holding back. He was now thirty-seven, and until the day of his first interview with Mariel last August when he had watched her walk across the plaza, he had almost decided he would stay single forever. Something about Mariel that day, her wit, her vulnerability, her valiant control over her temper, something had called out across the years to that part of him so dormant, and he had found himself at last willing to pursue a commitment.

He smiled a little ruefully as he watched her watching the game. Who would have thought she would be so elusive? Chalk one up to the foolish notions of a single man on the mission field! Pride had waited, patient as a tiger, to bring him flat on his face. His own conceit and overconfidence had unbalanced him.

Even so, after so long a wait, Adam would not back away no matter how much she resisted him. His vanity notwithstanding, he felt certain the fault lay not in himself, but in her, in the secrets she carried over her like a cloak, in the fears and guilt she bore like a hairshirt on her soul. Whatever her past faults, forgiveness waited. When she would let him, he would battle those demons with her and help her through to whatever reconciliation with God awaited her.

With her attention on the game, Mariel almost forgot he was there. The final game of the tournament was being played this year between the inter-island rivals, Taipei and Hudson, and looked to be the closest in the tournament. Unfortunately, though Hudson managed to stay within four or five points of the Taipei team, they never managed in the first half to even tie the game, much less pull ahead. Worse, three of the starters were in foul trouble by the half.

At the half-time buzzer, Mariel leaned back, caught Adam's eye on her, and shook her head. "Not good; not good at all. If either Buck or Tommy foul out, we have Barry to come in for them. He's a good forward, especially on rebounding. Garth will probably start him in the second half. Scott's a different matter. Our best back-up guard is Steven Williams."

"He's not up to it?"

"In a game like this? Even if his skills were good, which they're not especially, the pressure would get to him. It takes maturity to play well in a tournament final. A couple years ago in the NCAA tournament, in the final seconds of the final game, when Georgetown had a chance to score and go up by one, a younger player got confused, passed the ball right into North Carolina's hands, and Georgetown lost."

Adam rubbed his jaw thoughtfully. "You might be surprised. Steven has a lot of poise, probably from all those years with asthma."

"That's right. Katy told me about that. How does that develop poise?"

"Stress or outbursts of excitement often set off an attack. He learned to keep himself calm. "

"Steven doesn't still have asthma, does he?"

"No, he seems to have outgrown it."

She wondered if he knew about the health problems of all his students, but then he did seem like a father, she thought, remembering the night Jessie had been hurt. Would Mr. Gunderson's face have looked any more concerned if he had been there?

Just as she realized she was staring at him—and realized that he was smiling back—Katy leaned past Adam to say, "Mariel! Thanks for dinner at the Plume last night. What a treat!"

"The limousine ride?" Mariel asked, smiling.

"It's the only way to travel!"

Luke grinned over Katy's shoulder. "I told her she should have married Guthrie if she expects a Rolls Royce every time out."

From the way Katy snuggled into Luke's side, however, one hug from him equaled a whole fleet of fancy cars.

Seven minutes into the half, Scott fouled out, and Steven got his chance to play. Collectively, the Hudson crowd winced as he turned the ball over coming down the court and the opponents converted for two points. With the ball again on offense, he threw up a wild shot from the top of the key. On defense as well, he seemed overeager, making foolish fouls and bumping into his own men. Mariel began to rock slowly forward and backward, a mother's instinctive effort to calm a nervous baby.

"Slow down, Steven," she muttered softly. "Slow down. No

one expects you to win on your own."

A time-out, pats on the back, encouragement from the coach, and he did begin to play more reasonably, doing his part on defense, passing off quickly on offense, and once or twice making a clever assist. Now Mariel began to nod her head toward the court, punctuating Steven's possessions with a sharp, approving, "Yes!"

As time began to run out, Hudson pulled to within a point, then their center tipped the ball in to go up by one. For the first time in the game, Hudson was ahead. With everyone else, Mariel was on her feet, yelling, "Defense! Defense!" Adam, his eyes on Mariel's flushed cheeks, watched the excitement change abruptly to horror and turned toward the court in time to see a Taipei player sink a long shot. Taipei was up by one point.

As if one watcher, the Hudson crowd let out a long collective groan, then fell silent. Only eleven seconds remained. What could they do in so little time?

Mariel, who had seen so many NBA and NCAA games turn around in only a fraction of that time, felt gloom with the rest. Professional these boys were not; most would not even play college ball. Coach Wilson called time-out as the crowd, stoked by the cheerleaders, gradually built up steam again.

"How would you call this one?" Adam asked.

"Well, I don't know about Garth Wilson, but I can guess what the Taipei coach is saying: Try to grab the ball, especially off of Steven since he's shown his inexperience. If Taipei can get the ball away, they can hold for the win. If they foul Steven, they can probably count on him to miss."

"Sounds ruthless."

"It's a ruthless game."

"Garth might foresee that strategy and make sure someone else gets the in-bound pass."

"No way. If they're smart, Taipei will double-team the other players and leave only Steven free."

The buzzer sounded and Adam grabbed her hand. "We'll soon see."

As Mariel had said, Taipei put a full-court press on all the Hudson players except Steven. Steven caught the ball and began advancing down the court, his nervous, uneven dribbling torturous to watch. Three Taipei players descended quickly upon him. A more experienced player would have seen them coming, found Barry down court, and made a game-saving pass for a lay-up.

Instead, with the crowd screaming frantically around him, his teammates and the coach shouting instructions, Steven froze, dribbled in place for a moment as if waiting for the Taipei players to surround him, then made a bolting, jerking attempt to get through them into the clear.

In this, his erratic dribbling saved him. Reaching where the ball should have been, one of the Taipei opponents caught Steven's arm instead, clearly hooking it and twisting Steven roughly to the floor. With two seconds on the clock Taipei had stolen the ball, but Steven had drawn the foul and with it the chance to put his team ahead.

A sudden movement toward the exit caught Mariel's eye. Who could be leaving now? Looking down the bleachers toward the gymnasium door Mariel saw a white-faced Jessie first look up court toward Steven and then slip out into the hall. Moments later, as Steven stepped up to the line, Jessie's white face briefly appeared again from between the swing doors.

At the line, Steven bounced the ball, once, twice, three times.

Around him the gymnasium was oddly unbalanced, the spectators on the Taipei side chanting, "Airball! Airball!" and the Hudson side barely hazarding a breath. When he finally shot, the ball lifted gracefully into a perfect arc and fell cleanly through the net. The game was tied.

The balance tipped, with Hudson ecstatic and Taipei hushed. In the interlude, Jessie slipped through the doors, lifted her eyes slowly to the scoreboard and stayed rooted this time to watch the second shot, her face a poem of stunned incredulity, hands clasped together, face chalky with worry.

Adam heard Mariel gasp. "Oh, Jessie, don't faint," she said, as the second ball followed the first, catching only net again. Hudson erupted into deafening cheers. As spectators swelled toward the court in their excitement, Jessie retreated back against the wall.

Down on the court, Steven was brushing off the congratulations, his face looking with fear at the clock, apparently urging his teammates to take up defense. On the sideline, Coach Wilson shouted across the court, "Don't foul! Whatever you do, don't foul!"

Taipei didn't have a chance. One second to catch the ball, one to throw a frantic—and errant—missile downcourt. With the buzzer the loyal Hudson crowd swarmed onto the floor, lifted Steven and the other players onto their shoulders, cheering and hugging each other.

"So, no one expected it, but it looks to me like Steven did win the game for them!"

"He really did!" Mariel agreed. "The weakest player but still too strong."

But she spoke absently. Her eyes were on the door. She

frowned suddenly and caught Adam's arm. "Look," she demanded. Jessie stood almost defensively beside the swinging door, hugging herself to the wall, with her arms crossed before her. "Maybe someone should go down there."

"Someone is going down there."

Shrugging off his friends' congratulatory punches, slapping hands right and left, Steven began to move inexorably toward the swinging doors. Seeing him coming, Jessie's mask slipped and a mixture of fear and longing began to shine in her eyes. She stepped back abruptly when Steven stopped before her.

As far away as they were, Adam and Mariel could hear nothing of what Steven said, but they could see his hands come up slowly toward Jessie, could see Jessie look up with the same puzzled incredulity she had cast upon the scoreboard moments earlier. Her lips moved hesitantly. Steven grinned again (Mariel thought more widely than when he'd made the free throw) and he lifted his arms triumphantly. After throwing his arm around her shoulders, he led Jessie out into the hall.

"Oh, isn't that nice?" Mariel sighed.

Eyes twinkling, Adam fought down the impulse to mimic her wistful question, tried to effect a serious response, then howled in mock alarm when she kicked him. "I'm getting out of here!" he exclaimed. "Come on, Luke, let's get down there and strew around our share of congratulations!"

Twelve

Walking through the elementary building on her way home one afternoon in early February, Mariel turned a corner and found Adam waiting for her. He was sitting on a low wall beside a pillar. Seeing her, he stood up.

"Mariel! I've been waiting for you!"

Her steps slowed then stopped. A flicker of disappointment crossed his face, caused no doubt by her wariness, but having at least stopped her progress, he leaned against the nearby pillar and smiled. As usual, the warmth in his eyes flustered her, and she let her eyes drop from his face.

His arms were crossed over his chest, but his body was relaxed, giving the impression of power at rest. His taut shoulders pulled at the material of his shirt—Mariel knew from Hong Kong how firm those shoulders were; in fact, she had found herself remembering the feel of her cheek against them. Otherwise the shirt and his casual slacks had a loose, comfortable fit, masking the strength within. She let her gaze linger briefly on his hands, the one gripping his forearm, the other resting easily against his arm. She had thought about those hands, as well, remembering how they had held hers outside her hotel room in Hong Kong.

Her gaze drifted upward and a delicate flush rose in her cheeks as she realized he was still watching her, pleased to have her attention, weighing her response. She let her eyelashes fall, covering her thoughts.

"Mariel," he prodded gently, drawing her attention back.

"What?"

She was embarrassed and answered abruptly, but he only smiled, the humor causing his eyes to glimmer. When she finally looked up again, he asked, "How about putting your work aside tonight for a field trip in Chinese culture? Luke and Katy suggested we go downtown with them for the Chinese New Year's festivities."

"I should work," she responded.

Adam's jaw hardened momentarily and she thought he might object. Then he looked down at the ground and nodded. "I understand."

Did he? she wondered. *Could he begin to understand why she was hesitating? But then, perhaps he did.* "All right," she finally agreed. "What time?"

This time his smile was immediate and its effect on Mariel so devastating that she almost reneged. Giving her no chance to speak, he announced he would pick her up at 6:00 P.M. and then he cut back across the school grounds.

Continuing her way home, Mariel told herself not to get excited. So much had changed in the month since she returned from Hong Kong. Although Luke had moved in with Katy next door to Mariel, they had made their own world, and while she completely understood their desire for privacy, she found herself frequently at loose ends. Katy had come to Mariel one day and asked for permission to tell Luke about David and Annie, and Mariel had been grateful for Luke's warm hug later and for the closeness the shared knowledge gave them, but inevitably her contact with both Katy and Luke had lessened after their marriage.

How odd. In the previous years, she had held her isolation around her like a comforting cloak, resenting anyone who intruded too frequently. Now here she was, missing Katy. Was this the way God worked—creating the need and then withdrawing it, a constant feast and famine until she was forced to find her equilibrium in him alone? He was indeed a jealous God!

She had filled many quiet evenings listening to theology tapes Pastor Cartwright had lent her on the holiness of God and his providence and sovereignty. Somehow through those tapes she was gaining a picture—no, more an *awareness* of God as a pure, brilliant, burning spirit who filled her with awe and, frequently, fear. This God, although completely within his rights, would not hesitate to manipulate the circumstances of her life for his glory. Given that power, it scared her to be drawn so irresistibly to Adam. What role would he have in God's cosmic drama?

Adam had not approached her personally during January. She thought at first he would, especially since they were frequently at the same ball games, but seeing his knowing look when she almost refused his invitation just now, she thought she understood why he had been so patient. She might have gone to a basketball game with him in Hong Kong, but here, in Taichung, in full view of the entire student body? She certainly would have been uncomfortable.

She stole a glance at him later as he helped her into the taxi. He knew a trip downtown would be more acceptable to her.

Perhaps he knew as well how a lonely January would affect her. His insight into her reactions unsettled her. He was no young boy, this Adam Lyons, to be easily intimidated or influenced, but a man of keen intellect and practiced wisdom who brought tremendous resources of strength and stamina to any relationship.

He joined her in the back seat and began to tell her about the celebration they would find downtown, but she hardly listened. She supposed there could be a freedom in giving her welfare over to a man like Adam, but could she bear the loss of control? It was the same old dilemma—to rely on her untrustworthy self or risk trusting another who could so easily disappoint her.

They met Katy and Luke at a corner on one of the side streets and moved through the crowds toward the center of town. The Chinese New Year had taken over the area downtown from the train station to the park, to Wuchuan and Minchuan Roads. Dragon dances and parades wove through the streets, which were all decked in red—red clothes, red flowers, red streamers, cake, candies, and hundreds—no, thousands—of firecrackers and rockets.

Pointing to one of the many small red envelopes people were carrying around, Adam told her, "Those are *hungbao*, filled with money."

"Do you hear what they're saying?" Katy asked. *"Kunghsi Fatsai!"*

"Sounds like you're sneezing," Luke said, laughing. "Need a Kleenex?"

"It means 'Wishing you prosperity,' thank you anyway, and it's the only proper greeting for New Year's. The smart response, of course, is 'Hungbao nalai.'"

"Hand over a red envelope," Adam interpreted dryly. "People

in Taiwan hand around so much cash at New Year's that the banks often suffer shortages."

Katy said: "It's the custom for everyone to pay off their bills. It's very bad luck not to."

"The firecrackers?" Mariel asked. "What are they for?"

"To scare off evil spirits!" Katy said, clapping her hands loudly.

"Watch it," Luke said, pulling her up against his side, "or someone will think you're an evil spirit."

Through the evening, Katy and Adam kept Mariel and Luke entertained with Chinese tales, superstitions, customs and other cultural tidbits, and she went home thinking other outings would follow.

They didn't, not the way Mariel expected. The next Wednesday, a hint of spring drew Katy, Luke, and Mariel out onto the plaza for lunch and halfway through Adam joined them. He had never eaten with them before, but after that Wednesday, he did occasionally. As the weather warmed up a little, he also sometimes sat on the porch outside the two apartments, while Holly studied with friends in the library. Luke and Katy invariably came out when he was there so Mariel rarely saw him alone. Though he greeted her warmly at the Taipei game, the final event of the basketball season, he sat instead with out-of-town friends, so basketball season ended with only the one game in Hong Kong shared. At least his dispassionate attitude protected her from rumors and gossip. Adam never lingered with her in the evenings after Katy and Luke went in, and their conversation when they met on campus, though friendly enough, certainly would have given even Katy no cause to tease her.

Somehow none of this pleased her. Mariel felt herself slip into a period of melancholy. She blamed it on the absence of Katy and the time of the year. Nothing seemed new anymore. School was school, lessons were lessons. The basketball season was over. It wasn't time yet for anyone to look forward to the end of the year. Everything seemed so tedious somehow.

One day when she met with Pastor Cartwright, she asked, "Why is it good for us to feel hopeless? Rachel said that one day after you and I discussed something and I was feeling down. I've been wondering what she meant."

"Hopeless?" he said, clearly uncertain how to respond. "I'm not sure what Rachel meant. An ability to hope is crucial for me, that one day I will be in actuality the person God wants me to be." He thought for a moment and then nodded. "But of course Paul speaks of hope in Romans chapter eight, *after* he has established that we can't do anything to make ourselves right with God. Godly hope grows out of hopelessness, perhaps?"

"That makes hopelessness good?"

"When we can see how totally incapable we are of earning God's acceptance, when we realize we are already dead in our sins, then we can begin to understand his grace. Grace he gives freely. We can never earn it, we can never disqualify ourselves from it, we can never lose it. We can also never convince God to bestow this grace."

"We can only accept it?"

He nodded again, waiting this time for her to speak. When the silence lengthened, he asked, very gently, "Would you really rather have your salvation, your growth, your ability to obey, any of it, depend on you?"

"I'd rather he left me a little self-esteem! Does he have to take it all for himself?"

"Mariel." He shook his head slowly. "All undeserving, you are

215

still his beloved child. Sinful, you are loved; sinful, redeemed; sinful, forgiven; still sinful, made holy and brought into his glory. You'll have to find your esteem in that amazing string of events."

"I wish it could become real," she said, a little woefully.

"His grace can take care of that as well."

While the pastor's words were probably true, the session did little to alter her spiritual malaise. Even her students found her responses dull, she whose comments on their papers, if occasionally sharp, had also been frequently witty as well. Katy tried to cheer her up, thinking perhaps Mariel had slipped back into grief, but Mariel knew better. After David's death, everything had hurt so much that she purposely found ways to deaden the pain. Now she had trouble feeling anything. Worse, she didn't want to.

Then in early March, Adam joined her one day as she walked home, and this time stood on her porch when they reached her apartment, looking out across the fields. He said, "Of all the months in Taiwan, March suits me best. The sun is so sharp and bright, and the sky is so clear, almost as though the winter, with all its wind and rain, has wiped the sky clean and made this brilliance possible." He stood for a minute more, breathing deeply, and then turned toward her and grinned. "That's as poetic as I get, so don't ask for more!"

She smiled, and his eyes grew suddenly serious and thoughtful. He stood studying her a moment longer and then spoke. "Will you come to dinner with me this Saturday? Holly is spending the weekend down-island with some friends, so I'm on my own. Will you come out with me?"

After so many weeks of gray winter, how could she refuse the promise of spring, however many changes it threatened?

Mariel had no idea where Adam would take her or how she should dress. For a few moments as she stood before her closet she considered an aquamarine jumpsuit, which in spite of its utter simplicity, nevertheless emphasized her every feminine curve. No, not for Adam, she decided. Wrong tactic entirely. She drew out instead a brown Laura Ashley, its gentle lines and soft ruffles emphasizing even more dramatically—if a little less sensuously—her feminine side. A few strategic ringlets for her hair, a ribbon at the back, and she was ready.

When she opened the door, Adam didn't come in but leaned against the doorjamb and smiled with a hint of surprise in his eyes. "For the fairest flower," he said, holding out daisies. She retreated for a vase, glad of an excuse to hide her pleasure.

In the taxi, he said, "So tell me, have you eaten anything particularly memorable since you came to Taiwan?"

"Memorable? Definitely. The dinner with you and Holly at the Grand Hotel; I'll never forget that—thank you. I enjoy eating *jyaudz* with Katy and Luke. Wendy and I have eaten at several of the nicer restaurants. I've liked Chinese food for a long time, though I'm wary of sweet and sour pork now—"

"Too much fat," he guessed. "The Chinese seldom trim their meat."

"Actually, the only thing I've been unable to swallow—how Katy loves them so much I cannot imagine—are sourballs."

He threw back his head and laughed. "Definitely an acquired taste. Holly can eat bags of them."

"They taste like pure salt!" Mariel exclaimed. "What *are* they?"

"Plums soaked in brine and then dried."

She pulled a long face. "They're disgusting!"

"Well, we're going to try Mongolian barbecue tonight," he said. "Here's hoping you like it more than sourballs."

In the restaurant, long tables, covered with plastic cloths, sat diagonally under bright lights, and mismatched chairs offered poor seating. "Lacks something in atmosphere," he admitted, "but the flavor's an experience."

For her part, as skittish about being out with Adam as she was feeling, she was just as glad the lights were too bright for romance, the tables too close for privacy, and the waitresses too insensitive to encourage intimate conversation. After ordering, Adam stood and led her to a long row of stainless steel trays along one wall. Each propped up a sign to identify the thinly shaved, still partially frozen strips of meat below them: "Venison," "Beef," "Mutton," "Wild boar," and "Pork." Continuing on, signs also identified heaping mounds of fresh vegetables—"Onions," "Pineapple," "Cabbage," "Scallions," "Ginger," and "Garlic"—and sauces—"Wine," "Garlic Sauce," "Soy Sauce," "Ginger Sauce," "Sesame Oil," "Red Pepper Sauce," and "Water."

Mariel followed Adam's lead in filling her bowl, choosing carefully to avoid anything that would threaten her ulcer. She hesitated when she saw the amounts he was packing into his bowl. "Pile it in and pack it down," he advised her. "It shrinks quite amazingly when it's cooked."

With a bowl so full she had to use her right hand to keep it in, she followed Adam around a corner and into a small lean-to built against the main restaurant. Here chefs threw the contents of her bowl onto a grill, four feet across and so hot that it shot searing flames skyward. The oils spit and crackled; the meats sizzled in protest; the sauces fumed a pungent aroma. After a few quick swipes with his long bamboo tongs, a chef returned her bowl, barely full now with cooked meats and vegetables drenched in sauce. At the table, Adam showed her how to stuff the mixture into a tough, heavy pocket bread peppered with sesame seeds.

Adam watched her first sloppy bite. "Not bad," she muttered into her napkin and proved it by taking another bite.

"Eat as much as you want," he said, pleased. "This is a Chinese smorgasbord."

After they had both eaten their fill, he leaned back and asked, "How's the theology class going? What are the students writing about this year?"

"Oh, not at all what I expected. I imagined they would write on dispensationalism or amillennialism or other topics about the end times. Instead, everyone's being marvelously practical."

"Thanks to Thomas, I would think."

She nodded. "Yes. I thought at first it was only with me, this fixation he has on knowing God, but he pulls it out everywhere."

A question flickered across his face, and she paused, wondering what she had said, but he must have decided to let it pass. "Tell me about the papers," he said.

"Well, let's see. They're not all noteworthy, of course. Some are merely typical for high school seniors, some even typical of lazy seniors." He smiled. "The topics are varied enough, though. There are papers on prayer, reasons for evangelism, New Testament giving, even one on why Christian women should be strong leaders. Barry Jasper's paper on ethics is interesting. It seems secular ethicists generally fault religious ethics for being too prescriptive: They say Christians—well, any highly religious people—show their immaturity by citing God's absolutes instead of trying to figure out an ethical framework for themselves.

Instead of fighting this notion, Barry is showing how seldom God gives us rules in the New Testament, how much more often he gives principles and guidelines. At Thomas's suggestion, Barry's limiting his examples to the Sermon on the Mount."

"Some of that criticism is justified, of course. We do have absolutes."

"Yes, some actions are definitely wrong, some definitely right. But much is left to our discretion—no, discernment, Barry says. Isn't that a mature topic for a high school senior?"

"He has Thomas to help him, but yes, I'm impressed," Adam said. "What about the others?"

"Oh, there's Jessie's. She's writing on the place of gratitude in a Christian's life, about how much God must love to give and how often our response should be thankfulness. For someone like me who grew up in a home where gifts were given grudgingly, it's…it's hard to cope with the idea that God wants only gratitude in return for his generosity."

Mariel, thinking back, missed the small frown that again crossed Adam's forehead. "Your home was like that?"

"Yes," she said, looking up now, and to her relief she found it easy to speak about her childhood, the Christmases and birthdays that had so often disappointed. "It wasn't because I wanted more presents. I can't even say, looking back, that I realized something was wrong. I suppose I thought my father's reluctance was normal. It came as quite a shock to discover how much I enjoyed giving presents to my own—"

She stopped abruptly, let out a stunned breath, fumbled for a drink, and then, realizing that her hand was trembling, buried it in her lap again. What was it about this man that caused her to speak so freely? "Anyway," she trailed off weakly, "my home was like that."

His look was sharp, but what had she expected? He must know she was hiding something. Would he demand that she explain? After so many years as the chief administrator of a K-12 school, he certainly knew how to draw out information from even the most reticent person. His right to demand a response must by this time seem God-given, his authority habitual. How long could his patience last?

If only he knew how rarely she spoke even this much.

She saw him scowl and then close his eyes for a moment. When he opened them, he looked determinedly normal. "What were we talking about?" he asked.

The dinner went poorly from then on. At her apartment, when she asked him in for coffee, she expected him to refuse so that he had entered and was sitting on her couch before she fully realized his intention. She served coffee and then sat across from him in her armchair, nervous about what he might ask. Probably to forestall him, she blurted out, "Was it awful when your wife died?" The awkwardness of the question surprised even her.

Caught offguard, for a moment he didn't answer. When he did, he proceeded carefully, like a hiker picking his way across a rocky stream. "Yes. Awful. I felt disoriented at first, as though I'd lost my frame of reference. I'd built my adult life around her. Jenny and I were married four years when she died, but we had known each other six years before that. Without her I had to change habits that had grown over ten years of time. Then the way she died! You know she died in childbirth, didn't you? The baby died too."

At her sudden reaction, he stopped.

"The baby?" she said. "I thought...Holly..."

"No, we already had Holly. She came when I was in graduate school, a little bit of a surprise, but with the next baby we were on track. We were settled in Taiwan, things looked stable, our future was laid out. We were so excited about a big family. Suddenly, I lost them both, the baby and Jenny. At my worst moments, I felt like I was in a carnival fun-house, my subconscious bringing up the expected happiness of childbirth and a new baby, then my conscious mind hitting me again with the truth."

Lost in memories, he had a hard set upon his face, as if even now he rebelled against the travesty. Something deep within her twisted painfully. She hesitated to break in, then finally suggested, "Wouldn't it have hurt less if you had gone back to the States? Started again, left those memories behind?"

Adam looked again at Mariel, as if refocusing. "Oh, I thought about it. Even though the mission board would have let me off, I decided I should stick out my term. I didn't want my students to think quitting was okay or that running away would solve anything. As the years passed, I saw how good the mission life was for Holly, so I stayed."

Looking across to where Mariel snuggled down in an armchair, he watched her steadily and his eyes narrowed. "Why do you ask me, Mariel?"

Somehow, something inside her lightened, and she found herself smiling impishly. "Because you're such an enigma, Adam Lyons. How is it you've eluded marriage all these years? More than one person warned me that mission fields have far more single women than single men!"

Keeping a straight face, but not trying to mask the laughter in his eyes, he replied smoothly: "What you mean is, what brings me up to the standard of women, I alone among men, able to survive on my own?"

"Oh, Adam," she groaned, "I suppose I deserved that!"

"Yes, you did," he drawled. Then he leaned forward, as inquisitive as she could have feared. "Let me ask you, Mariel, something I've been wondering for a long time. Why were you so nervous during that first interview with me?"

"Nervous," she said, hoping for time.

"You know you were."

"I *was* afraid," she said, and then couldn't go on.

This time he was ready. He leaned across the stout coffee table to take her hand. "Don't, Mariel, don't draw back! Finish what you were going to say, please."

"Because of how I felt about God," she blurted out. "I thought you'd send me back if you knew how difficult everything was for me spiritually. When I came, I couldn't pray, Adam. I hadn't read the Bible in over a year, hadn't gone to church for ages. I even questioned my salvation. If you had known all that, wouldn't you have wanted me to leave?"

He hesitated. "I don't know. Probably not. I would have been more cautious with you." His eyes narrowed again. "Has it changed now? Is it better between you and God?"

"A little."

He drew a deep breath and she could almost feel the tension building inside him. Finally, he came around to sit on the table and took her hands in his. "Will you explain the trouble to me, how it happened, what caused the problems?"

The hands holding hers felt warm and coaxing, and Mariel knew if she could only speak she'd tell him everything—David, her anger, Pastor Cartwright, Rebecca—but she couldn't speak without crying and the thought of that paralyzed her. Habits of composure and pride, of dignity and poise bound her like cords, and especially tightly when she was with Adam. She couldn't let him see her cry. She couldn't! So she sat there and shook her head, silent, tense, stricken.

Adam stood abruptly, clearly disappointed and frustrated. He muttered a goodnight and left without glancing back, missing the tears that fell anyway.

Adam came to her the next Friday night, arriving at her door before supper. In the course of their activities during the week, their paths were not likely to pass often, and she hadn't seen him until Thursday in the faculty lounge. He must have realized how self-conscious she felt, for he smiled reassuringly at her before going on with his work, and here he was tonight.

"Adam?"

"I hope I'm in time for supper," he said and held up Chinese food. "I've brought my own."

"Oh! Of course. Come in." Somewhat awkwardly, she hurried to set an extra seat.

"I'm glad to see you weren't expecting someone else!"

At this, she laughed, and a little of the tension vanished. "No, Adam. I'm sure you would have heard if someone else asked me out. No less than junior high boys have asked me how our date went. What is it about this place?"

"I'm afraid I knew this would happen. I haven't taken you to any school functions for that very reason, but you see how it is. In such a small community, gossip abounds."

"What about the banquet? You did ask me to that."

"Ah, but you didn't come."

Unsure of how to respond to that, Mariel began to serve the food.

Adam reached out so that she stopped and looked at him. "They can jump to whatever conclusions they want," he said, "but why let them affect us? I would like to know you better. If nothing ever comes of it besides us being friends, they'll have to deal with that. Besides," and he pulled a long face, "I'm the one who'll have the worst of it in their stories if you leave at the end of the year. I'll be the poor jilted widower, spurned in love, left lonely and wan—well, you can imagine!"

A smile hovered momentarily on her lips and then she laughed. "They'll be delighted to see you rejected and you know it. The sisterhood of females reaches even to the mission field."

His voice tightened. "About last weekend—"

"It's okay, Adam. It was my fault."

"No, much more mine. I'm afraid being a superintendent has tricked me into thinking I should always have my way. You'll tell me in your own time."

"Then you'll still get your way," she said loftily, but smiling.

He put on a wounded expression. "I don't think you realize how much that patience will cost me," he said, "or you'd be showing me a little more admiration!"

"I am grateful," she said, much more seriously. "And…thank you for coming tonight."

"We'll do it again next Friday, if it's okay."

She nodded, and so began a habit for them. The following weekend they went out for dinner and a movie, then came back to Adam's house where they talked late—about where each had lived, why she had chosen to teach writing, he math, what her favorite hobbies were, authors, food.

The next Friday Katy and Luke invited them for pizza. Mariel wandered over early to Katy and Luke's house and, assured that she couldn't do anything to help, stood in the doorway of the small kitchen as Katy chattered over her cooking.

"It was so nice of you and Adam to come for dinner, Mariel!"

"Why? Is your cooking so bad?"

"Ha, ha," Katy scoffed, and then snuck a sly look at Mariel. "It sounds like you and Adam would rather be alone these days. What has it been—dinner dates and fireside chats?"

"Katy...you promised! Adam's off-limits. Instead tell me about you and Luke. Is marriage as good as you hoped?"

Katy stopped washing the lettuce and sighed, a dreamy look coming over her. "Sometimes I walk across campus and see him coming out of his room and that old feeling of longing overwhelms me—you know, the one I never recognized, where I want him to be in love with me. Then he looks up, and he *is*. I can see it in his eyes. Belonging to each other is incredible! I can touch him whenever I want to, ask him what he's thinking and he'll tell me, reach out for him and know he's there. Is marriage as good as I hoped? Mariel, how could I ever live without him?"

For a few moments, Katy's question lingered between the two women in the kitchen, and then Mariel's rueful smile registered with Katy. "Oh, Mariel, I'm sorry! That was so thoughtless of me."

"I asked," Mariel said, lifting a hand to block Katy's apology. "In spite of what happened to me in the past, I still love hearing about you and Luke."

Katy frowned and then lifted inquiring eyes to Mariel. "What did happen between you and David, really? Were you happy?"

"At first." Mariel paused, considering. "Yes, we were very much in love. Then things got hard, and we began protecting ourselves. He was—well, whatever he was, I certainly expected too much of him. I wanted him to fall in with my plans, and he wouldn't. People rarely do." Mariel shrugged. "Anyway, it scares me now—this need to think of others. I'm not sure I can."

"Oh, Mariel, that's not true! Look at how much you've helped Luke and me."

Mariel's smile was full of regrets. "Katy, that didn't cost me anything. I loved being in on your romance! That's the fun part of love, and I had a front-row seat. Now it all gets hard. You'll have to start caring for Luke even when he's not thinking about you. It's the way men are, you know—they pursue us, but once they have us, they feel like we should be their support while they get on with the important business of their lives. How will you react when you're feeling a little neglected, looking forward to an evening with Luke, and he calls to say he's staying late at the lab? He'll put his work first a lot. David certainly did."

"I don't know what I'll do," Katy answered. She thought for a moment and nodded, acknowledging from the memories of her parents' marriage how true Mariel's words were. Her own father had frequently taken her mother's love for granted, counting on Rebecca to free him from distractions so he could work. It didn't seem right, but it had certainly happened—often. How difficult to have Luke do that! Then Katy's face cleared. She lifted confident eyes to Mariel. "Seeing my mother care for my father has been my meat and drink since I was born. It's like you said. She does put his needs first. She always has. But she's genuinely happy. Maybe she made his work her own, a sort of team effort. Or maybe Dad had his own way of making her feel special and loved. I don't know how it all worked, but they are happy. I think Luke and I can do that."

Mariel nodded. "I think maybe you can, Katy. As for me, I was spoiled. Knowing it, I'm more than a little nervous about trying again."

Katy turned back to the lettuce, tearing it quickly and slicing some other vegetables into the bowl. She didn't say anything, just shook her head regretfully.

Mariel leaned back against the doorjamb and after a few thoughtful minutes looked up again at Katy. "I think maybe it's God," she said and hearing her own words, smiled sheepishly. "You see how completely Thomas has altered my thinking? God has invaded everything for me. But it's just this—it's so easy to think of ourselves as alone. We pushed off from God when we sinned; we gave up his protection. Without God, we're on our own out there, at risk. We have to watch our backs constantly. If we could only realize that now we're back in his fold, and he's watching out for us, maybe we could spare a thought for someone else. Oh, dear, I'm rambling, but you can see I've been thinking about this."

Katy had stopped her work again and was watching Mariel in surprised wonder. "I can't believe you said all that. You've really changed, Mariel!"

"You mean about God?" Mariel shook her head. "No, not really. The knowledge is there. The words. I have more of the theory or theology or whatever you want to call it. But have I actually changed? Not that I can see. I still want to protect myself. Even worse, I still see God as an adversary—not always, but sometimes."

Katy crossed to the doorway and gave Mariel a warm hug. "That's the way it works, Mariel. We're all *being* transformed. Surely you can see God's hand in your life?"

"Not always."

Katy made an incredulous sound. "Well, even if you can't," she said, "I can and Luke, too. As for Adam, he always saw something special in you." Katy waggled her eyebrows. "The eyes of love, you know."

Mariel threw a piece of lettuce at her. "Stop that, or I'll develop a headache, and your little foray into matchmaking will end before it begins!"

Katy laughed, then turned to greet Luke as he entered. Mariel could see what Katy was talking about: There shone on Luke's face a flash of joy and wonder as he gathered Katy into his arms. Mariel turned and bit her lip, and through the evening Adam found her strangely silent.

The next Saturday, however, Mariel was in wonderful spirits. Adam got her up early for a walk across back roads between the rice paddies to a cold stream that came down from the mountain. He brought a backpack for the picnic lunch she had packed.

Seeing her skirt, he hesitated, then nodded. "You'll do. In a skirt, you can wade if you want to. For some reason, most people do. Come on!"

The day was gorgeous: the sky deep blue, the air so clear, and the sun warm as a kiss. Mariel felt curiously free and unencumbered, and Adam, seeing the bounce in her step, smiled with deep satisfaction. An imp seized her. When he held out a hand to help her step onto one of the dikes that divided the paddies, she laughed and tugged him toward the water.

"Don't you dare!" he said, pulling her close, and she caught her breath, wondering if he would possibly kiss her in open daylight. He didn't, just smiled lazily, but he tucked her hand under his arm in a warm grip, challenging her with slanted eyes to refuse his claim. She laughed and meekly followed after him.

Her light heart lingered, and after lunch she spent a sunny

hour with Adam exploring among the huge boulders that lined the stream. He refused to go in the water with her, and when she stepped bare feet into the frigid stream she understood why. After a few well-aimed splashes toward the low boulder where he sat, she climbed out and joined him.

"I see what you mean about Taiwan in March," she exclaimed to Adam after their picnic. He was sitting on the rock, his arms stretched out behind him, and she was leaning against him, her back against his side. She could feel the steady beat of his heart and the rhythmic rise and fall of his chest, and she knew he was watching her, his breath warming her hair. Dangerous, even perilous to be so close, but she just couldn't bring herself to move. A deep lassitude came over her as she pressed her cold feet against the warmth of the rock, reveling in the pure sensation of the moment. Almost, almost she could forget everything here. She sighed. "This is so beautiful, Adam!"

He didn't say anything at first, and she thought maybe, perhaps, that she felt his lips kiss her hair. "We could come again," he murmured, and then she was sure.

This was not fair to him, she informed herself, but refused to let anything intrude on the magic of the day.

Back at Hudson, however, she didn't allow any such moments of closeness, keeping everything determinedly friendly. Somehow he was willing to accept her terms.

He told her, one evening, about his work. "The hardest part of my job," he admitted, "is facing the parents after their children have gotten into trouble. A few years back two of our brightest students had to be suspended for shoplifting. Under duress the city police agreed not to press charges, but only on the condition that the boys be sent home for the rest of the semester.

"And there's always Hong Kong," he said. "It's our biggest gamble, setting all those teenagers loose in that city. Who knows what the kids do without our knowing? We see only the tip of their transgressions, I'm afraid, and it worries me."

"Such as?"

"Oh, one year three of our first-string varsity basketball team turned up at the first morning game incapacitated."

"Sick?"

"Hung over."

"Oh, dear." Mariel could picture the coach's embarrassment. "What did you do?"

"Suspended them from playing for the rest of the season."

"Adam, you must have been very unpopular with the students!"

"Not as unpopular as I was with a few of the parents! Missing the chance to see their sons play basketball was too cruel a punishment—especially since they held the coaches and me responsible."

"But those seem like small transgressions compared to public schools back in the States. I faced hangovers there many mornings, not to mention drugs and the threat of violence. I don't think I had a class without at least one girl pregnant."

"We've had a few pregnancies here, I'm sorry to admit. One of our girls almost had an abortion, too. Her best friend warned their PE teacher in time for her to forestall it. We convinced her that she not only might eventually decide she'd made a tragic mistake, but more immediately that the medical care she'd receive here might kill her. She finally told her parents."

"And?"

"She went home to stay with an older married sister and gave the baby up for adoption."

"So sad."

"Sadder still for it to happen here," he said grimly. "We are supposed to be providing the best possible environment. You can see why I have no patience with teachers who complain that the school leaves them too little time for ministering to the nationals. Being a missionary kid is not that easy. Our kids need all the attention the teachers can give them."

She smiled at him, wondering if the students appreciated Adam's concern for them. Probably not.

CHAPTER

Thirteen

In early April, the school had a week of spring break. Wednesday afternoon Mariel went to Adam's house to pack her knapsack for a climb up Yu Shan, the highest mountain in Taiwan. With Mariel and Adam were Holly, Luke, Katy, Wendy, and a few assorted high school students, packing together so they could split up the food.

Adam, who had climbed the mountain twice before, convinced Mariel to join the group. "Missionaries on the island call it Mt. Morrison after Robert Morrison, the 19th century missionary to China," he told her, "but its official name is Yu Shan or Jade Mountain. They say the top of the mountain looks like white jade, though it's always looked more like snow to me."

Now, watching Mariel squeeze warm clothes, rain gear, extra socks, a plastic bottle for water, canned stew, trail mix, dry cereal, and dried Chinese noodles into a borrowed knapsack, Adam looked a little concerned. "Sure you can carry that?"

"I think so," Mariel said.

"You know the climb better than we do!" Luke said. "Tell us again how it goes."

"We take the morning train to Chiayi, then switch to another train," Adam began.

"A little one," Holly said, "almost like a toy."

"Left over from when the Japanese were here in World War II," Adam explained.

Katy continued: "We take that up into the mountains to Ali Shan, the Chinese people's most popular resort. You'll see why, if it's not raining."

"Okay, okay, but when do I start carrying this pack?" Luke wanted to know.

"We stay overnight in Ali Shan," Adam said, "and take an early, early train over to a logging camp, and that's where we start climbing Yu Shan."

Katy leaned back against a wall and grinned. "That's when you can feel free to play the gallant husband, Luke, and carry my bag for me."

"And let you betray your sex? How could I ever stoop to that?" Luke objected. Even so, Mariel noticed that both Luke and Adam put the heavier canned goods into their bags and gave the women the lighter foodstuffs.

Katy came over to Mariel's apartment later that evening and flopped down on the couch. She cast a sly look at Mariel. "You're in for some big trouble, lady!"

Mariel sat down in the armchair and considered Katy. "Exactly how will I have trouble? Is there something you haven't told me?"

"No," Katy said, all innocence. "But for almost three whole days, you're going to be in Adam's constant company. Fresh air, privacy, tired muscles—"

234

"Oh, very romantic," Mariel scoffed. "Are blisters and sweat on your list as well?"

"Uh-uh-uh. Tired muscles can easily lead to shoulder massages and the trail has plenty of curves and twists, just perfect for stealing a forbidden kiss!"

Mariel let out a long, slow breath and stared across at Katy. "Are you trying to discourage me? I could still bow out."

"Why?" Katy objected. "You do...care for Adam, don't you?"

Mariel lifted her shoulders, unable to respond.

"And David, Annie? Have you told Adam about them?"

Mariel slid her eyes away from Katy's and shook her head. "No." One word; a whole volume of fear.

Katy jumped up from the couch and gave Mariel a big hug. "Don't worry!" she exclaimed. "You'll know the right time, and Adam will be okay, you'll see."

Mariel sighed. Was there ever a time to admit such duplicity?

Standing beside Adam at the railroad station the next morning, Mariel decided quite suddenly to tell Adam everything as soon as possible. She was ready to put it behind her. This was Adam, after all: no abstraction, not at all theoretical, just Adam, a little dictatorial and very decisive, patient and perceptive, thoughtful and kind as well. The idea of marriage still frightened her. Commitment entailed risk, and nothing in her past allowed her to imagine a rosy future with him. Yet, overwhelmingly, here and now, she wanted to lean her head against his chest and let him bear her burdens with her.

He looked down to find her watching him and must have sensed something of what she was thinking, for his eyes filled with tenderness. "You don't look ready for this, Mariel!" he said.

"Could I leave now if I wanted to?" she asked, her words heavy with meaning.

Concern flickered across Adam's face. "Mariel?"

Fortunately, Katy and Luke arrived then and kept conversation going easily, helped by the students who gravitated naturally to Katy's enthusiasm. Still worried about her decision, Mariel hardly noticed the scenery on the first leg of the journey, but once on the smaller, narrow-gauge train track, she curled up against a window and watched as tropical banana groves, rice paddies, and sugar cane fields around the bottom of the mountain gave way with the plains to a lush, closely woven carpet of evergreens, cedars, and cypresses. Chugging valiantly, the little train climbed an increasingly steep grade up the mountains, emerging from each tunnel to reveal ever more distant sunshine upon the trees, ever more threatening clouds. When the track curved ahead she caught occasional glimpses of the engine and found herself charmed.

"It's even painted blue," she commented to Adam. "The little engine that could!"

It came back to her, then, how often that story with its repetitive phrasing had finally lulled Annie off to sleep. *Would Annie still have liked it now?* she wondered.

Ahead, the engine let out a shattering whistle as they entered a tunnel, and when they emerged, they drew into Ali Shan. And into the rain.

The clouds and hillsides around the little town cut off the scenery so that the town seemed to inhabit its own densely packed microcosm, isolated, smothered, and remote.

"Oh, my," Wendy exclaimed, coming to peer out the window. "Don't tell me we're going to have to do this through the rain tomorrow!"

"Perhaps not," Adam said. "The weather changes very quickly up here in the mountains, and don't forget we have the trip by train tomorrow to the logging camp. Chances are, the rain's already gone through there."

The group accomplished the transfer to the hotel with much loud complaining. The Japanese-style hotel had wall-to-wall tatami mats in the small sleeping rooms and walls so paper thin that Mariel thought she could poke her hand through them. Thick cotton comforters, or *pugais* as they were called, had been piled in the corner of the room, a welcome sight to Mariel who already felt chilled in the mountain air.

The afternoon dissolved away, helped along with hot Chinese noodles and tea, and when the rain finally stopped, Mariel and Adam took a leisurely walk around the small town, more rain a constant threat.

Once away from the busy, crowded restaurants and shops, from the tourists' conversations and the obligatory blaring radio, Mariel found Ali Shan primitive and secretive. The secluded mountain paths wound through centuries-old cedars and cypresses, guarded by thick walls of fog, hidden under a heavy roof of green, impervious to all other life. She found herself doubting that any place but this little spot in the mountains even existed. Her claustrophobic reaction was a trick of the fog and the moisture dripping around them, she told herself, but words alone couldn't lift her melancholy.

Later, sitting with Adam, Katy, and Luke in the garden grotto behind the resort's leading hotel, Luke commented on how many Chinese tourists were milling through the town.

Adam said, "The Chinese love the mountains and won't go long without their *teng shan,* their climbs to high places. According to custom, the life force or energy rises in the air, like cream in milk. This wet stuff looks like mist; it's really the vital essence of life. Coming up here will strengthen your virtue, help you live longer. In fact, the Chinese character for immortal—*hsien*—combines the symbols for man and mountain."

"Sure, but they don't come only for their virtue," Katy said mischievously. "The mountains are said to be an aphrodisiac, as well. Check out those tourists; they're not sorry it's been raining. According to an old Chinese story, clouds are the female, rain the male, and all this moisture's their progeny. See that stump over there? It's labeled the 'Heavenly Couple'; that one over there's 'Forever United in Love.' As you can imagine, this is a favorite honeymoon spot."

Mariel shuddered. What was she *doing* here?

Luke said, "Christians also use rain to signify God's blessings."

"Like in the hymn, 'Immortal, Invisible,'" Adam agreed. "It has a line about clouds of goodness and love."

Restless beyond her control, Mariel stood and walked to the very edge of the garden, leaning against the rail and looking out into the blanketing fog. *Let them continue their talk of honeymoons and God's goodness without her!*

Soon after this Katy and Luke left, and Adam came to stand beside her. He must have seen how she was feeling, for he said, "What is it, Mariel? What are you thinking?"

"That song you mentioned. It used to be a favorite of mine and then..." she paused. She knew she should tell him now about David and Annie. They were alone, and she had time. She couldn't. Not when she felt so trapped.

"Then?"

"Something happened," she said, "and now the only line that

seems to mean anything to me is the one about us withering and perishing. Don't you sometimes feel…incidental, Adam?"

He took her hand and discovering how cold it was, he put his arms around her. "You're getting chilled, Mariel. Much too cold. Let's go back to the hotel and get some hot tea, shall we?"

More than anything she wanted to turn and burrow her face into his neck and gather warmth from his strong arms around her and let that microcosm shrink to only include them. Why did she have to bring all her troubles with her wherever she went?

"Where are we?" Mariel asked the next morning as she stepped down from the train, perched precariously on the edge of a steep hillside, and looked around her. On boarding the train earlier that morning, she had fallen quickly into a fitful sleep, waking now and then as the Alpine logging train creaked its way across from Ali Shan to Tengpu, the logging camp on the side of Yu Shan. She had woken as the train stopped completely, heard Katy's yelp, and leaned out to see the small Chinese man running down beside the train toward them.

"We're not at the logging camp, are we?" Mariel asked.

"No," Wendy said. "Not for another half hour or so."

Outside, Katy and Adam walked a few train cars forward to a small Chinese man who gestured frantically toward the front of the train, speaking so loudly and vigorously that even from a distance they could hear him. Luke watched with amusement. He said, "What's gotten him so excited?"

"Let's go find out," Mariel said.

"He says there's a tree across the tracks," Katy explained when

239

they reached her. "They can't go on. We either sit here for hours or walk on ahead."

"A tree?" Luke repeated.

"From the storm yesterday," Adam explained. "We got the remnants in Ali Shan of a bad thunderstorm up here."

"They won't take us back?" Mariel asked.

"No. This is a logging train, after all, not a passenger liner. They've got to go up there for a load, even if it takes all day."

By now the others in the party had gathered around.

"So let's get going," Steven Williams said, glancing at Jessie for her approval.

"I agree," she said. "What's an extra couple of miles?"

"An extra five miles, climbing," Adam corrected her, "and that's only to the logging camp. After that, we have more climbing, and harder, up the mountain. It's nine now, we'll be cutting it close to get up there by dark. I think we should wait it out."

Wendy broke the ensuing silence. "Come now! Faint hearts never won anything! We're made of stern enough stuff here. Let's get going!"

Under a chorus of cheers, Adam shrugged resignedly. "All right, then," he said. "Here's the plan. We walk up the tracks to the logging camp. We'll wait there until 1:00 P.M. at the latest for any stragglers, and then we go up the mountain together. Wendy, you go with the lead group; Katy and Luke, stay somewhere in the middle; I'll bring up the end, in case anyone has trouble. Any questions? Then let's get going—and pace yourself, folks!"

Climbing over the wreckage, Mariel could well believe the train would be stuck for hours. Adam and Mariel waited for everyone else to go ahead, the group quickly stretching out in twos and threes in front of them. At first she enjoyed the walk. Yesterday afternoon in Ali Shan she had felt confined. This morning with the world quite literally at her feet she could almost sense the mythical essence in the sparkling mountain air. The sky arched a deep cloudless blue above her, the sun shone bright and warm, and in the forest on the hills around them, the birds sang joyfully.

Increasingly sensitive to her reaction, Adam saw her take a deep breath of fresh air, and he relaxed with her.

"It's beautiful up here," she said, smiling at him.

"Very beautiful," he responded, looking only at her. Seeing the expected color rise in her cheeks, he grinned and touched her cheek with a gentle thumb. "And colorful, too."

The tracks beneath them turned a slow, sloping corner in front of them, then around a jutting rock. At first Mariel didn't notice anything odd, and then she stopped abruptly, her mood shattered. Before her, across a chasm deep enough to swallow a scream, stretched a train trestle, fifty or sixty planks across, no sides, seemingly no supports, gaping holes between each plank.

"Adam, I can't!"

"I know," he said sympathetically. "I remember that heights bother you. It looks precarious, Mariel, but it's not." Stepping out onto the first trestle, he bounced his foot heavily upon it. Mariel drew him back as sharply as she would have a child from a cliff.

"Stop that!" she demanded. "Adam, you don't understand. I'm not just scared of heights. I'm dysfunctional. Feel my hands. Cold as ice."

Adam looked sympathetic but adamant. "You can't turn

241

back; you can't stay here. Take my arm, if that'll help."

She drew back in horror. "No, Adam, I can't! If I fall, then you will as well."

He said, so firmly that she had no option but to agree, "Look, hold onto my knapsack, right here at the tether." He took her hand and physically wrapped it around the cord. "Now you can let go if you need to. Watch my feet; step where they step. Don't look ahead, don't look down, don't look back. Look only at the wood; that will get you across."

So they went, step by step, across bridges so numerous that Mariel forgot the mountains around her, the air, the birds, the beauty. She barely heard what Adam was saying. She concentrated only on his foot ahead of hers and the wood of the trestle beneath.

When they finally reached the mining camp at Tengpu, even though she knew the path would now climb far more steeply and that physically the hike would become much more difficult, she didn't care. The worst was behind her. Adam pulled her away from the group and said, "I'm proud of you. I know that was hard." The warmth in his eyes surprised her.

She didn't bother pretending. "I wouldn't have done it for anyone else."

"God made us to need each other, Mariel," and she knew he wasn't talking only about the hike.

The others, having had to wait for Mariel and Adam, set off almost immediately, this time with Katy and Luke leading the pack. Adam wanted to take a break, but Mariel wanted to press on. The mountain path was about five or six feet across and wound steadily up the mountain. At least with the path's good construction and upkeep, it was safe.

Adam, Wendy, and Mariel soon caught up with the first stragglers. From the expression on Gracie Wilkins' face, Mariel decided Adam had been right to question the wisdom of adding any extra hiking.

"Feet hurt, Gracie?" Wendy asked.

"Oh, Miss Engstrom! I have such bad blisters."

While Wendy applied some first aid, Adam lightened Gracie's knapsack, and so began a familiar routine, with the small group adding more and more tired travelers as they went. Unfortunately, the hardier climbers had scrambled on ahead, and Adam couldn't carry the entire load of the stragglers.

Worse, night fell early in the mountains. Long before they reached the hostel near the top of the mountain, darkness had added its burden to the weary hikers. In the gathering night, when Mariel was having trouble remembering why they had come, the band heard a rowdy crew ahead on the track, their singing growing louder as they came closer.

"We've come to help you along!" Luke announced. Behind him tramped Barry, Bridget, Jessie, and Steven, grinning sympathetically. Gratefully, tired hikers passed over their knapsacks, and with that relief, found within themselves the energy not only to continue but to join the singing as well.

Later, after a hot supper and a foot rub from Gracie, who had become quite a talented athletic trainer, Mariel crawled under her *pugai*. Because of the lingering trauma of crossing the trestles, she thought she might sleep poorly, but her last thoughts were of Adam's voice encouraging her, his hand clasping hers in praise. He must have banished her fears, for she slept peacefully.

❧

The next morning, after a stick-to-the-ribs breakfast of oatmeal and hot cocoa and a glance outside to see the sunshine slipping invitingly through pine boughs, Mariel decided to go with the others to climb to the top of the mountain. It would only take an hour, Katy assured her.

The group soon met a thin layer of snow, enough to cover the rocks strewn over the mountainside. Katy, Mariel, and Holly quickly fell behind, hindered by Holly's shoes slipping across the snow packed onto the path. She was wearing typically charming sneakers, with black spots and a big-eyed cow face hanging over the lacings.

"Are you sure your father wants you to climb up here with those shoes?" Katy asked Holly. "They look pretty slick on the bottom."

Holly shrugged. "Oh, he got me boots, but they're new and don't feel good. Besides I like my cow shoes. He won't care, Miss Martin. Really."

"Well, take short steps," Katy cautioned, "and be especially careful on the snow. We're almost there."

Mariel looked gratefully down at her own sturdy hiking boots.

When they approached the peak itself, Mariel paused to wave at a few of the faster hikers already at the top, Adam among them. From where she stood, she could see that the path led once more around the peak before climbing to the summit. Seeing how narrow the path was, perhaps only a foot wide in places, she thought longingly of the wider path from Tengpu. At the summit, there were no rails or guards.

"We'll get everyone up here," Adam was saying, "take a picture, and get back down as soon as we can. Everyone stay away from the edge, and no jokes about pushing anyone off!"

"You coming?" Katy asked Mariel.

Mariel paused to let Holly go ahead. "Maybe."

"Well, be careful if you do," Katy warned. "The path is very slippery."

Mariel began to follow, looking cautiously over the edge. On the side from which they had approached, the mountain fell away at a fairly gradual slope, but on this other side it dropped off much more precipitously. Below her, after a short hill, the mountain dropped almost immediately to a sheer cliff. She was glad to see a flimsy wire fence along the path below, but doubted it would hold anyone falling from above.

Slowly, more nervous than she'd want anyone to realize, she advanced toward the top. The path narrowed to no more than ten inches across, the guide wires ended, and only the mountain against her right side continued. She hugged it like a child does her father on the first day of school. A few more steps and she'd be directly above the cliff.

"Mariel?"

She stopped, fearful of slipping, and looked up cautiously. She had come shoulder-level to the flat summit, perhaps twenty feet across, crowded now with hikers. She wondered why the government didn't put up a sturdy fence around the summit, but then maybe the constant snow cover made that impossible. *Besides,* she reminded herself, *most people who were afraid of heights have enough sense not to come up here!*

Adam leaned on one knee directly above her. "How are you doing?" he asked, and she wrinkled her nose at him. After yesterday he knew very well how she was doing.

Then Holly, only a few feet in front of Mariel, stumbled. She tried to keep her balance, but her inadequate tennis shoes slipped across the icy snow and carried her off the path. Ahead of Holly, Katy made a frantic swipe at Holly's arm and missed, the falling tones of her warning call matched by Holly's sharp descent toward the cliff beneath.

Holly bounced into the flimsy fence that stood above the cliff, bending it away from the path. She caught at a metal post, but this too bent over so that Holly lay precariously hugging the small hill above the cliff, the flimsy wire her only protection against falling.

Over the startled silence on the mountaintop, one sound pierced the air: "Daddy!" Holly screamed. Over and over: "Daddy! Daddy!"

Mariel didn't think. She slid clumsily down the gentler incline behind her, grinding her feet into the snow and catching desperately at the rocks to slow her descent, twisting and turning to come as close as she dared to the steeper side of the mountain. In a rocky avalanche, she fell awkwardly onto the path, stumbled around to where Holly hung, and pulled her up to safety.

Adam arrived moments behind her. He knelt beside them both, holding them tightly in his arms. This was how the group found them: Holly sobbing hysterically into Adam's shoulder, Mariel limp against his arm, and Adam's head bowed over them both.

"You're bleeding!" Katy exclaimed, though it was hard to say to whom. All three showed red.

It turned out that the rocks Mariel had used to break her fall had also left deep gashes in her hands, and when pulling Holly to safety and later clinging to Adam, she had stained them too. Mariel looked down at her mutilated hands. She felt no pain at all.

Luke put his arm around Mariel. "Let's get you back to the hostel," he suggested gently.

Holly had suffered no injuries except a bad bruise where she had landed on the path, but she was badly shaken, and Adam half-carried, half-guided her down the mountain behind Luke and Mariel.

Mariel would need stitches; everyone agreed about that. Whether to linger an extra day or hike back to Tengpu that afternoon as planned, that was a different matter. Holly bounced back quickly. Mariel faced the greater challenge.

"All right, it'll be rough," she admitted, "but my hands need treatment. Let's eat lunch and go. If I take it easy going down, I'm sure I'll be fine."

She and Adam walked slowly and soon lagged far behind the others, for Mariel found that once the shock had worn off, her hands bothered her more than she'd anticipated, and the motion of walking aggravated them.

At one point, when she had stopped to rest on a large boulder, Adam said, "I'm not sure how to thank you—"

"Don't," she pleaded. "What else could I do?"

"After those trestles yesterday, sliding down that mountain must have been every nightmare come true. You know as well as I do that you could have overshot the path."

Mariel sat looking at her hands, bound in bandages red with blood. "What sacrifice would have been too much? I heard her calling, 'Daddy! Daddy!' and I didn't even think. I would have given anything to stop that fear, can't you understand that?"

Adam knelt before her so she could rest her throbbing hands on his. He wouldn't let himself say anything to prompt her. She had her head turned away from him, looking out across the valley beside them. Silence settled over them, broken only by birds, the wind rustling the trees, and far ahead of them on the path, the song of some hikers.

When she finally did speak, her voice sounded numb and distant, and Adam wasn't sure she remembered his presence. "My own little girl said that," she murmured slowly, "the night she died. They had her in the emergency room all taped up with needles and monitors and then suddenly her eyes opened and she started calling, 'Daddy! Daddy!' I couldn't get through all the nurses and doctors. I couldn't touch her, couldn't hold her. I was helpless—she couldn't even hear my voice." Her shoulders sagged and then she finally looked down at Adam, lifting her hands in entreaty. "Can't you see? When Holly cried out the same thing, what else would I do, Adam, when this time I *could* save her?"

"Your...daughter?"

"She was two. Her father was driving her."

A daughter. A father. So...married. She must have been married. Adam's entire being seemed to contract down to this one singular shock. Was she still...?

A slight, painful breath, a pause, and then: "Where is he?"

She looked away again. "Dead. He died...afterwards."

He felt his hands tremble under hers, his thoughts a painful mixture of relief and shock, sorrow for her and then sudden fear.

"Not from the accident?"

She began to shake her head, slowly, reluctantly, the tears streaming down her face, and somehow once begun she couldn't stop the movement. Adam bit back his instinctive response, but couldn't stop the frown. It all seemed hopeless. If her guilt involved her husband's death, how could she ever overcome that?

What grace could reach that far?

She must have seen his frown, for she stopped shaking her head and was looking out across the valley again. He realized she had been silent too long. She wouldn't leave him with only this, would she? He wanted to put his hands on her shoulders, shake her, beg her, grovel, barter—coax her with any and every means available to make her continue. Yet wisdom granted him only this: that he hold his breath, send out a silent, desperate prayer, and then wait for her choice.

She didn't begin immediately, in fact waited far longer than he thought he could bear, crouched there in front of her, afraid to move, afraid even to breathe, but when she finally spoke she told him everything, the whole unhappy story. Her words flowed quickly and mechanically, and when she finished she pulled her bloodied hands away from his, stood up, and went to lean against a tree on the other side of the path, her head bent over in abject weariness.

He came to stand behind her, wrapping his arms around her and pulling her back to lean against him, wanting to enfold her so completely in his strength and freedom that somehow her pain could become his, his assurance hers. "Mariel," he said, so gently, and kissed her hair. "Mariel."

She waited for some other response from him, but he was silent and she finally brushed some tears away and then stiffened, knowing he would step back. "I suppose we should go," she said.

They walked most of the way in silence. She would have liked words—words of inquiry, understanding, reconciliation, even words of curiosity, but he didn't give them, so she took comfort instead in his hand beneath her elbow, his care as he guided her, and his concern during the walk.

After supper that night, she followed him outside. "Adam!"

"You should go straight to bed," he said. "You're exhausted."

"I can't!" she exclaimed. "We have to talk. Please let's walk down the road." When they had gone a little way, she asked, "Are you angry?"

He gave a short, sharp sigh and shook his head. "No, Mariel. No. Not at all."

"Then what?"

"Surprised. I knew there was something, of course, but I never supposed this."

"What?" she asked breathlessly. "What did you think had happened?"

He frowned, obviously reluctant to answer. Finally, he said, "I thought it must be a man. You're so beautiful, Mariel, how could there not be a man somewhere in your life?" He paused and shrugged. "But then there wasn't anything to say this man would love you well. I thought perhaps he had hurt you, and then when you reacted so painfully to the little Reston girl, I thought perhaps—"

"Yes," she prompted him, after a moment. "You thought..."

"That there was a child. Perhaps abortion. I didn't know."

She had stopped and was looking at the ground, her forehead creased thoughtfully.

"Mariel?"

She looked up, and he saw tears glittering on her lashes. "You weren't far wrong, were you? Except about David—*I* was the one who didn't love well!"

He took her hand and touched a finger to a tear that had fallen down her cheek. How could he convince her she was wrong? "You really must go in now, Mariel. You're too tired to be thinking along these lines."

She let him lead her back to the Tengpu Hostel, telling herself not to be disappointed. After all, what had anyone ever been able to say to her that made a difference? Who had ever been able to drown out her own voice relentlessly, terribly dictating the undeniable truth?

CHAPTER

Fourteen

Mariel's hands healed slowly and steadily. In the following weeks, she came to know how gentle and caring Dr. Schwartz was under her rough facade. Adam, she saw as usual on the Friday after the hike.

At first they were both tense. Then after supper she asked, "Would you like to see a picture of Annie?" and they sat side by side on the couch looking back through her album. It had been a very long time since she had done so, and she was surprised to see how young David looked. So much time had passed, and she realized that she could see David now as part of a different life, herself a different woman.

But not Annie. Did a mother ever stop mourning for her child?

Adam touched a picture of Annie. "She's so much like you," he said. "Serious, and look—there's that same tilt to her head that you have when you're wondering something. And here she's smiling! She's beautiful, Mariel." He didn't try to hide his regret. "I'm so sorry."

She nodded. "I would be a better mother now," she said, and he put his arm around her and held her head to his shoulder. After a few moments, she said, "Let's go see a movie. A funny one. Please?"

It started to rain during the movie, the heavy, sloshing rain so common in Taiwan, so that even though the weather was beginning to warm up to the summer's intensity, Mariel began to shiver a little in the taxi coming home. Running to her apartment, Adam put his arm around her to shield her as much as possible, and they arrived laughing at the enclosed stairway leading up to her second-floor apartment.

"I'm soaked," she said, pushing her hair away from her face and trying to wipe away the rain that continued to run down her face.

He took a dry handkerchief from his pocket and began to help her, but in the darkness of the stairway, with only the vague lights of the nearby apartments upon them, their laughter vanished. His hand on her cheek stopped, and his thumb rubbed lightly over her lips. She had never seen his eyes so dark.

"You're so beautiful," he said, and then kissed her.

After he left she still trembled, but not from the cold.

After the climb up Yu Shan, no one pretended anymore that they didn't know Adam was dating Mariel. In fact, while visiting the Martins at the end of spring break, Rebecca sat Mariel down at a quiet moment and informed Mariel that Gladys Carlton had visited her the weekend before.

"Mrs. Carlton? In Tainan? I didn't realize you were such good friends."

"Oh, we're not. She and Chet were on their way down to Olanpi, a beach on the southern tip of the island. She said she stopped to say hi, but that was just an excuse. She really came to pump me about you!"

"Me!"

"You and Adam, of course. The whole island's buzzing. Adam Lyons's love life has been one of our favorite hobbies, you know."

"I thought his love life wasn't much to talk about."

"It wasn't! That was the whole problem! All these years, not a spark of interest from him. You're an answer to prayer, Mariel!"

"Well, keep praying. I'm not at all sure I'm ready to get married again."

"You mean you wouldn't stay, Mariel, even if Adam asked you to marry him?"

"You're such a romantic, Rebecca. Adam hasn't asked me, and maybe he won't. Maybe he knows I don't want him to."

"Call me romantic if you want, but you'll break more hearts than Adam's if you leave at the end of the year. We're already discussing what to wear to your wedding."

"You have to be joking! You *are* joking aren't you?"

"Only partly," Rebecca said. "What do you expect? It's seldom enough that we get any kind of romance on the mission field. Of course we're interested!"

Wendy said the same thing the next week when she stopped by Mariel's apartment on an errand. "You're the object of both envy and delight, Mariel. We wouldn't be women if we didn't feel that way."

"But what will happen if I say no—not that he's asked me, of course. This puts me in a terrible position."

Wendy laughed. "Don't feel sorry for Adam Lyons, for goodness' sake. Trust him to fall for the one woman on the field who won't fall at his feet!"

In bed that night, Mariel thought about what Wendy had said and wondered if she really were unwilling to marry. Staying on the mission field with Adam offered the security of a society devoted to spiritual matters, surrounded by people who had made God the focus of their lives. But staying single seemed so much safer! Marriage meant adjustment, risk, possibly heartache and loss. Back in the States, without the friction of a life shared with someone else, wouldn't she be more likely to make peace a reality in her life?

In this confused state of mind she entered the Holy Week and took from it two lingering memories. First, at the Maundy Thursday service, Luke sang "Oh, the Deep, Deep Love of Jesus."

Hearing the song ignited in her such an urgent desire to feel that glory, to know herself becoming like Jesus, lifted to his standard, his perfection, for only a moment to shine back to God the perfection he meant for her, that she went away from the Maundy Thursday service more shaken than at any other time since coming to Taiwan.

In the end, was even his desire for glory somehow to her benefit? Did he know that she came closest to joy only as she reflected back to him some of his perfection? If so, what had seemed to her his selfishness was actually his goodness. What had seemed demanding, showed his kindness; cruel, his care. What had so frightened her about his character should actually have drawn her most irresistibly to him.

Yes, he did love on his own terms. He offered no compromises, bent not at all to meet her expectations, refused absolutely to yield at any point. Unflinching standards he certainly had; unfailing love as well—she had to admit it.

The second memory was of Saturday afternoon, the day before Easter, when Mariel discovered it would be her last session with the pastor. "The year's almost over," he said. "We've talked a lot about God, about his attributes, his actions, the role he wants in your life. In another six or eight weeks, you'll be heading back to the States. I want you to have a few weeks for this all to settle, fill in all the cracks so to speak, and still have the chance to ask me any questions that might come up."

Mariel swallowed uncomfortably. "I'm...I'm not sure..." She bit her lip. "I'm stunned."

Gently he answered, "Did you think your troubles would be over now? That I could answer all your questions? Mariel, I can tell you from years of following our Master, he does not include comfort and contentment in our covenant. He keeps presenting us with challenges, especially spiritual challenges, because only when we find ourselves at the end of our resources do we turn completely to him."

"His power is made perfect in weakness."

"It's true. Right now, in your life, he'll be strongest when I'm gone. I can't let you lean on me any longer. God covets that role in your life."

Perhaps, after all, the pastor did know what he was talking about, for it was a few days after her last counseling session that she had her most stunning revelation about her relationship with God.

≈

"Have any idea what you're in for tonight?" Adam asked as he helped her out of the car.

"No," Mariel answered. They had come with Holly to Peikang for the annual celebration honoring the goddess Matsu. While temples honoring Matsu covered the island, two temples boasted the largest celebrations, the one in Peikang and the larger temple in Tainan.

"It should be memorable," Adam promised, "if a little troubling at the same time."

"You won't believe the noise!" warned Holly. "The parades are bad enough and the music, but the firecrackers! You've never heard so many—and so close."

"More than New Year's?"

"More than any other time of the year," Holly promised.

Indeed, after they parked and approached the center of the small town on foot, Mariel could hear the din from several blocks off. She stopped and looked at Adam apprehensively.

"We warned you!" he laughed, putting his arm around her briefly. "Don't worry. You'll be safe."

Then he turned to Holly. "Where are you meeting the Gundersons? At the temple? Great. You'll be going home with them, right? Then come on, Mariel, let's walk around a bit and then get something to eat."

He led her straight through the melee. The night was already warm and muggy. As they turned a corner, a further wave of heat came up to meet her and a blurred impression of color, noise, and movement, and smoke so thick with the scent of gunpowder that she could hardly breathe. Hundreds of people, sometimes six deep, lined the sidewalks and quickly closed in around Adam and Mariel. Bands moved constantly through the streets,

257

punctuated briefly by men weaving a paper dragon beside them, around them, and even over their heads. Street vendors hawked their wares, children shouted, and endlessly, endlessly, the firecrackers exploded around her. What surprised her most was the dust and debris in the air, so dense she couldn't see across the street. Because of the noise, she motioned to Adam, who leaned his head close to hear her question. "Why is it so smoky?"

"Those," he shouted back, his breath warm against her cheek, and pointed to a string laden with firecrackers hanging from a storefront. As the chain reaction exploded the firecrackers, starting at the bottom and going up the string, smoke and paper sprayed into the air. All around, people were hanging similar strings, one after another. No wonder the air was so thick!

Adam pointed along the street walkway to where onlookers were throwing handfuls of small firecrackers onto the street, often right at the feet of the bands. Seemingly oblivious, with little more than a twitch as the firecrackers exploded beneath them, the parade members marched on.

Mariel leaned toward Adam. "Isn't it dangerous?"

He smiled and shrugged. "Probably."

She wrinkled her nose, covering her ears for relief. With his arm across her shoulders, Adam led her down the street toward the temple, pushing through the people to make a path. It stood in the center of town, with all major roads leading toward it, intersecting with a circular drive around it. Tonight, with so many people on the streets, the bands and dragon dancers, the vendors and tourists, only the most foolhardy taxis dared to intrude. Foolhardiness being common among that intrepid breed, the constant beeping of taxi horns added to the scene's confusion.

Inside the temple, the noise receded abruptly and the streams of people became more orderly. Mariel whispered, "Why all the firecrackers, Adam? Won't they get hurt?"

He drew her back against a wall so they could watch before answering her. "First, they're not as dangerous as you might think. Those little ones they throw make more noise than anything, noise *and* smoke. People stand away from the hanging firecrackers. Why so many? Here, at the Matsu Festival, the firecrackers welcome the gods and the people's ancestors to the celebration. At funerals, firecrackers scare the evil spirits away!"

"Ancestors? Evil spirits? Do these people really believe that?"

"Yes, these do, I believe. Does that surprise you?"

She wondered why it did. "Perhaps because the country's so industrialized," she said. "They work so hard. They seem so much in control of things. How can they believe something so...primitive?"

"Good question. But while it's true that over the past thirty-five years Taiwan has changed from agriculture to industry, even so, their folk beliefs haven't weakened. Instead, the people have changed how they practice their religion. For example, the next time you're in a taxi, check out the rear view mirror. You might see a small, red packet hanging there. This is a *hsiangbao,* made by wrapping the ashes from the incense over there—" he pointed toward the altar, "in a piece of yellow paper that has characters written on it, and then tying them up in the red cloth. Long ago, they used the same talisman whenever they went anywhere, certainly when they journeyed here from the mainland. Now they use the *hsiangbao* to protect them in their cars or buses or trucks."

"It's not for luck, like a rabbit's foot? They actually believe these ashes will protect them?"

"Look over there," Adam said, nodding toward a middle-aged Chinese woman, dressed in the customary wear of a moderately well-off Chinese, neat cotton skirt, plain blouse edged with lace. She stood beside a large furnace, and she held in her hands two four- or five-inch stacks of what looked like money, some gold and some silver.

"What is she doing?"

"She's waiting to burn that money. It's paper money, not real. She bought it specifically to burn here, the gold money for the gods, the silver money to provide for her ancestors. Many Taiwanese believe that when a person dies, he goes to a sort of Hades. There he needs a place to live, clothes, food, and money. Only that person's living relatives can provide these things."

"So the money's for the dead?"

"Though not only for the ancestors' sakes. At least, not normally. That woman probably thinks that if she doesn't keep her ancestors happy, their spirits will wander around causing harm to people and especially her. Unfriendly spirits whose descendants haven't provided for them are the ones firecrackers are supposed to scare away."

"She really believes this? How sad to be *afraid!*"

As the woman passed her money to the temple priest to burn, her face bore such an earnest expression that Mariel was left with no illusions as to the seriousness of her belief. Mariel wondered how receptive the Chinese were to Christ, whethei ministering here was difficult.

"They're very receptive," Adam told her, "until they realize how jealous God is. They would gladly add Christ to their other gods, with the thinking, I suppose, that the more gods they worship, the better their chance of preserving their good life. For them religion means bartering: They do this, their god does that. They're in a constant effort to placate their gods, either placate or coerce. Given the suffering they've experienced—the plagues and famines and wars—they are willing to do anything to keep things peaceful. That's why the Taiwanese observe so many different religions—Buddhism, Taoism, Confucianism, animism—they add them all together in an eclectic hodgepodge. When they realize that our God is a jealous God, that he will not share them, that's where the problems start."

"What is the incense for?"

"When the incense is burning, the gods are here." He nodded now toward a new petitioner entering the temple. "Watch him. First he puts his offerings before the gods, then he lights the candles. The three cups of tea are for the gods, and he adds his own incense, asking the god to listen to him. Now he adds a cup of wine to his offering."

"What about the blocks he's throwing on the ground?"

From where she stood, Mariel could see the man throw two pieces of wood—perhaps bamboo, she thought—onto the floor. The wood had been carved into the shape of a quarter moon with one side flat, the other side convex.

"They're holy or divining blocks. The convex is the yin side; the concave is the yang side. He asks the god for something, then throws the blocks. If one comes up yin and the other yang, the god agrees. If both come up yin, the god is angry. Both yang, and the god's laughing at the petitioner."

"They don't know how their gods will react?"

"How could they? Their gods are unpredictable, constantly changing. People in Taiwan spend an inordinate amount of time looking for auspicious days when the gods might look more favorably down on them. They plan weddings and business activities around these days, and trips and everything else."

"Some days the gods favor them and other days not?"

"It gives new meaning to the word *capricious*, doesn't it?"

The man finished his ritual worship. At the sight of his face in prayer, so intent, so serious, Mariel shuddered and shrank against Adam. She didn't know to what the man prayed; she did know it couldn't be God. Never imaginative enough to write fiction, rarely overcome by fantasies, she had always shunned horror movies or Gothic suspense novels, thinking herself above their emotional sensationalism. Here, the worshipping petitioners ritually moving before her and the aroma of incense swirling around her, the methodical click, click of the blocks falling on the floor and the priest droning questions, the lights from the candles shifting over the wall and the smoke drifting in from the street, here unexpectedly a feeling of malevolence and foreboding settled over her so powerfully that she clutched Adam's hand, grateful beyond words to have him beside her. "Let's go," she urged him, reaching up to grip his other hand holding her shoulder. "This is terrible."

This time he led her away from the temple, far down one of the main streets leading up to it, and then across to where tables and chairs had been set out, a local restaurant owner's attempt to accommodate the sudden surge in business. Even so they had to wait a few minutes for a place to sit. Adam went inside and returned carrying two steaming bowls.

"Hope you're not too hot to eat *mien!*" he said, but although the noodles looked delicious, she couldn't eat more than a few bites. He smiled sympathetically.

"I'm beginning to understand why people become missionaries," Mariel said. "How…pathetic. To feel at the mercy of a being so erratic."

"And frightening, too, since these powers seem to have so much power," he admitted. "Here in Taiwan, we don't have to go far to see some pretty graphic demonstrations of that demonic power. There are powerful enough demonstrations here at the Matsu Festival. Would you like to see what I mean?"

She drew back. "Is it safe?"

"Come on. You'll see."

Adam led her back toward the temple, then off to a far side, squeezing her into a crowd of onlookers. Someone in the crowd moved, stepping aside, and she saw a man, short, well-muscled, wearing no shirt, and—she froze. A knife. No, a ten-inch spike, in his right hand. He was sinking it into the fleshy part of his arm, slowly and calmly, like a skewer into a piece of meat. She drew back in horror, not only at the mutilation, but at the man's expression. His erratic eyeballs jittered back up behind his eyelids, and his body, too, swayed unsteadily, as if dangling chaotically from unseen strings. Mariel shuddered. What sadistic being held those strings, making this man's face a mockery of human features, deceiving his body, blurring his mind?

Adam's voice, close to her ear, broke through her revulsion. "This man is a *chitung*," he explained from close beside Mariel. "He's a spirit medium in touch with the netherworld."

He turned her slightly and led her about six feet through another group of onlookers. "Here is another one," Adam said.

This man was flailing himself with a spiked mallet—an iron ball studded with one-inch spikes. The crowd watched in curious wonder as small drops of blood ran down his back. He was inflicting damage to his skin, and yet he showed no signs of pain, but was actually grinning, his teeth bared in obvious sadistic amusement and his eyes bright with a malevolent glow. To Mariel's horror, his head began to turn, his gaze intent, watchful, ominous, his eyes searching through the crowd, hunting, probing, and then they pierced hers and stopped. His eyes narrowed, his teeth bared their pleasure again, and then he began to move unmistakably in her direction, his legs stepping delicately and unerringly in a line toward her, as if to a beat that only he could hear. The crowd pressed excitedly in around her, thickening and tightening, until she was pushed up firmly against Adam's chest, and still the man came, closer and closer.

"Adam," she moaned, barely getting the word out.

He felt her fear, stepped quickly in front of her, and the man backed off, scornfully calling out what was obviously ridicule in Chinese. Adam hugged Mariel for a moment and then let the crowd enfold them, slipping away from the *chitung* onto the sidewalk.

"Are you all right?" he asked her when they were well away from the men. He brushed her hair back and let his comforting hand linger on her cheek. She barely felt it.

"It's awful!" Mariel said, shuddering in dismay. "How can they do those things?"

He shook his head, more concerned about her fear than about answering her question.

"*Why*, Adam? What do they gain?"

"Money, of course. And respect. With their feats they show their power over the natural world. They are tapping into spiritual power."

"Demonic?"

"Don't you think so?"

She leaned back against the concrete wall of a shop that lined the street, fighting nausea. The dust and noise and crowds were becoming too much for her; the sounds and fumes swirling dizzily around her. She was losing control, losing and gaining, the clouds of smoke concealing and revealing, everything so confused and yet so clear. "They found the god I feared," she whispered.

Seemingly without volition she turned and reached out a stunned hand to Adam's face. His eyes were kind, so worried and concerned, his smile tentative and yet generous. When he put his hand over hers and warmed it with his cheek, she knew he was thinking about her, hoping to help her, wanting to shield her from whatever was causing her such distress, and she knew that everything, all of his deliberate love and compassion, the sum of his humanity, had come from God. God made the love possible.

She sagged back against the wall, her hand still on Adam's cheek but her head twisted around to see what she could of the men, their figures moving like wraiths through shifting shadows. "They mock the cross, mock his death, mock sin and holiness and grace. I...I...Oh, no! They're so obvious, but I do it, too." She let her hand fall from his face and gripped the front of her shirt defensively. "Oh, Adam!" When he didn't respond, she raised challenging eyes to him and saw his frown.

"Mariel, it'll be okay."

"You don't understand, Adam!" she exclaimed. "You can't! I wanted to reject—no, destroy *everything* he did for me. I wanted to be my own judge, my own savior. I've been bitter and hateful and I wanted him to suffer. To *suffer*, Adam!"

"Mariel, stop. Nothing's as bad as you think."

"Yes it *is* and even worse." She stared up at him for a moment, searching for something, and then she pushed away, turning her face from him. "You just don't know what I've tried to do."

He put his hands on her shoulders, holding her so firmly that she couldn't escape, and his voice was stern and unwavering. "I'm sorry, Mariel, but God is bigger than your efforts. Even those men can't thwart him. He doesn't give up. He won't change his mind."

"Oh, stop," she cried.

His hand on her face was gentle again, his breath on her forehead as tender as a blessing. "With them, it's his wrath, Mariel, the smell of death, but not with you. Can't you accept life? Love?"

Life. Love. The words echoed through her thoughts, pulling the air out of her lungs, and she collapsed against him, tears streaming down her face. Come to give life. Life to the full. She drew in an agonizing breath and then another, deeper this time, and somehow, in spite of all the smoke and grit and dust in the air, the breath felt fresh and clean and vital. She took another and another and when she could finally manage it, whispered, "I don't know. I want to." She shuddered. "I'm sorry. I've messed everything up."

"You haven't messed *anything* up. I promise. *He* promises!" Roughly, Adam pulled her into his arms. "The measure of our sin is the measure of his love. While we were still sinners...Mariel, *trust* him."

Mariel let herself lean against Adam. She felt utterly drained not only of energy but of so much more. What had she told herself so long ago at Christmas? God is good. Gracious and good and generous. She *could* trust him. Even more than Adam, standing so strongly against her, God would not back away and leave her bereft. "I think, maybe you're right. No, you *must* be right. It's incredible that he still cares. That he ever cared." She looked back again at the men. "I feel so sorry for them, Adam. What will happen to them?"

"God knows. Even they are in his hands."

They stood together for a few minutes more, letting the crowds swirl around them, and then she gathered the shreds of her stamina and stepped away from him. "Adam, let's go home now, please. I've had enough."

The ride back to Taichung was quiet and the distance between them miles wide. She knew he felt cut off from her, but she couldn't bring herself to say anything more. Mariel didn't want to lean on him, not now, not for a long time. God had to come first. Would Adam understand that? She was too weary to find out.

At her door, Adam gently lifted her chin to see that she was all right, but she pulled back.

He sighed. "We'll talk tomorrow," he said.

She didn't respond except to turn her face away.

"Mariel—"

"Not tonight."

He nodded reluctantly, kissed her on the forehead, and said goodnight.

As Mariel prepared for school the next day, she was almost surprised to see the same face looking back at her from the mirror. She was glad she had fallen asleep so quickly the night before, spared the introspective tangle her thoughts would have trapped her in. What was left for her anyway in those dark nights, if she could no longer denigrate herself, piercing herself with accusations and condemnation, seeking a way to explain her unhappiness? She felt disoriented. At her feet was an unexpected cliff where yesterday familiar pathways of thinking had offered themselves, as if an earthquake had suddenly shifted her internal landscape. She smiled briefly—along a fault line. The thought amused her. Was the Spirit smiling? Had he given her the pun? Well, good. At least he understood, but she wasn't sure that Adam would. She dreaded seeing him.

She knew what was coming. The school year was ending. No one had ever questioned his intentions. He was too honorable to pay her so much attention and not be hoping to marry her. Did he think now, because she had cried with him, that she was ready? After being so patient, did he have to rush things now? Or was it she who was pushing the issue?

That evening, Mariel couldn't get out of eating dinner with Adam at Luke and Katy's apartment. They were all three too clever to miss the tension in Mariel or the deliberate way she worked her plans for leaving Taiwan into the conversation. As the meal progressed Adam became quieter and quieter. Mariel would have hurried off alone after the meal, but when she stood to leave, Adam stood as well. Holding Mariel's arm, he told the other two goodnight and walked her back to her own apartment.

"You don't have to manhandle me!" she said once they were inside. She refused to move from her position by the door, hoping he would take the hint and leave.

Adam's eyes narrowed. "I had the idea from your behavior at dinner that if I gave you much choice, you'd have gone with Katy and Luke." When he saw the confirmation in her eyes, he shook his head grimly. "I thought as much. What's the matter, Mariel?"

"Nothing," she said. "I'm fine."

His eyebrows promptly went up. Taking her arm, he guided her to the couch and indicated that she should take a seat. As he had earlier in the spring, after their Mongolian barbecue, he sat on the coffee table and took her hands in his. "Tell me what's wrong, Mariel."

"Really. I'm fine."

"I don't think so."

Mariel sighed forcefully and frowned. "If you're thinking of last night, I know I sounded emotional and dramatic. I'm sorry if that worried you, but I'm all right. Really."

Adam said gently, but firmly: "Being all right, you don't want to talk about it?"

Mariel didn't answer immediately, and the silence stretched between them like a chasm, growing deeper and broader, until it seemed impassable. Finally she looked up and found in his eyes the same concern she had seen as he prepared to lead her over the trestles at Yu Shan.

So he did understand. It didn't make it any easier to speak. Stalling for time, she pulled a hand away from his and ran her thumb across the couch upholstery, watching as an impression briefly appeared on the tablecloth and then vanished. She did it again and then again, until at last a slight groove remained.

"Mariel."

She sighed, this time in resignation. "Okay, Adam. What do you want to know?"

"Mariel!" he exclaimed, holding up his hands in exasperation. "You came here with serious reservations about God, and now he seems to be working things out for you. Shouldn't I want to know about that?"

"You want me to explain...about God?"

"Would that be so hard?"

"I suppose you deserve that," Mariel said eventually. "It might help you understand...everything."

Clasping her hands tightly together on her lap, she spoke, the words spilling out haphazardly: what the year had been like for her, her anger, doubts, and questions at the beginning, her talks with Rebecca and the pastor, her slow comprehension of grace and God's goodness. "I never had much of a faith to begin with," she finally admitted. "I never knew the God that Pastor Cartwright introduced me to. No one could love or trust the God I imagined. It's been very slow, my getting to know this God, but the more I do, the more I realize how empty life would be without him. I want to know him better, Adam. I want to force myself to rely on him. I still can't see him." She paused. "Can you understand that?"

"He plays in ten thousand faces, Mariel. Didn't you know that?"

"What?"

"Can't you see him in Rebecca and Katy and Thomas?" Adam reached across the table and touched her cheek, running a finger down her jaw and briefly across her lips. "I see Christ in you, Mariel, and I love you all the more because of it. He gives us that: a chance to know him through those around us and to make him known ourselves."

"I...I want more. I want to trust him, not Pastor Cartwright or Rebecca." She bit her lip, then added: "Or you."

Adam didn't move, but his eyes narrowed, and then what she was trying to say must have sunk in, for he leaned back and crossed his arms.

Mariel rushed on: "Can't you see why I need to leave at the end of the year?"

"No, I can't." His jaw tightened. "I love you, Mariel, don't you know that? I want you to stay here as my wife."

After one agonizing perusal of Adam's face, Mariel turned away from him. "You can't know what you're saying."

He seemed to hold his breath for a moment, then an almost imperceptible sigh escaped from him, and he shrugged. "I see. No chance."

"No, Adam! That's not true. I do care for you, I care very much. I *wish* I could say I love you. How easy that would make everything! But I can't!"

She could hardly bear to look at him. He seemed to have turned to stone, ceased moving, ceased even breathing. Finally he said, "Go on, then. Try to explain."

"I can't stay, Adam. I've thought a lot about you and how I feel and nothing makes sense except that I have to leave Taiwan. Rebecca thinks I'm being selfish, leaving to avoid the...the necessary adjustments of a marriage. She's never said so, I'm guessing, but she might be right. The pastor thinks perhaps I'm afraid to trust God, that my misconceptions about his character have led me into a fear of punishment from him. And Katy—she's in love. She says that I'm crazy to even think of leaving." Mariel shrugged. "The truth is maybe they're *all* right, Adam, but I still feel I must go. Please forgive me."

"We wouldn't have to marry, not until you were ready."

"No, I have to get away. I can't pretend anymore, not after David, that God will let me..." she paused, groping for words to explain a feeling she could barely define to herself, even subconsciously, much less to him. She began again. "I don't know."

271

"So you are scared to trust God."

She saw the tension in his face and knew she had hurt and disappointed him. "I'm not afraid to trust God; I just don't know if I *can* yet. If I don't know that, doesn't anything else seem premature?"

"So there's nothing I can say." Adam leaned back. The words he spoke next carried a tinge of bitterness. "Nothing I've ever known of God could prepare me for your attitude, this God as a jealous rival, but if that's the way you see things, I'll go."

Mariel winced. He moved stiffly, standing in front of her, and walked toward the door. She barely looked at him, but it took only a glance at his face when he looked back one last time to confirm her worst fears. The weeks ahead seemed ominous suddenly, his silence and distance, everyone's response to their break. She felt awful.

Yet, on Monday evening, there was Adam again, bringing a supper, talking over the meal about his week, his plans for the summer, all as he had so often. Only after helping her wash the dishes did he bring up their conversation. He said, "I want you to understand that I'll keep hoping you'll change your mind, praying that even if you don't love me now—and I think you do, Mariel—that somehow, some way, you will."

"Thank you."

"What are your plans?"

"I'm going to graduate school. Everything has gotten so mixed up since David's death. I've left too many things undone and finishing my degree is one of them."

"You will write," Adam said, sounding like his old arrogant self.

Mariel's answer came slowly. "No promises, Adam."

He grinned. "That's okay. I'll make the promises to myself, then, and they'll be enough for both of us. Now, how about a movie?"

School finished on schedule. A rush of final assignments to grade, the drama of commencement, a flurry of farewells, and then the silence that settles so uncomfortably over a school in the summer. It was a silence so sudden, yet so complete, that it made Mariel almost wonder if any of the previous year had actually happened, if she wasn't now seeing the grounds for the first time as she had last August with Adam.

Fifteen

Mariel left Taiwan on a sunny day in early June, her route from Taipei to Hong Kong first and then on to the States. She chose the route perversely, against the travel agent's advice, because of an overwhelming desire to visit Hong Kong again. She would have two days there before flying on to Texas to visit her mother.

Leaving Katy and Luke, Rebecca, the pastor, Steven and Jessie, and all the others was terribly difficult. Katy threw her arms around Mariel. "We'll be at Texas A&M next year for Luke's graduate school," Katy told Mariel. "When you're in Dallas visiting your mother, please come see us."

Then there was Adam. He went with her to Taipei, getting a promise from her that she would call him from Dallas. "The world's much smaller now. You can do that, Mariel. Please?" She glanced back before getting on the plane and wondered why she had to make everything so difficult for herself.

Adam haunted her arrival in Hong Kong, especially at the Peninsula. As she walked into the lobby, instead of registering immediately, she had the bellhop stow her luggage for a moment, and she made her way across to the chairs where she and Adam had talked so many months before. Running her hand over the place where his head had leaned, touching the arm of the chair that had held him, a rush of longing swept over her and she felt she really understood for the first time how difficult it was for her to leave Adam. She couldn't remember then why she had left. What unfinished business had been so urgent that she had to flee his presence?

The need to escape had driven Mariel this far. She discovered she couldn't go any further. If something within her had called for a departure from Taiwan, well, she had left. That done, it occurred to her that she had no idea what came next. Her plans for graduate school were far from firm. She hadn't applied anywhere yet and certainly had no teaching position to support herself in graduate school. What had she been thinking? She wasn't even sure where she would live, she who was always so cautious and deliberate.

She would stay here for a while at least, think things through. Perhaps she could regain a little perspective on what she wanted—no, what God wanted. Now that the past was cut off behind her, she needed to decide what lay ahead of her.

She couldn't stay at the Peninsula, that she knew. The hotel booked its rooms too far in advance for her to lengthen her stay. Apologizing, she asked the receptionist to recommend another hotel. He booked her into the Shangri-La for a week. She also canceled her ticket to Texas and phoned her mother to explain her change in plans.

The first few days she wandered aimlessly around Hong Kong, going in shop after shop, looking at nothing in particular, until finally the futility of this activity pressed in upon her, and she retreated to her hotel room.

There she tried to write about the last year: what she had learned, what she would take away from the year. She wanted to make some sense of the myriad experiences and impressions she'd had, lectures she had heard, conversations she had taken part in, people she had met. *I'm a writing instructor, after all,* she thought. *By trade and training, I should be able to distill this year into a few memorable lessons.*

She found it impossible. The year refused to coalesce into a neat little list of steps on how to be right with God.

Abandoning that approach, she began to do what she should have done so long ago. She prayed first, trying to find within herself an image of the father she'd longed to have as a child, a caring, interested, accepting father, and haltingly, stumblingly sought this Father God in her prayers. She began to write again, about her past, her lingering questions, her feelings for Adam, her fears for the future. She faced all the anguish, turmoil, anger and even despair of the past three years.

She also read the Psalms, searching out the times David revealed this Father she sought, through his poetry, his praise, and proclamations. One thing she became convinced of—based on the psalmist's relationship, this Father could handle all manner of tirades, questions, doubtings, and distress. He would not have turned from her, whatever her behavior.

She also fasted, certain in her heart that she did so not in penance, but in a genuine, heartfelt desire to honor God.

On the third morning, she rose early from her prayers and began to write again. This time it came more naturally. She wrote about Moses, for like Moses on the mountain she had long had the vision of what she might be; as with Moses the vision had faded rapidly away when she had gone down into her own valley. The memory of her long nights, weary questions, bitter anguish seemed already distant and she realized how far God had brought her since that night last fall when she first called the pastor. God had been with her all along.

She wrote about Paul, too, for like Paul, she had passed from glory to glory, leaving behind her misconceptions of a law she could never keep. What she would become now she thought she knew. The Bible said she would be like Christ. This time her hope depended on no ephemeral vision of what she wanted, no temporal image of who she should be, no personal longing or determination, instead on reality—a Savior in whose face shone the knowledge of the glory of God, a Spirit who helped her in weakness and guaranteed what was to come, and a Father who called her his child.

When she put down her pen after two hours, she knew she had on paper what she wanted, not only what the year had given her, but enough to insure her confidence for the future as well. If more suffering and hardship lay on her horizon, if questions and doubts would again assail her, she could accept them now and know at the very least that he would take her across the chasm. Nothing was finished, but then hadn't Thomas said that God would keep challenging her? For this moment at least, she could accept that morning had come and with it joy.

After calling her mother, Mariel ate a light breakfast, went to the reception desk to make her travel arrangements, and then found herself with a free day ahead of her. The choice was easy. The past days, rich in spiritual nourishment, had nevertheless taken their physical toll. She would spend some time in the sunshine.

As she had with Adam in December, she took the Star Ferry across the channel, boarded the Victoria Tram, and traveled to the peak, but she had underestimated the effect of three days without food. Climbing from the tram, she felt light-headed and dizzy and barely made it to a bench without fainting. She gratefully leaned her head into her hands.

"Mariel?"

Opening her eyes slowly, Mariel saw first a pair of stout walking shoes, a plain cotton skirt, simple blouse, and then the astonished faced of Gladys Carlton.

"Why, I thought that was you!" Mrs. Carlton exclaimed. "I said to Chet, 'Doesn't that look like Mariel Forrest?' And sure enough it was!"

Mariel lifted her hand. "Good morning, Mrs. Carlton, Mr. Carlton."

The older woman held Mariel's hand for a moment longer than necessary, then said, decisively, "We were going over for tea, weren't we, Chet? Quite expensive, of course. Absolute nonsense, what they expect tourists to pay. But then they do have a captive audience up here, don't they?"

As she spoke, Mrs. Carlton propped a hand under Mariel's elbow and led her forcibly toward the tea house. "You come with us," she commanded, "and tell us what you're doing here."

Only after she drank the tea Mrs. Carlton had thrust upon her—much too sweet, Mariel thought petulantly—did Mariel's mind clear enough to see the look of genuine concern in both the missionaries' faces. Through the impromptu party, which Mariel became increasingly convinced had occurred only for her sake, the couple talked energetically about their visit to Hong Kong, their favorite sights, restaurants, and shopping haunts.

"We're off to the beach this afternoon," Mr. Carlton informed her.

A hurriedly exchanged questioning glance passed between the two, then Mrs. Carlton asked, "Just what you need: sun, sand, and surf. Wouldn't you like to come, too, dear?"

Impulsively, Mariel reached across the table to clasp their hands. "You are kind!" she exclaimed. "And so gentle with me. I...I know I look awful. I feel awful, too, though much better now since drinking that tea. You've been my Good Samaritans this morning, you know. I can't thank you enough, but I think I'll head back to my hotel now. I'll be leaving Hong Kong in the morning, and I think I should rest until then."

Mr. and Mrs. Carlton insisted on escorting her back to the Shangri-La, a courtesy Mariel accepted gratefully. She collapsed into a sound sleep almost immediately upon returning to her room, waking to eat a light supper, then sleeping again.

At eight the next morning, having eaten breakfast in her room, Mariel made her way downstairs to check out. Feeling better, she decided that rather than staying in her room all morning, she would shop for a few presents. She needed something to fill the time, she was so restless.

Halfway across the lobby she stopped. Adam stood by the door watching her, a guarded look on his face.

She hurried to him. "Adam! What are you doing here?"

He stood still and studied her for a moment, unsure how to react to her greeting. Then he said, "Gladys Carlton."

"I don't understand."

"She called Rebecca yesterday morning, informing her that you were still here in Hong Kong, that you looked on the edge of death, but would be leaving today anyway. She wondered if perhaps Rebecca should warn me?"

Mariel could understand the hard set of his jaw now. What

man would want Gladys Carlton meddling in his affairs?

Adam continued. "I knew something had happened, of course. You were supposed to call days ago from your mother's in Dallas. So what has it been, Mariel? Have you been sick?"

"Come sit down," she said, pulling him toward a couch. "No, I haven't been sick. I've been trying to get a few things firm in my heart before I leave Hong Kong, doing some thinking that I should have done long ago."

"You are leaving this morning?"

"Yes," she admitted, slowly. "I am."

Adam lifted his chin sharply, as if he had been hit. His face became still, his eyes like the darkness of a sky before dawn. "I see."

"No, you don't!" Mariel exclaimed, her eyes sparkling now with laughter. "Look at my ticket, Adam."

He flipped the folder open almost reluctantly, barely glancing at it, and then looked closer. "Taipei?" he said. "You're going to Taiwan this morning?"

"My plane leaves at one, actually."

His face was frozen in confusion. He finally shook his head. "You're right! I don't understand at all."

"Adam," she said gently, "I got to Hong Kong and realized I couldn't leave you, not for good. I had some things I needed to get straight in my mind, so I stayed here to see them through. Now, if you still want me, I would like to come back. I want to marry you, if you'll have me."

For one stunning, memorable moment, Mariel saw the joy gloriously dawn on his darkness, and then Adam leaned his head back against the couch and closed his eyes. "So you would have come back on your own?"

"Yes."

Adam groaned. "A man in love is a perfect fool," he said, and then turned his face toward her. Lazy eyelids still low, he reached for her hand and kissed the open palm. "Don't expect these high romantics every day, my love! I'm usually a very practical man."

Mariel dropped her head slightly and smiled, and Adam realized he had never seen her look so happy. The thought filled him with a rush of pleasure and a sudden desire to hold her close. He stood up abruptly, thrusting his hands into his pockets, and looked rapidly around the lounge.

"What's the matter?" Mariel asked, rising herself. "Where are we going?"

"Anywhere we can be alone."

Though he kept a respectable distance from her, his hands safely tucked away, there emanated from Adam such an unmistakable eagerness that Mariel couldn't help laughing.

"I haven't checked out yet. We could go to my room," she said helpfully, well aware of how he would respond.

"No," Adam said slowly, "I don't think that's a good idea."

"Then…" Mariel glanced around, too. "We could get a taxi, go on out to the airport."

"A taxi." He nodded. "That would do."

Adam called the airport to reserve a seat on Mariel's flight, then waited patiently as she checked out. In the taxi, however, having given the cabby a vague instruction to drive through a nearby park, all patience vanished.

Adam put his hands on her shoulders and looked down into her laughing face with a threatening gleam. "Fair warning: I've wanted to do this for a very, very long time!" Then he was kissing her, tenderly at first and then with increasing urgency, and at some point it occurred to him—she was giving him kiss for kiss, matching his eagerness, and holding as tightly as he was. Joy erupted in laughter.

"Mariel, you're a fraud," Adam declared, his eyes brimming with tenderness. "You've thought about this, too!"

She reached up and took off his glasses. "Of course I have. Now kiss me again, Adam! We've wasted enough time!"

The taxi driver, obviously a romantic at heart, kept his eyes discreetly averted, but he wasn't surprised when he was told to drive through the park a few extra times before being told to stop.

Once in the park, Adam and Mariel settled themselves on one of the benches.

Mariel told him first about the last four days. "I knew I wanted you, Adam. I knew when I left that all the romantic feelings were in place. I just couldn't bring myself to accept that God would let this happen. Once away from you, though, once I'd cut everything off, I was able to see that I was more than in love with you—I really needed you. God was giving me your love as a gift, freely, because you would bring me closer to him." She paused then and dropped her eyes, too embarrassed suddenly to continue.

"There's more?" he said. When he used a gentle finger to lift her chin, she found his eyes warm and curious and—yes, she really saw it—brimming with pleasure at the freedom to pursue her secrets. "Go on, Mariel," he coaxed her. "Tell me what you're thinking."

She touched his face, running a finger across his forehead, over his lips, and across his cheek. "Oh, Adam, I love you. It's easy to believe that God sees you as a gift, as precious and worthwhile and necessary, but..." She paused again, and he gave her a brief kiss to give her courage. "After so long thinking about my own needs," she continued, "these last few days have been like coming out of a tunnel and of course I thought of you. It occurred to me that perhaps—this sounds so incredible—perhaps I am God's gift to you! Perhaps I'm part of a plan for *you* and not the reverse! It's humbling not to see myself at the center anymore, but gratifying, too, because it must mean that you need me as well. I want you to be happy. That's why I was coming back."

Adam lifted one of her hands and placed it palm to palm against his own as if in prayer. "We're neither of us at the center, Mariel; he is. We exist for him—that's the secret of the universe—and though he doesn't need us, he does love us and enjoy us. Together we'll reflect his glory back more brightly and that will be our blessing."

Mariel felt an unmistakable sense of pleasure within her, *not* her own and yet so powerful that it seemed literally to fill her heart and her lungs and spread throughout her. God's? A God who smiled? *I'm happy, too,* she whispered silently to him. *I'm happy, too!*

Adam drew her closer and she heard laughter hovering in his words. "We shouldn't be surprised that he drew us to each other! He's the original matchmaker after all!"

Mariel leaned closer to Adam. His breath was warm against her temple, the stubble of his unshaven chin rough against her face, his nearness a precious promise. She knew Adam was right; God had brought them together. Yet she had to ask: "After all these years, why fall in love with me?"

"Fishing for compliments?"

"No! I really want to know."

He leaned away from her to get a better look at her expression, saw how serious she was, and sought an answer. "I suppose I should have found someone years ago, really. I knew life on the mission field would be easier for me if I married, and I can't deny that once or twice since Jenny died I have considered a sort of marriage of convenience. But every time it seemed possible, things would get hectic, I'd become involved in school work, something would happen in Holly's life, and the chance would pass. Then you came along and nothing distracted me from you! Far from it. You distracted me from everything else I was supposed to be doing!"

"But when did you know, really know, that you loved me?"

"Almost from the beginning; I reacted to you differently than to any woman I had ever met. I began with a campaign to get to know you, but you made it almost impossible. It was even more difficult given my position at the school. I found every means I could to see you away from campus."

"I thought so, except for the banquet. That puzzled me."

"Ah, but I knew you were going with Luke."

"Adam! How deceptive of you!"

He laughed. "Not really. I wasn't trying to deceive you; I was trying to make something clear. How else could I show you how interested I was?"

"Oh, you did that! I almost passed out when Katy said you never brought anyone to the banquets with you. I was doubly nervous around you after that."

"Of course, I also got Holly to ask you to go shopping in Taipei with her."

"Holly? She knew way back then how you felt?"

He laughed, his chuckle relaxed and happy. "No! But it was easy to manage. Our battles over clothes are legendary. Since

Holly had never made any secret of how much she admired your clothes, when I said it was time for her to get some new things, I simply added how unfortunate it was that I knew so little about fashion. She responded on cue by suggesting that you accompany her."

"I'm impressed," Mariel said. "Is this ability to manage her something you picked up from trying to stay ahead of adolescents all these years?"

"No. This isn't from being a superintendent. This is just a father who knows his daughter. You'll see how it is: If not with Holly, then with our other children."

"Oh!" Mariel sat back abruptly and gazed up at him in shock. "Children?"

"Don't you want children?"

"I don't know!" She took a few deep breaths and then smiled, enchantment filling her face. "I...I hadn't even thought about a baby." She lifted a searching hand to his face, running a finger down his jaw. "Oh, Adam. Your little boy. Can you imagine?"

"Yes, and I have for a while." Seeing her lips so close to his and remembering his new-won freedom, he pulled her close and kissed her. "Ummm. Where were we? You asked when I really knew. It was at Double Ten, when you saw the Reston girl. I realized then how important your happiness was to me. I wanted so much to take all that anguish away. Here in Hong Kong, seeing you across the lobby at the Peninsula, so incredibly beautiful and so maddeningly unattainable—that's when I began to lose sleep! How hopeless it has seemed at times!"

She couldn't respond completely to the laughter in his eyes. "Problems don't vanish overnight or even over a year, Adam. I won't ever be easy to live with."

His laughter vanished. "Let me decide that," he whispered, close again. "When I saw you leave on that airplane, I thought I'd lost a part of myself forever. I won't forget that."

"But there's still so much I'm working through. You can't possibly know—"

Adam covered her lips with his fingers. "*You* don't know, Mariel, how much I love you. That's what I want to show you."

Mariel thought back over the year and saw so many ways he had already cared for her. He said he had known at Double Ten, so long ago, and yet he had been so patient, demonstrating both wisdom and strength, loving her and yet denying himself for her sake. His care would be the shelter in which her newfound knowledge of God could take root and flourish. Her concern for him would be the firstfruit of her new confidence in God.

She lifted her eyes to his again. "It's all been so hard for you, I know, Adam. Please forgive me."

He grinned. "Now, now, don't forget how long the women back in Taiwan have wanted to watch me eat humble pie. This has all been very satisfying for them."

Mariel winced. "Oh, Adam—"

He kissed her before she could say anything else. "No more apologies," Adam declared, and she smiled and nodded.

"I'm just surprised that you came to Hong Kong."

"Gladys said you looked sick. I knew you hadn't made it to Dallas. I had to come."

She gripped his hand more tightly.

"Shall we stay in Hong Kong?" Adam murmured against her temple. "We could get married here. Ummm…it's a nice place for a honeymoon."

"Is that what you want?"

"Dear love, of the many things I want right now, some quite profusely, the most important is to make you happy."

"Then I'd rather wait," Mariel said, bending her head again to his shoulder. "I want to be married in the Martins' garden by Pastor Cartwright, with Holly there beside us, and Luke and Katy and all our other friends. I have only two requests."

"Anything," Adam promised her.

So it was that later that month, Mariel had her first wish: Gladys and Chet Carlton were among the friends present at the garden ceremony, their role in the romance a bond to the couple.

Mariel's mother came out for the wedding and, with Rebecca and Katy, helped Mariel dress. In her mother, Mariel saw concern and a caution that Mariel only now recognized. She wondered again how she could convince her mother to come for a long visit. Grandchildren, perhaps. Or surely there was a job around Hudson she could do? Then perhaps her mother could meet God as Mariel had done.

In Rebecca's eyes, however, Mariel saw only genuine selfless joy, as if no personal pleasure could possibly bring her more happiness than Mariel's. When Mariel stepped out into the early morning coolness of the garden, that same joy shone from all the faces around her—Luke, Katy, Holly, and many others. Mariel paused, took a deep breath, and let the sunshine warm her. Her wedding day!

Then she looked across the garden and froze, suddenly understanding why brides walk down the aisle on their fathers' arms. If only she had accepted Spence Martin's offer!

For there stood Adam across the garden, looking as formidable and imposing as that first day she met him last August, his face inscrutable and his will beyond hers. Her old familiar doubts came crushing down on her. This man, in this strange place? How could she ever be what he needed? Did he comprehend the risk?

She cast panicky questions across the garden, seeking his assurance, and then he smiled and somehow he was her own Adam again, her patient suitor and gracious friend. There came back from him such a rush of strength and confidence that she wanted to cry, and against all instructions, all plans, he began walking toward her, threading his way down the aisle, his eyes steadfast on hers and his hand reaching out. Enchanted, Mariel smiled and then shook her head quickly, so that after only a few steps down the aisle he stopped and waited.

She would come to him. She would put her future in his hands and join her life to his, just as God planned. She walked forward, feeling as if she were floating, and when she reached him and put her hand in his, with wonder and delight she saw what she had missed from across the garden.

More than confidence and strength, his eyes shone with gratitude, and Mariel knew to whom Adam directed that recognition. She smiled again and nodded. They would enter this marriage knowing where their strength came from.

So Mariel's second request became all the more fitting: In the hushed, sacred moments after Adam and Mariel said their vows, Luke lifted his guitar and sang as their wedding prayer:

Great is Thy faithfulness, Oh God our Father.
There is no shadow of turning with Thee.
Thou changest not, Thy compassions they fail not.
As Thou hast been Thou forever wilt be.

Dear Reader,

How exciting that Mariel and Adam will have a chance to live in your imagination! I hope you also meet God in a new and meaningful way within the book.

We tend to think of God as part of our lives. Far from it. Instead we are a part of his world: "In Him we live and move and have our being." May you meet this great God in Mariel's story, bringing his will to pass in her life and becoming more real to you in the process. If so, thanks are due to pastor Andy Seidel, authors J.I Packer and R.C. Sproul, and my husband Randy Kok. (I hope I got it right—any mistakes in theology are mine.)

My missionary father died when I was two. With great courage and confidence in God, my mother, Neli Grubbs, returned to India with her five children. She later moved on to Taiwan, serving as a teacher at Morrison Academy, a missionary kids' school like Hudson. With all my heart I thank her. She granted me a childhood filled with unique and colorful experiences, and gave me the privilege of living among that complex breed of Christians known as missionaries. In Taiwan I met my future husband and his wonderful family. Randy and I live in Decatur, Illinois, now, with our six children.

Missionary schools like "Hudson" are always looking for good teachers. If you are interested, please call InterCristo at 1-800-426-1342. This Christian Placement Network knows of openings around the world in missionary schools and will be glad to help you.

With thanks to Him,

Marilyn Kok

Marilyn Kok
c/o Palisades
P.O. Box 1720
Sisters, Oregon 97759

Palisades...Pure Romance

Refuge, Lisa Tawn Bergren
Torchlight, Lisa Tawn Bergren
Treasure, Lisa Tawn Bergren
Secrets, Robin Jones Gunn
Sierra, Shari MacDonald
Westward, Amanda MacLean
Glory, Marilyn Kok
Love Song, Sharon Gillenwater (May)
Cherish, Constance Colson (May)
Betrayed, Lorena McCourtney (June)
Whispers, Robin Jones Gunn (June)
Angel Valley, Peggy Darty (July)
Stonehaven, Amanda MacLean (August)
The Garden, Shari MacDonald (August)
Hidden, Lisa Tawn Bergren (September)
Antiques, Sharon Gillenwater (September)
Echoes, Robin Jones Gunn (October)

Titles and dates are subject to change.